# Multicultural Perspectives in Customer Behaviour

*Edited by*

**Maria G. Piacentini and Charles C. Cui**

 Routledge
Taylor & Francis Group

LONDON AND NEW YORK

 Westburn Publishers Ltd

First published 2012
by Routledge
2 Park Square, Milton Park, Abingdon, Oxon, OX14 4RN

Simultaneously published in the USA and Canada
by Routledge
711 Third Avenue, New York, NY 10017

*Routledge is an imprint of the Taylor & Francis Group, an informa business*

This book is a reproduction of the *Journal of Marketing Management*, volume 26, issues 11-12. The Publisher requests to those authors who may be citing this book to state, also, the bibliographical details of the special issue on which the book was based.

*British Library Cataloguing in Publication Data*
A catalogue record for this book is available from the British Library

ISBN13: 978-0-415-62890-7

Typeset in Times New Roman
by Taylor & Francis Books

**Publisher's Note**
The publisher would like to make readers aware that the chapters in this book may be referred to as articles as they are identical to the articles published in the special issue. The publisher accepts responsibility for any inconsistencies that may have arisen in the course of preparing this volume for print.

Printed and bound in Great Britain by the MPG Books Group

# Contents

# Notes on Contributors

**Anne Broderick** is a Principal Lecturer in Marketing at De Montfort University in the UK. Her research interests include role and social-identity perspectives in services marketing, relationship marketing, and ethical and social developments in consumption. She has published in services marketing journals, and is co-author of *Relationship Marketing: Dimensions and Perspectives.*

**Louise Canning** is a Lecturer in Marketing at the University of Birmingham, UK. She held various international sales and marketing posts before embarking on a career in higher education in 1993 at UWE Bristol, joining Birmingham Business School in 2003. Her current research interests include inter-firm relationships, environmental management, and sustainability, on which she has published nationally and internationally.

**Charles C. Cui** is a Senior Lecturer in International Management and Marketing at the Manchester Business School, University of Manchester, UK. His research focuses on international marketing and consumer behaviour, with a special interest in managerial and consumer behaviours in cross-cultural contexts. He has published his work in international journals such as *Asia Pacific Journal of Marketing and Logistics, Industrial Marketing Management, International Marketing Review, Journal of Business Ethics*, and *R&D Management.*

**Andrea Davies** is a Senior Lecturer in Marketing at the University of Leicester in the UK. Her research interest focus on contemporary and historical aspects of consumer behaviour as they inform brand theory, advances in marketing research methodology, and cultures of consumption. Recent publications attend to identity performance, motherhood and consumption, persuasion knowledge in advertising, consumer research methodology, and cross-cultural consumer behaviour. Her work has been published in *Journal of Macro Marketing, Consumption, Markets and Culture, Marketing European Journal of Marketing, Journal of Marketing Management, Advances in Consumer Research*, and *Journal of Consumer Behaviour.*

**Claudio De Mattos** is a Lecturer in International Business & Management at Manchester Business School in the UK. His research interests focus on international business negotiations, in the context of strategic alliances and mergers & acquisitions, as well as cross-cultural differences and similarities in International Business, including their impact on international business negotiations and international branding. He has published in internationally recognized journals such as

*International Journal of Operations and Production Management, Thunderbird International Business Review,* and *European Management Journal.*

**Christine Ennew** is a Professor of Marketing at the University of Nottingham, UK, and Pro Vice Chancellor with responsibility for the University's international strategy. Her research interests lie primarily in the area of services with a particular interest in service consumers in financial services and tourism. She is author of a range of academic and non-academic books and articles on the subject of marketing. Recent publications have appeared in the *European Journal of Marketing, Journal of Business Research, Journal of Business Ethics* and the *Journal of Public Policy and Marketing.* She has published some 90 articles in refereed journals, presented over 50 refereed conference papers and produced 4 books.

**James A. Fitchett** is a Reader in Marketing at the University of Leicester in the UK. His research focuses on critical readings of consumption and consumer behaviour. He has published work on consumer empowerment, consumer research methodology, and consumer identity in the *Journal of Marketing Management, Journal of Macromarketing, Marketing Theory, European Journal of Marketing,* and *Consumption, Markets and Culture.*

**Pervez N. Ghauri** is full Professor of International Business at Kings College, University of London in the UK. He has had books and articles published in leading international marketing journals including the *Journal of International Business Studies* and *European Journal of Marketing.* He consults to a wide variety of UK and European companies.

**Margaret K. Hogg** is a Professor of Consumer Research at Lancaster University in the UK. Before joining LUMS in 2004, she was reader in consumer behaviour at Manchester School of Management, UMIST. Her research interests are around the issues of identity, self, and consumption. Her work has appeared in refereed journals including the *Journal of Advertising, Journal of Business Research, Journal of Marketing Management,* and the *European Journal of Marketing.* She has presented papers at a number of international conferences including European Marketing Academy (EMAC) and US and European meetings of the Association for Consumer Research (ACR), and AMA Marketing and Public Policy.

**Katerina Karanika** is Lecturer in Marketing at the University of Exeter, UK. Her research interests are around consumers' desires, distastes, identity projects and symbolic (anti-) consumption as well as around cultural aspects of identity and consumption. She has presented papers at a number of international conferences including Consumer Culture Theory Conference (CCT), European Marketing Academy (EMAC) and European Advances in Consumer Research (EACR).

**Kannika 'Mink' Leelapanyalert** is a Lecturer in Marketing at Birkbeck College, University of London in the UK. She obtained her PhD in International Business from Manchester Business School, The University of Manchester. Her research investigates the factors influencing internationalisation of retailing firms and cross-border retailing activities. She has published her works in *Advances in International Marketing.*

**Pauline Maclaran** is a Professor of Marketing and Consumer Research at Royal Holloway, University of London in the UK. Her research interests focus on cultural aspects of contemporary consumption. Her publications have been in internationally recognised journals such as the *Journal of Consumer Research, Psychology and Marketing, Journal of Advertising*, and *Consumption, Markets and Culture*. She is also editor-in-chief of *Marketing Theory*, a journal that promotes alternative and critical perspectives in marketing and consumer behaviour.

**Peter Nuttall** is a Lecturer in Marketing in the School of Management at the University of Bath, UK. He teaches in the areas of international marketing and marketing communications, and is also a visiting associate professor at Malta University. His publications have been focused primarily in the field of adolescent and young consumer behaviour. More specifically, his research has explored the consumption and use of popular music as a means of expressing identity, and the impact of family structure and peer-group affiliation on this consumption behaviour. Consultancy work has centred on consumer market research in the charity and not-for-profit sector.

**Elizabeth Parsons** is a Reader at Keele University, UK. Her research interests bring critical and ethnographic perspectives to two key areas: the cultures of consumption, in particular the marketing and consumption of the non-new, and the construction of gender and identity in organisational life. Her publications are strongly interdisciplinary, spanning journals in marketing, retailing, consumer research, geography, and voluntary sector studies. She co-edited the Sage three-volume major work on nonprofit marketing, and is assistant editor of *Marketing Theory.*

**M. Teresa Pereira Heath** is a Lecturer in Marketing at Nottingham University Business School (NUBS), in the UK. Her publications and research interest focus primarily on consumer behaviour, sustainability and critical marketing. She was awarded an Emerald Citation of Excellence in 2008 for a paper published in the *Journal of Marketing Management* and was recently granted an Academy of Marketing Research Funding award. She completed her PhD at NUBS, with a scholarship granted by the Portuguese *Fundação para a Ciência e Tecnologi*a. Until January 2011, she was a lecturer in marketing at the University of Minho.

**Maria G. Piacentini** is a Senior Lecturer in Marketing at Lancaster University Management School, UK. Her research focuses on the consumption behaviour of vulnerable consumers, with specific interest in the coping strategies employed by consumers in difficult situations. She has published her work in a number of journals, including the *Journal of Business Research*, the *Journal of Marketing Management*, *Advances in Consumer Research*, the *Journal of Consumer Behaviour*, the *International Journal of Non-Profit and Voluntary Sector Marketing*, and the *International Review of Retailing, Distribution and Consumer Research.*

**Laura Salciuviene** is a Lecturer in Marketing at Lancaster University Management School in the UK. Her research is multidisciplinary and focuses on cross-cultural consumer behaviour and virtual worlds. She has had articles published in international journals, including *International Journal of Cross-Cultural Management, Advances in International Marketing*, and *International Business Review.*

**Rudolf R. Sinkovics** is a Professor of International Business at Manchester Business School in the UK. His research centres on inter-organisational governance, the role of ICT, and research methods in international business. He received his PhD from Vienna University of Economics and Business (WU-Wien), Austria. His work has been published in international business and international marketing journals such as *Journal of International Business Studies*, *Management International Review*, *Journal of World Business*, *International Business Review*, and *International Marketing Review*. Born in Austria, he now lives and works in Manchester, UK.

**Stephanie Slater** is a Senior Lecturer in International Marketing, Strategy and Business at Cardiff University, UK. She is also Associate Editor for the *Journal of Marketing Management*. Her research focuses on the role of culture in international marketing, strategy and business and the central issues include the determinants of relationship quality in international business strategy, and exploration of the effects of culture and trust-based relationships on management style and infrastructure. Dr Slater has published in international journals such as *International Business Review*, *Management Decision*, *International Marketing Review*, *Journal of Marketing Management*, *Asia Pacific Journal of Business Administration* and *Multinational Business Review*.

**Ruth Salomea Streder** is an international PR consultant working for a leading global tech PR agency in London in the UK. Her academic research interests focus on international PR, international marketing, consumer behaviour, and branding.

**Luping Sun** is a Lecturer at Shandong University Foreign Language School in Shandong, China, which she joined in July 2008. Before commencing her academic career, she worked as an assistant manager in the Shanghai Volkeswagen Dealership, in Zaozhuang, Shandong. Luping completed her MA degree in Marketing at Nottingham University Business School. Her undergraduate degree in Management Studies was awarded by Waikato University in New Zealand. Her research interests include consumption meanings, self-gift consumer behavior, cultural differences in consumption and relationship marketing in cross-cultural contexts.

**Isabelle Szmigin** is a Professor of Marketing at the University of Birmingham, UK. Her research has been focused upon understanding and conceptualising consumers' behaviour, and includes publications examining the behaviour of older consumers, families, ethical consumption choices, online behaviour, and the use and meaning of credit and debt. In addition to her book *Understanding the Consumer*, she has published over 50 refereed research papers and a number of book chapters.

**Amandeep Takhar** is a Lecturer in Marketing at the University of Bedfordshire in the UK. Her research interests focus on consumption, ethnicity and identity construction. Recent publications have looked at the role of computer culture within the Indian Diaspora and social comparisons to the globalised Bollywood film medium. She has published in the *Journal of Marketing Management* and *Advances in Consumer Research*.

**Julie Tinson** is a Reader and Director of the Research Centre for Consumers, Cultures and Society. Her research focuses on adolescent consumer behaviour. It is motivated by a genuine interest in the relative impact of transition on consumption and identity formation. Her work centres on the inter-relationships between adolescent consumer behaviour and the social factors that affect the consolidation of identity positions. She has published widely on consumer behaviour in relation to families and children, and has recently written a book on how to research with children and adolescents.

**Caroline Tynan** is a Professor of Marketing at Nottingham University Business School in the UK, President of the Academy of Marketing, and a Visiting Professor of Marketing at The University of Ljubljana in Slovenia. She currently represents the discipline of marketing for the UK research assessment exercise REF2014. She is a Fellow of the Chartered Institute of Marketing and a Chartered Marketer. Her research interests focus on consumption meanings, experience marketing and managerial marketing practice and she has published in a number of journals including the *Journal of Business Research*, the *Journal of Marketing Management*, the *European Journal of Marketing*, and the *Journal of Strategic Marketing*.

**Fangfang Wang** is a Marketing Officer in China Oil and Foodstuffs Corporation (COFCO Group) in Beijing, China. Before joining COFCO Group, she served as a Brand Communication Officer in Lenovo Group. She has awarded MA Marketing degree from Nottingham University Business School. Her professional interests are brand communication, advertising and consumer behaviour.

**Mo Yamin** is a Professor of International Business at Manchester Business School in the UK. His research focuses on the organisational and managerial aspects of the multinational enterprise. He received his PhD in economics from the University of Manchester. He has published in international business and international marketing journals such as *International Business Review, Journal of International Management, International Marketing Review, Journal of World Business, Critical Perspectives of International Business*, and *Advances in Consumer Research*. Originally from Iran, he now lives in Manchester.

**Mirella Yani-de-Soriano** holds an MBA from Bryant College, RI, in the United States, and a PhD from Keele University in the UK. Her international academic experience spans two decades, and she has also held management positions at several business corporations. She teaches consumer behaviour to postgraduate students at Cardiff Business School, Cardiff University, UK. Her research focuses on cross-cultural consumer behaviour in three main areas: the interplay of emotions, cognitive style, and behaviour in consumer choice; attitudes and behaviour in a societal marketing context; and technology-based-services consumer behaviour. She has published her work in a number of publications, including *Journal of Business Research, Journal of Applied Social Psychology, Journal of Retailing and Consumer Services, Journal of Consumer Behaviour*, and *Journal of Management History*.

# Introduction

Maria G. Piacentini, *Lancaster University Management School, UK*
Charles C. Cui, *Manchester Business School, UK*

With globalisation taking centre stage in the business world and multiculturalism affecting markets and societies, there is a need to understand the ways that customers respond to the changing marketplace from international and multicultural perspectives. This special edition comprises a set of papers on the theme of 'Multicultural Perspectives in Customer Behaviour', emerging from the 6th Customer Research Academy Workshop Series (CRAWS) hosted by Manchester and Lancaster Universities in April 2008.

This special edition is timely in addressing important themes raised in the most recent marketing literature, such as: *global consumer culture*, and the impact of Western culture on consumer behaviour in other countries (Cleveland & Laroche, 2007); *consumer acculturation processes*, and the impact on identity conflicts and the strategies people use to manage them (Askegaard, Arnould, & Kjeldgaard, 2005; Jafari & Goulding, 2008; Oswald, 1999; Penaloza, 1994; Ustuner & Holt, 2007); *globalisation vs. localised strategies*, and the interaction of local and global influences on customer behaviour (Belk, 2006); *climate change and global warming*, the impact on consumer behaviour, and the implications for social responsibility (Lash & Wellington, 2007); and *cross-cultural customer research*, including important methodological questions around the application of sociological, group-level measures to psychological, individual-level phenomenon in marketing contexts (Bearden, Money, & Nevins, 2006; Lass & Hart, 2004; Salciuviene, Auruskeviciene, & Lydeka, 2005; Shavitt, Lalwani, Zhang, & Torelli, 2006; Singh, Kwon, & Pereira, 2003).

The papers in this special edition address those themes, reporting on studies from a range of countries, including Germany, Greece, China, and Austria, and a number of cultural groups in the UK. These papers draw on quantitative and qualitative methodologies, reflecting the full range of methods employed in contemporary consumer research.

Our opening paper, by Andrea Davies and James Fitchett, focuses on the processes of becoming part of a new culture, specifically how visiting residents in the UK for less than three months cope with cultural fracture (defined as the thoughts and feelings that individuals associate with an acculturation situation in which they must modify their previously held and accepted skills, expectations, behaviours, values, and competencies from 'home'). Davies and Fitchett examine the proposition that immigrant consumption may constitute an important type of cultural learning, an intriguing and original perspective on consumption in multicultural contexts. This is different from earlier models of acculturation and consumption whereby a new culture is often considered an antecedent of acculturation and consumer competence. Rather, Davies and Fitchett demonstrate that consumption activities and attitudes facilitate the development of cultural knowledge and understanding, and indeed potentially aid those individuals as they cope with their experiences of cultural fracture. They also highlight the importance of understanding this issue alongside an understanding of materiality and possession centrality (i.e. how skilled and confident the individual is in aspects of consumption), and find that visitors possessing higher levels of possession centrality experience less cultural fracture than those with lower levels of possession centrality. Overall, they conclude that '*individuals who live in consumer cultures and have therefore developed abilities to read, encode, and interpret consumption symbolism are likely also to be better able to cope with the transnational movement*'. This has important implications for companies and organisations who serve consumers who are likely to spend extended periods of time in other countries (such as overseas students, business travellers, international teachers, etc.). For instance, apart from cultural factors identified in conventional marketing models derived from acculturation theories, marketers may benefit from researching such types of consumers' consumption experience, capabilities, and preferences in their home culture, and how these factors affect their response to a new cultural environment, and hence how companies could better serve their 'acculturated' consumption behaviours.

The paper by Rudolf Sinkovics, 'Mink' Leelapanyalert, and Mo Yamin explores consumer decision styles in Austria in comparison with reports about other countries in the literature. The authors argue that when approaching complex purchasing decisions, consumers' mental orientations characterise particular information search, learning, and decision patterns, which are crucial to the actual purchasing behaviour. In this context, the authors examine the concept of consumer decision styles and its measurement using the Consumer Styles Inventory (CSI) (Sproles & Kendall, 1986) in Austria (an unexplored country context). The authors concur with the view about the danger of simply using 'borrowed scales' (Douglas & Nijssen, 2003) in cross-national research and urge further replication and extension studies of consumer research instruments to minimise the detrimental effects of wrong conceptualisation and operationalisation. Despite the fact that replications are not very popular in marketing, consumer behaviour, and advertising research (Hubbard & Armstrong, 1994; Madden, Easley, & Dunn, 1995), they argue that from an epistemological perspective replications are vital to scientific progress (Collins, 1985; Evanschitzky, Baumgarth, Hubbard, & Armstrong, 2007) and make an important contribution to the advancement and generalisation of marketing results (Koçak, Abimbola, & Özer, 2007). Supported by this view, the authors explore the dimensions of CSI by replication of this instrument in the Austrian consumer context and compare their results with previous studies from Germany, the UK, the United States, South Korea, and China.

The dimensions of CSI have been found to deviate slightly in some studies. For example, the 'time–energy conservation' dimension is found in Korea and China, while 'variety seeking' is found in Germany. From their Austrian sample data and comparison with other studies, Sinkovics et al. report some interesting patterns from their analysis. For example, the dimensions 'Perfectionist', 'Brand Conscious', and 'Confused by overchoice' occurred in most countries, including the Austrian case. Their results confirm Mitchell and Bates's (1998) finding that 'confused by overchoice' occurs in most countries because of overloaded information and too many product choices (Klausegger, Sinkovics, & Zou, 2007). An important point raised by Sinkovics et al. is that *'issues observed in multicultural societies may not only reside within culturally diverse societies but can also arise in cross-cultural communication and understanding activate within a culturally homogenous society'*. The arguments and results from their study lend strong support to the view that marketing instruments must be validated by replications in the cultural contexts to be applied to, and marketers should not overlook the fact that homogeneity at a local scale such as Austria is not equivalent to the homogeneity at the global level, and, vice versa, heterogeneity perceived at the global scale should not be seen as exclusion of homogeneity at a local scale.

The third paper, by Laura Salciuviene, Pervez N. Ghauri, Ruth Salomea Streder, and Claudio De Mattos, pp. 1037–1056 has identified an important research gap where inconsistent findings are reported with regard to foreign brand names and their effects on brand preferences. To contribute to filling this gap, they employed the congruity and categorisation theories and examined the effects of incongruity between brand names in foreign languages and country of origin on hedonic perceptions and preferences of services. Salciuviene et al.'s study is timely and important in that marketers are challenged by the increasing diversity in conditions that dictate different consumer perceptions and choices. As the authors claim based on their review of the literature, country image's influence is higher than brand when consumers are not familiar with the brand. In such a case, it is expected that services from a country that has a hedonic image may be perceived as more hedonic than those from a country that has no perceptions of a hedonic image. On the other hand, the change of the market factors, such as the increasing use of the Internet and products being designed in one country but manufactured in another, has resulted in the diminishing importance of country boundaries, and hence the difficulty in identification of country of origin in consumers' perception of product and service. This has given rise to the importance of increasing attention to brand names, especially use of brand names in foreign languages.

Their findings suggest that: insurance services branded with French names are perceived as offering higher hedonic values than those with German or English brand names; services associated with a country with a hedonic image (e.g. France) are perceived as more hedonic; brand names in languages other than the language of the home country of origin (i.e. incongruence) increase consumer preferences for those services; and that incongruence between the language of a brand name and country of origin of utilitarian services leads to a stronger perception of the suitability of those brand names. The authors found the role of gender in choices of services branded in foreign languages is inconclusive and suggest further investigation.

The results from their study suggest that incongruence between a brand name in a foreign language and the country of origin (either home country or a foreign country associated with prior knowledge) of a service represented by this brand name may lead to increased perceptions (consistent with their prior knowledge) for the service represented by such a brand name. In other words, marketers need to be aware that the effect of the country of origin is not absent but functions in a different way through the association with the foreign language used with brand names. For academics and marketing practitioners, this study inspires attention to new important issues such as: whether or not the country-of-origin notion is still relevant in the current age of diminishing country boundaries in the product/service supply chain; how consumers gain their knowledge of the country of the language used in brand names; and how bilingual/multilingual consumers perceive brand names differently from monolingual consumers in a multicultural society or the global market.

A major theme in recent consumer acculturation studies has been that of identity conflicts and the strategies people use to manage them (Askegaard et al., 2005; Jafari & Goulding, 2008; Oswald, 1999; Penaloza, 1994; Ustuner & Holt, 2007). This is developed in a number of papers appearing in this special issue, including the paper by Amandeep Takhar, Pauline Maclaran, Elizabeth Parsons, and Anne Broderick. Their paper is about Indian cinema culture (i.e. Bollywood), and the paper focuses on the ways that the wider processes of globalisation and acculturation play out through this medium and how, in turn, this may impact on the identities of its young audience at the local level. This paper shows how Bollywood films function as a cultural medium through which it is possible to explore changing identities, values, and expectations of young British Sikhs negotiating a position for themselves. A novel methodology is adopted, drawing on the netnographic approach (Kozinets, 2002), but also combining offline interviews. The first author was immersed in the research site (an online Sikh matchmaking service) in the search for a partner herself. The Bollywood characters provide a way for these third-generation British Sikhs to self-categorise their social identity (Hogg & Terry, 2000; Turner, 1987), and in this way reconnect with this part of their social history and culture. Bollywood films enable a form of re-engagement with their Sikh values, which may be weaker for this group of third-generation British Sikh community members. For these young people, Bollywood film provides a powerful way for them to connect to their British Sikh ethnic identity, and facilitates their constructions of the romantic self. However, the participants were 'torn' between their Western selves (with the accompanying identity values that accompany being Western) and their more romanticised selves that aspire to the romance as presented in the Bollywood genre (a similar finding to that of Jafari & Goulding, 2008, in their study of consumption practices of UK-based young Iranians, and the conflicts and dilemmas they experienced between their Iranian and UK identities). For Takhar et al., these films represent the British Sikh ethnic identity as less uncertain than perhaps it in felt in their everyday lives, and the Bollywood films at times reflected some of their pressures and helped them to engage with the issues in their everyday life.

The paper also makes interesting contributions around social identity theory, and the authors conclude that Bollywood represents a 'subtle social function . . . a valuable narrative space of negotiation in which young British Sikhs can "remoor" their ethnic identity'. Consumption of Bollywood offers an opportunity and place for young British Sikhs to explore and negotiate their conflicting identity positions, especially in terms of their possible and potential selves (Markus & Kitayama, 1991) and ultimately can lead to a 'remooring' of ethnic identity.

On a similar theme, Julie Tinson and Peter Nuttall look at the fascinating phenomenon of the American high-school prom, and explore the ways in which this ritual has been adopted or adapted as part of youth culture in the UK. They demonstrate that the high-school prom in the UK is becoming increasingly integrated into the fabric of youth culture, an illustration of 'glocalisation' (global practices reworked to fit local contexts) that gives the young people in their sample an opportunity for differentiation from others. The major contribution of this paper is that it builds on the work of Kjeldgaard and Askegaard (2006) to demonstrate consumers' appropriation of globalising cultural rituals, and shows in more detail how youth culture is indeed a 'glocal' phenomenon that depends on a dynamic cultural process of adoption and adaptation. In doing so, they build on the emerging body of literature on this area, but in particular move beyond previous studies (e.g. Ger & Belk, 1996) that allude to globalisation and appropriation but have tended to provide examples of brand-related products. This paper contributes to the understanding of appropriation by illustrating the extent to which homogenisation and heterogenisation are interconnected processes (Robertson, 1994; Robertson & White, 2005) and that there can be varying degrees of appropriation (e.g. global, local, or glocal) even for the same ritual practice. The authors provide insights into how the prom rituals are appropriated and adapted to fit with existing local practices, and emphasise that the US prom ritual has not completely replaced previous traditions associated with celebrating the rite of passage associated with leaving school. The authors add support to Giulianotti and Robertson's (2007) point that that the creation of localities is a standard component of globalisation.

Tinson and Nuttall provide some intriguing insights into the prom, as performed in the UK context, commenting on the role of technology in supporting the way that performance is managed (especially in terms of displaying popularity and general social position), and providing additional insights into the role of performance authenticity in the context of the prom rituals and how young people negotiate authenticity (Arthur, 2006). Additionally, they comment on the role of agency in this context, that is, the ability of individuals and groups to transform and play with meaning (Ger & Belk, 1996). They develop understanding of adolescent agency through their focus on the way in which co-creation is influenced by both a dominant force (US producers) and conformist behaviour.

The sixth paper, by Katerina Karanika and Margaret Hogg, is entitled 'The inter-relationship between desired and undesired selves and consumption: The case of Greek female consumers' experiences'. The authors report on phenomenological interviews with Greek women, which focus on their consumption experiences that are linked to positive and negative aspects of the self. Greece represents an interesting empirical context as consumers' identity projects in Mediterranean and non-American cultures have been relatively neglected; and most consumer studies about identity projects and identity conflicts were conducted mainly with American consumers (e.g. Ahuvia, 2005; Cherrier & Murray, 2007; Fournier, 1998; Holt & Thompson, 2004; Murray, 2002; Thompson, 1996; Thompson & Haytko, 1997; Thompson Locander, & Pollio, 1990). The paper makes cross-cultural comparisons and reports similarities, as well as differences, in symbolic consumption in Greece and the United States. As expected, the Greek women in their study did experience identity conflicts, and this did shape their consumption experiences. However, in contrast with Ahuvia's work where US respondents managed to create a sense of self-coherence without solving their identity conflicts by combining conflicting standards through consumption of loved objects, the Greek respondents were more uncomfortable with the difficulties they faced in constructing a coherent sense of self and with their identity conflicts. These women strived to achieve a compromising balance between opposing identity positions (similar to the consumers in Thompson, 1996) or to compromise with one identity position while often aspiring to overcome the identity conflict in the future. The Greek women experienced the desire for a coherent self that often left them with a sense of 'baffled self' (Miller, 2009) when coherence was not attained. Interestingly too, Karanika and Hogg identified more ambivalence in the emotions surrounding consumption than previous work (Ahuvia, 2005; Cushman, 1990; Firat & Venkatesh, 1995), identifying a range of different strategies used to cope with their identity conflicts related to consumption.

The paper by Caroline Tynan, M. Teresa Pereira Heath, Christine Ennew, Fang Fang Wang, and Luping Sun reports their study that extends research on self-gift consumer behaviour (SGCB) into China, a cultural context that is distinctly different from other contexts in which SGCB is examined in the literature. The authors have identified an important research gap where calls were made for understanding of SGCB in collectivist culture such as China and cross-cultural settings but no research in such contexts were reported in the literature. Based on their argument that the nature and role of SGCB is culturally specific, the authors attempt to reconsider and redevelop existing understandings of SGCB that have emerged from North America.

The authors point out that in Western societies, the self is not associated with obligations to fulfil the needs and expectations of others, and individuals are encouraged to be proud and reward themselves for their own achievements (Mesquita & Karasawa, 2004). By comparison, individuals in Chinese society are interdependent and self is a relational entity because the individual's social obligation to family and other networks is prime. The authors argue that the important aspects of Confucian cultures such as the human universals, face-saving, and shame and thought are crucial in explaining much behaviour in Chinese society. They also identify family orientation (Qian, Razzaque, & Keng, 2007), *guanxi*, *renqing*, face, harmony, and reciprocity (Zhou & Guang, 2007) as salient aspects of Chinese cultural values that influence gift-giving behaviours. Following from those important cultural aspects, the authors used interviews with consumers to establish the existence of self-gifting behaviour in China, particularly in the motivations for this behaviour in positive contexts, and further compared motivations for and the emotions associated with SGCB in the UK and mainland China.

From their interviews, the authors found SGCB existed in China and in the UK but with important differences in the preferred self-gift occasions, the gifts chosen, and the emotions experienced after self-gift giving. For example, they found Chinese SGCB to be particularly affected by the importance of the family, group-association orientation of the self, and the "face" concept. Contexts related to work, holiday, or receiving money are the main positive circumstances for self-gift giving. But for UK participants, these self-gifts are noticeably perceived as deserved by the self-attribution of the achievements, while for the Chinese, the gifts chosen are often not purely self-oriented. The findings from this study bear implications beyond SGCB. Interpersonal communication and relationship (i.e. Chinese *guanxi*) play a crucial role in initiating, facilitating, and sustaining business in China. For this reason, marketers targeting China may benefit from understanding important aspects of SGCB, as this study reported, for planning and executing communication approaches when interacting with Chinese customers.

The eighth paper, by Louise Canning and Isabelle Szmigin, 'Death and disposal: The universal, environmental dilemma', makes a very interesting contribution to this special issue by focusing on the disposal of the dead and relating this to environmental concerns in marketing and consumer behaviour. Few authors in the marketing and consumer behaviour have addressed issues around death and dying (few notable papers include the work of Bonsu & Belk, 2003; Gabel, Mansfield, & Westbrook, 1996; Gentry, Kennedy, Paul, & Hill, 1994; O'Donohoe & Turley, 2000, 2006), and yet decisions regarding the disposal of the dead do form part of the consumption cycle, and from a consumer culture theory perspective could be considered a 'neglected experiential, social and cultural dimension of consumption in context' (Arnould & Thompson, 2005, p. 869) worthy of further investigation. Discussing the disposal practices that dominate in different countries, the authors draw attention to the very real environmental challenges associated with the disposal of the dead. There are concerns around resources and substances associated with the disposal process (e.g. chemicals for embalmment, wood for coffins, energy requirements for cremations) and issues around land (and sea) use for disposal. The authors offer some fascinating insights into cross-cultural practices around the disposal of the dead, and adopting a consumer culture theory approach (Arnould & Thompson, 2005), they demonstrate the impact of cultural, social, economic, and market contexts on the way that consumer demand is managed. They also draw attention to the impact of disposal processes on the maintenance of identity beyond death, contrasting the symbolism of the various cross-cultural practices. They conclude by discussing the issues around natural burials, and how they go some way to addressing the range of environmental concerns, as well as more personal reasons to do with the identity of the deceased and how they are memorialised (Clayden & Dixon, 2007).

The final paper, by Stephanie Slater and Mirella Yani-de-Soriano, turns to methodological issues that are critically important for researching consumers across countries or in multicultural societies. The authors point out that many theories have rarely been tested in cultures with different languages and traditions, and confronted with diverse environmental conditions, such as Asia, Africa, and Latin America. By chronological reflection, they note that a trend in asserting the generalisability of received consumer behaviour theories and findings emerged in the United States during the 1980s and continued into the 1990s. An important factor for the increasing attention to cross-cultural marketing research is the globalisation of marketing activities and the cross-cultural use of advertisements (Malhotra, Agarwal, & Peterson, 1996; Manrai & Manrai, 1996). The authors highlight that a major methodological issue arises regarding either examining and understanding behaviours or concepts from within a specific culture (known as the 'emic' approach) or making generalisations across cultures by taking into account all human behaviour beyond the specificity of an individual culture (known as the 'etic' approach) (Berry, 1990; Douglas & Craig, 1983; Trandis, Malpass, & Davidson, 1971). The difficulty in choosing between these two perspectives is known as the 'emic–etic' dilemma, and this has been the main challenge to international marketing academics and practitioners. By reviewing the literature, the authors report on efforts in searching solutions to tackle the 'emic–etic' challenge for cross-cultural consumer research. In addition, the authors argue that, in fact, it can become difficult to differentiate the emic from the etic (Sekaran, 1983) when people around the globe have been adopting to similar values and behaviours (Nasif, Al-Daeaj, Ebrahimi, & Thibodeaux, 1991) as a result of globalisation and rapid technological advances. A related viewpoint (Cleveland & Laroche, 2007) is that it is no longer appropriate to use countries as the cultural unit of analysis or market segmentation, since most of the world's countries are already highly multicultural. Thus Slater and Yani-de-Soriano concur with the view that the borders among cultures are becoming blurred due to cultural diffusion (or cultural convergence), therefore the samples taken from different cultures might not be independent, leading to biased results (Yeganeh, Su, & Chrysostome, 2004). On this point, they remind us of the early literature (e.g. Naroll, 1961; Strauss et al., 1975; Tylor, 1889) on Sir Francis Galton's argument that if sample independence could not be achieved or methods of correction were not applied then the research findings were of no value (known as Galton's problem). The authors note conflicting views as to whether or not Galton's problem is solvable and some suggestions for solutions (e.g. Denton, 2007; Naroll & D'Andrade, 1963; Strauss et al., 1975).

Slater and Yani-de-Soriano also introduce some most recent methodological literature that take into account the current trend in utilising the Internet and web-based data-collection methods. Several new issues are noted in this Internet-specific context such as participant behaviour (e.g. drop-out rates for panels, incomprehension, response set bias, low response rate, and subject fraud), data integrity (e.g. caused by technical problems), and ethics (keeping privacy, anonymity, confidentiality, and avoiding stress related to sensitive questions).

Slater and Yani-de-Soriano's paper suggests that the twenty-first century marketing is challenged by an increased pace of globalisation, the exponential growth of the Internet, diversity of marketing-research contexts, and growing multicultural societies. This paper highlights the problems, issues, and advancement in solutions for better understanding such challenges and better approaches to research methodology for cross-cultural research. It represents a worthy attempt to encourage researchers towards a more sensitive awareness of the methodological issues when conducting cross-cultural research at the global context and/or within individual multicultural societies.

## Reviewers

All papers within the special issue were subject to a double-blind peer-review process. Many thanks to the following academics who contributed their time and expertise to the review process:

*Temi Ambibola, Warwick University*

*Susan Auty, Lancaster University*

*Emma Banister, Lancaster University*

*Shona Bettany, Bradford University*

*Michael Bosnjak, Free University of Bozen-Bolzano, Italy*

*Iain Black, University of Edinburgh*

*Andreas Chatzidikis, Royal Holloway, University of London*

*Mark Cleveland, University of Western Ontario*

*Sue Eccles, Bournemouth University*

*Guliz Ger, Bilkent University*

*Sally Hibbert, Nottingham University Business School*

*Paul Hewer, University of Strathclyde*

*Gillian Hogg, Heriot-Watt University*

*Gillian Hopkinson, Lancaster University*

*Gavin Jack, La Trobe University, Melbourne*

*Hans-Rüdiger Kaufmann, University of Nicosia, Cyprus*

*Ben Kerrane, Bradford University*

*Dannie Kjeldgaard, University of Southern Denmark*

*Debra Laverie, Texas Tech University*

*Mike Lee, University of Auckland*

*Nick Lee, Aston Business School*

*Andrew Lindridge, Open University*

*Marius Luedicke, University of Innsbruck*

*Morven McEachern, Lancaster University*

*Peter McGoldrick, Manchester Business School*

*Dominic Medway, Manchester Business School*

*Stephanie O'Donohoe, Edinburgh University*

*Stan Paliwoda, University of Strathclyde*

*Andrew Pressey, Lancaster University*

*Stuart Roper, Manchester Business School*

*Yasmin Sekhon, Bournemouth University*

*Avi Shankar, Bath University*

*Deirdre Shaw, Glasgow University*

*Edward Shiu, University of Strathclyde*

*Geoff Simmons, University of Ulster*

*Andrew Smith, Nottingham University Business School*

*Darach Turley, Dublin City University*

*Ekant Veer, University of Canterbury, New Zealand*

*Cleopatra Veloutsou, Glasgow University*

*Rick T Wilson, Hofstra University*

## References

Ahuvia, A.C. (2005). Beyond the extended self: Loved objects and consumers' identity narratives. *Journal of Consumer Research, 32*, 171–184.

Arnould, E.J., & Thompson, C.J. (2005). Consumer culture theory (CCT): Twenty years of research. *Journal of Consumer Research, 31*, 868–881.

Arthur, D. (2006). Authenticity and consumption in the Australian hip hop culture. *Qualitative Market Research: An International Journal, 9*(2), 140–156.

Askegaard, S., Arnould, E.J., & Kjeldgaard, D. (2005). Post-assimilationist ethnic consumer research: Qualifications and extensions. *Journal of Consumer Research, 32*, 160–170.

Bearden, W.O., Money, R.B., & Nevins, J.L. (2006). Multidimensional versus unidimensional measures in assessing national culture values: The Hofstede VSM 94 example. *Journal of Business Research, 59*, 195–203.

Belk, R. (2006). The meaning of cool: Transformations within global consumer culture. Paper presented at Lancaster University Management School, 5th May 2006.

Berry, J.W. (1990). Imposed etics, emics and derived emics: Their conceptual and operational status in cross-cultural psychology. In T.N. Headland & M. Harris (Eds.), *Emics and etics: The insider/outsider debate* (pp. 84–89). Newbury Park, CA: Sage.

Bonsu, S.K., & Belk, R.W. (2003). Don't go cheaply into that good night: Death-ritual consumption in Asante, Ghana. *Journal of Consumer Behaviour, 30*(1), 41–55.

Cherrier, H., & Murray, J.F. (2007). Reflexive dispossession and the self: Constructing a processual theory of identity. *Consumption, Markets and Culture, 10*(1), 1–29.

Clayden, A., & Dixon, K. (2007). Woodland burial: Memorial arboretum versus native woodland? *Mortality, 12*(3), 240–260.

Cleveland, M., & Laroche, M. (2007). Acculturation to the global consumer culture: Scale development and research paradigm. *Journal of Business Research, 60*(3), 249–259.

Collins, H.M. (1985). *Changing order: Replication and induction in scientific practice*. Beverly Hills, CA: Sage.

Cushman, P. (1990). Why the self is empty: Toward a historically situated psychology. *American Psychologist, 45*(5), 599–611.

Denton, T. (2007). Yet another solution to Galton's problem. *Cross-Cultural Research, 41*(1), 32–45.

Douglas, S.P., & Craig, C.S. (1983). *International marketing research*. Englewood Cliffs, NJ: Prentice-Hall.

Douglas, S.P., & Nijssen, E.J. (2003). On the use of 'borrowed' scales in cross-national research: A cautionary note. *International Marketing Review, 20*(6), 621–642.

Evanschitzky, H., Baumgarth, C., Hubbard, R., & Armstrong, J.S. (2007). Replication research's disturbing trend. *Journal of Business Research, 60*(4), 411–415.

Firat, F.A., & Venkatesh, A. (1995). Liberatory postmodernism and the reenchantment of consumption. *Journal of Consumer Research, 22*(3), 239–267.

Fournier, S. (1998). Consumers and their brands: Developing relationship theory in consumer research. *Journal of Consumer Research, 24*(4), 343–373.

Gabel, T., Mansfield, P., & Westbrook, K. (1996). The disposal of consumers: An exploratory analysis of death-related consumption. *Advances in Consumer Research, 23*(1), 361–367.

Gentry, J.W., Kennedy, P.F., Paul, K., & Hill, R.P. (1994). The vulnerability of those grieving the death of a loved one: Implications for public policy. *Journal of Public Policy and Marketing, 13*(2), 128–142.

Ger, G., & Belk, R.W. (1996). I'd like to buy the world a coke: Consumptionscapes of the less affluent world. *Journal of Consumer Policy, 19*, 271–304.

Giulianotti, R., & Robertson, R. (2007). Forms of glocalisation: Globalization and the migration strategies of Scottish football fans in North America. *Sociology, 41*(1), 133–152.

Hogg, M., & Terry, D. (2000). Social identity and self-categorization process in organizational contexts. *Academy of Management Review, 25*, 121–140.

Holt, D.B., & Thompson, C.J. (2004). Man-of-action heroes: The pursuit of heroic masculinity in everyday consumption. *Journal of Consumer Research, 31*, 425–440.

Hubbard, R., & Armstrong, J.S. (1994). Replications and extensions in marketing: Rarely published but quite contrary. *International Journal of Research in Marketing, 11*(3), 233–248.

Jafari, A., & Goulding, C. (2008). 'We are not terrorists!' UK-based Iranians, consumption practices and the 'torn self'. *Consumption, Markets and Culture, 11*(2), 73–91.

Kjeldgaard, D., & Askegaard, S. (2006). The glocalization of youth culture: The global youth segment as structures of common difference. *Journal of Consumer Research, 33*, 231–247.

Klausegger, C., Sinkovics, R.R., & Zou, H.J. (2007). Information overload: A cross-national investigation of influence factors and effects. *Marketing Intelligence and Planning, 25*(7), 691–718.

Koçak, A., Abimbola, T., & Özer, A. (2007). Consumer brand equity in a cross-cultural replication: An evaluation of a scale. *Journal of Marketing Management, 23*(1), 157–173.

Kozinets, R.V. (2002). The field behind the screen: Using netnography for marketing research in online communities. *Journal of Marketing Research, 39*, 61–72.

Lash, J., & Wellington, F. (2007). Competitive advantage on a warming planet. *Harvard Business Review, 85*(3), 94–102.

Lass, P., & Hart, S. (2004). National cultures, values and lifestyles influencing consumers' perceptions towards sexual imagery in alcohol advertising: An exploratory study in the UK, Germany and Italy. *Journal of Marketing Management, 20*(5/6), 607–623.

Madden, C.S., Easley, R.W., & Dunn, M.G. (1995). How journal editors view replication research. *Journal of Advertising, 24*(4), 77–87.

Malhotra, N.K., Agarwal, J., & Peterson, M. (1996). Methodological issues in cross-cultural marketing research. *International Marketing Review, 13*(5), 7–43.

Manrai, L., & Manrai, A.K. (1996). Current issues in cross-cultural and cross-national research. *International Journal of Consumer Marketing, 8*(3/4), 9–22.

Markus, H.R., & Kitayama, S. (1991). Culture and the self: Implications for cognition, emotion and motivation. *Psychological Review, 98*, 224–253.

Mesquita, B., & Karasawa, M. (2004). Self-conscious emotions as dynamic cultural processes. *Psychological Inquiry, 15*(2), 161–166.

Miller, T. (2009, May). *Engaging with the maternal: Tentative mothering acts and the props of performance.* Paper presented in the Motherhood, Consumption and Transition, 2nd seminar, Lancaster University, UK.

Mitchell, V.-W., & Bates, L. (1998). UK consumer decision-making styles. *Journal of Marketing Management, 14*(1), 199–225.

Murray, J.B. (2002). The politics of consumption: A Re-inquiry on Thompson and Haytko's (1997) 'Speaking of Fashion'. *Journal of Consumer Research, 29,* 427–440.

Naroll, R. (1961). Two solutions to Galton's problem. In F. Moore (Ed.), *Readings in cross-cultural methodology.* New Haven: HRAF Press.

Naroll, R., & D'Andrade, R.G. (1963). Two further solutions to Galton's problem. *American Anthropologist, New Series, 65*(5), 1053–1067.

Nasif, E.G., Al-Daeaj, H., Ebrahimi, B., & Thibodeaux, M.S. (1991). Methodological problems in cross-cultural research: An updated review. *Management International Review, 31*(1), 79–91.

O'Donohoe, S., & Turley, D. (2000). Dealing with death: Art, mortality and the marketplace. In S. Brown & A. Patterson (Eds.), *Imagining marketing: Art, aesthetics and the avant-garde* (pp. 86–106). London: Routledge.

O'Donohoe, S., & Turley, D. (2006). Compassion at the counter: Service providers and bereaved consumers. *Human Relations, 59*(10), 1429–1448.

Oswald, L.R. (1999). Culture swapping: Consumption and the ethnogenesis of middle-class Haitian immigrants. *Journal of Consumer Research, 25,* 303–318.

Penaloza, L.N. (1994). Atravesando fronteras/border crossings: A critical ethnographic exploration of the consumer acculturation of Mexican immigrants. *Journal of Consumer Research, 21,* 289–294.

Qian, W., Razzaque, M., & Keng, K. (2007). Chinese cultural values and gift-giving behaviour. *Journal of Consumer Marketing, 24*(4), 214–228.

Robertson, R. (1994). Globalization or glocalisation? *Journal of International Communication, 1*(1), 33–52.

Robertson, R., & White, K.E. (2005). Globalization: Sociology and cross-disciplinarity. In C. Calhoun, C. Rojek, & B.S. Turner (Eds.), *The Sage handbook of sociology* (pp. 345–366). London: Sage.

Salciuviene, L., Auruskeviciene, V., & Lydeka, Z. (2005). An assessment of various approached for cross-cultural consumer research. *Problems and Perspectives in Management, 3,* 147–159.

Sekaran, U. (1983). Methodological and theoretical issues and advancements in cross-cultural research. *Journal of International Business Studies, 14,* 61–73.

Shavitt, S., Lalwani, A.K., Zhang, J., & Torelli, C.J. (2006). The horizontal/vertical distinction in cross-cultural consumer research. *Journal of Consumer Psychology, 16*(4), 325–342.

Singh, N., Kwon, I.-W., & Pereira, A. (2003). Cross-cultural consumer socialization: An exploratory study of socialization influences across three ethnic groups. *Psychology and Marketing, 20*(10), 867–881.

Sproles, G.B., & Kendall, E.L. (1986). A methodology for profiling consumers' decision making styles. *Journal of Consumers Affairs, 20*(2), 267–279.

Strauss, D.J., Orans, M., Barnes, J.A., Chaney, P., de Leeuwe, J., Ember, M., et al. (1975). Mighty shifts: A critical appraisal of solutions to Galton's problem and a partial solution. *Current Anthropology, 16*(4), 573–594.

Thompson, C.J. (1996). Caring consumers: Gendered consumption meanings and the juggling lifestyle. *Journal of Consumer Research, 22*(4), 388–407.

Thompson, C.J., & Haytko, D.L. (1997). Speaking of fashion: Consumers' uses of fashion discourses and the appropriation of countervailing cultural meanings. *Journal of Consumer Research, 24,* 15–42.

Thompson, C., Locander, W., & Pollio, H. (1990). The lived meaning of free choice: An existential-phenomenological description of everyday consumer experiences of contemporary married women. *Journal of Consumer Research, 17,* 346.

Trandis, H.C., Malpass, R., & Davidson, A. (1971). Cross-cultural psychology. In B. Siegel (Ed.), *Biennial review of anthropology* (pp. 1–84). Stanford, CA: Stanford University Press.

Turner, J.C. (1987). A self-categorization theory. In M. Hogg, P. Oakes, S. Reicher, & M. Wetherell (Ed.), *Rediscovering the social group: A self-categorization theory* (pp. 42–67). Oxford: Blackwell.

Tylor, E. (1889). On a method of investigating the development of institutions applied to the laws of marriage and descent. *Journal of the Royal Anthropological Institute, 18*(3), 245–272.

Ustuner, T., & Holt, D.B. (2007). Dominated consumer acculturation: The social construction of poor migrant women's consumer identity projects in a Turkish squatter. *Journal of Consumer Research, 34,* 41–56.

Yeganeh, H., Su, Z., & Chrysostome, E.V.M. (2004). A critical review of epistemological and methodological issues in cross-cultural research. *Journal of Comparative International Management, 7*(2), 66–86.

Zhou, C., & Guang, H. (2007). Gift giving culture in China and its cultural values, *Intercultural Communication Studies, 16*(2), 81–93.

# Material man is not an island: Coping with cultural fracture

Andrea Davies, *University of Leicester, UK*
James A. Fitchett, *University of Leicester, UK*

**Abstract** Consumer acculturation is important to visitors crossing cultural borders, but the role of possessions on visitors' ability to cope in a host environment is less well understood. Two-stage structural equation modelling is employed to understand the relationship of possession centrality, lifestyle behaviours, purchases, and possession ownership on cultural fracture experiences. The possessions that educational visitors bring from home and goods they purchase once in the host culture relate positively to cultural fracture, demonstrating possible anchoring effects of possessions brought from home and the culturally disorientating effects of making purchases in a host cultural space. Possession centrality, or the skill and confidence in aspects of consumption and possession use, is principal in alleviating the experiences of cultural fracture. Visitors possessing higher levels of possession centrality experience less fracture than those with lower levels of possession centrality. This study highlights how consumption-related competencies function as acculturation mechanisms.

## Introduction

In a globalising world, where goods, capital, information, and people are more able to move between cultural spaces, an in-depth understanding of the experiences of crossing cultural boundaries is increasingly necessary (Andreasen, 1990; Cleveland & Laroche, 2006; Cui, 2001; Penaloza & Gilly, 1999). Acculturation is the process of learning about, and adapting to, norms and behaviours of new host cultures. It is not a single response to transition but an umbrella term used to describe many different possible responses (Berry, 1997; Bhatia & Ram, 2009) from assimilation and integration to isolation, separation, and segregation (Lerman, Maldonado, & Luna, 2008). More recently, research has sought to critique and move beyond assimilationist accounts to focus of a number of post-assimilationist perspectives (Askegaard, Arnould, & Kjeldgaard, 2005; Üstüner & Holt, 2007). People moving between spaces negotiate between competing cultural values and reconstruct new identities in which their ethnicity is used as a salient and resonant category. The immigrant's behavioural

disposition towards a cross-section of lifestyle behaviours will likely impact the extent of cultural fracture. One of the main objectives for examining acculturation has been to establish procedures and support structures that enable transition periods to be less traumatic and disorientating for individuals moving between cultural spaces (Rudmin, 2009). For example, reducing the stress and anxiety that international students experience because of crossing between cultural environments has been shown to have a significant impact on level of academic achievement (Gmelch, 1997; Jackson, 2009; Nolan, 1990). Similarly, organisations have made extensive efforts to understand further acculturation processes for international and expatriate workers (Shaffer, Harrison, & Gilley, 1999; Stroh, Dennis, & Cramer, 1994). One of the main ways to examine acculturation has been to map immigrant lifestyle. Acculturation is not seen as an outcome or goal, but rather as an ongoing process with a number of responses (Berry, 1997; Wallendorf & Reilly, 1983). Immigrant lifestyles have been classified in terms of assimilation, negotiation, and affirmation. These show how immigrants manage the comforts and contradictions of their ethnic home culture and a new culture, sometimes integrating the two in some unique way to create a 'new' (sub)culture.

## Cultural fracture

Cultural fracture are those feelings and thoughts individuals associate with an acculturation situation in which they must modify, appropriate, and in some instances relearn their previously held and accepted skills, expectations, behaviours, values, and competencies from 'home'. Individuals have described different levels and types of experiences, including anxiety, elation, excitement, disorientation, and frustration, and these experiences have been categorised into three basic types: emotional, symbolic, and functional (Aycan, 1997; Davies & Fitchett, 2004; Yavas & Bodur, 1999). Emotional fracture includes aspects of psychological adjustment, such as feelings of loneliness, feeling able to maintain aspects of ones own typical behaviour and norms, the ability to make friends and establish new social relationships, and being able to establish group membership (Ethier & Deaux, 1994; Fritz, Chin, & DeMarinis, 2008; Ward & Kennedy, 1994). Symbolic fracture includes sociocultural adjustment, such as abilities to understand and interpret social rules, understanding the types of behaviour appropriate to adopt in particular social situations, and overcoming communication problems (Chataway & Berry, 1989; Triandis, 1989). Functional fracture includes pragmatic or procedural aspects of adaptation, such as getting used to public transport, new working arrangements, and sorting out personal financial arrangements.

Understandably, considerable attention has been given to explaining cultural fracture so as to enable the design and management of programs to facilitate positive acculturation. Factors including the situations and institutions of the new 'host' environment (e.g. O'Guinn & Faber, 1985; Penaloza, 1994), the cultural history of the visitor (e.g. Chataway & Berry, 1989), their expectations of what life will be like in the new host culture (e.g. Shaffer et al., 1999; Stroh et al., 1994), their intended length and purpose of stay (Doran, 1994), and their ability to learn and appropriate relevant language and social skills (Berry, 1997; Doran, 1994) have been shown to mediate the experiences of cultural fracture. Little attention has, however, been given to the impacts of consumption and market-based activities in helping individuals cope with cultural fracture. This represents a potentially significant omission, which is important for understanding better material culture and consumer behaviours. This paper explores the hypotheses that possession centrality (a consumer-related attitude) and the purchase and ownership of possessions (market-based activities) can ease the experiences of cultural fracture.

## Consumption as a process of learning about a host culture

There is substantial support for the logic of our investigation: consumption is conceptualised as a core cultural information system through which categories of culture are made visible and stable (Douglas & Isherwood, 1978; Miller, 1995); people in consumer societies are known to use their consumption behaviours and other marketing technologies (such as brands) as resources to construct identity (Belk, 1988; Elliott & Wattanasuwan, 1998; Escalas & Bettman, 2005; Vanitha, Page, & Gürhan-Canli, 2007); and, especially in the case of global consumer brands, consumption symbolism often has transnational signification. Thus there is a strong argument to suggest that consumption and material possessions are some of the most accessible forms of cultural knowledge available to individuals moving from one cultural context to another. For example, individuals may find getting to know people, making friends, sorting out official documentation, and working out how the transport system works to be a highly disorientating experience, but they may find that the basic process of shopping, including where to shop for various items, recognising brands, selecting goods, exchanging money, and assessing product choice, as easier to negotiate (Michon & Chebat, 2004). The point to emphasise here is that markets, marketing, and consumption may provide the most global and cross-cultural sign system available to visitors faced with an unfamiliar environment. This suggests that visitors' ability to participate in market- and consumer-related activities might be a key factor in reducing cultural fracture, and studies of materialism may useful in this regard (Belk, 1985; Ger & Belk, 1990, 1999; Kilbourne, Grungahen, & Foley, 2005).

Learning about consumption values within a given culture is generally referred to as consumer acculturation and is recognised as an important aspect of acculturation (O'Guinn & Faber, 1985; Penaloza, 1994; Wallendorf & Reilly, 1983). However, studies to date do not fully appreciated the role that market structures and consumption activities may have as a means of learning about the broader (i.e. non-consumption-based) norms, values, and traditions of a host culture. Penaloza's (1989) study of consumer acculturation argues that immigrant consumer behaviour involves more than a simple assimilation of established consumption patterns. She shows that consumer acculturation is an eclectic process of learning and selectively displaying culturally defined skills and behaviours. The ability to appropriate and master certain types of cultural knowledge is thus identified as the key antecedent of consumer acculturation. One problem with this conceptual premise is that it denies that immigrant consumption may in fact constitute an important type of cultural learning.

This study aims to establish whether consumption activities and attitudes are an important means of learning about a host culture. Rather than locating culture as an antecedent of consumer competence and acculturation, this study explores whether it is right to position consumption as an important antecedent of cultural knowledge, that is, consumption activities and attitudes are a vehicle that provides access to cultural knowledge and understanding. In this sense, consumption-related activities have the potential to aid individuals as they cope with their experiences of cultural fracture.

## Possessions and possession centrality

A rationale for locating consumption activities and attitudes as important antecedents to acculturation is supported by social psychological insights into consumer behaviour. In the absence of concrete evidence to answer abstract questions about who we are, Belk (1985, 1988) suggests that surrogate forms of evidence are typically drawn upon, including the things we do and the things we have. Crossing culture is a disorientating experience that potentially threatens to dismantle a familiar sense of self, and continuity is often sought through consumption and market-related institutions (Mehta & Belk, 1991). The importance of possessions (the things we have) in maintaining a positive self and social identity is believed to be more pronounced in consumer cultures (Belk, 1985).

Possession centrality is a measure of the importance and significance that possessions have for an individual's sense of self and identity (Cleveland, Loroche, & Papadopulous, 2009; Richins & Dawson, 1992). People with high possession centrality are more materialistic than those with low possession centrality. Richins and Dawson (1992, p. 304) state that 'materialists place possessions and their acquisition at the center of their lives'. For Richins and Dawson, acquisition or possession centrality is the first of three themes of materialism, along with acquisition as the pursuit of happiness, and possession-defined success. Ger and Belk (1996) provide a corroborating account for possession centrality, finding that 'materialists are thought to excessively or obsessively value acquiring and keeping possessions'. Possession centrality does not necessarily account for the amount of possessions owned or the desire to acquire more or specific types of possessions. Research shows that that some people turn to materialism and therefore have higher possession centrality when they experience uncertainty (L. Chang & Arkin, 2002).

It is important to note that measures of materialism implicate the meanings of consumption and not just specific buying processes (e.g. Wallendorf, Belk, & Heisley, 1988). It is not just a matter of whether people chose to buy or not to buy particular goods, but the centrality of possessions to an individual's sense of self and judgements of others. Materialism is not a behavioural disposition but a consumption-related attitude that guides behaviour (Cleveland et al., 2009). It is possible to conceive of individuals, for example, who engage in the market but who attach little meaning or significance to their purchases. There may be individuals who are highly materialistic and have an aptitude for using material possessions in their expression of self but who, for various reasons, limit the amount and type of purchases they make. As such, to take the ownership and purchase of possessions as an indicator of materialism would be an error.

To argue that visitors who hold more materialistic attitudes and feel competent with consumption-based market structures and information are better equipped to deal with, and overcome, aspects of cultural fracture more effectively than visitors who are less materialistic is consistent with the theory outlined here. Visitors who feel particularly competent in using material possessions and reading the symbolic meanings of material culture are likely to access/acquire more easily an understanding of their host culture, and as such report lower levels of cultural fracture experience, when compared with visitors who are less competent in using material possessions or symbolic skill.

Materialistic attitudes as consumption-based skills are distinguished from possession ownership in this study, which then seeks to examine the ability of both possession centrality and possession ownership to reduce cultural fracture and facilitate acculturation. Specifically, our research examines the impact of possessions and purchases, possession centrality, and lifestyle behaviours on the experience of cultural fracture.

# Empirical study

## Study administration and sampling

The marketing and business discipline has recognised that there are many types of international visitor. Penaloza (1989) postulates that the least 'naturalised' acculturative change would result from a novel experience in a foreign culture, such as a vacation, whereas the most 'naturalised', or assimilating, mode of acculturation would result from an extended stay in another country. Elsewhere, attention to short stay and particularly to students as international visitors has been the focus for the theoretical development of cultural shock and acculturation (e.g. Furnham & Bochner, 1986). Common queries associated with the use of student samples are less relevant for acculturation research, as a strong case can be put forward to suggest that they form an important and sizable migrant group. There are currently an estimated one million international student movements worldwide. Whilst the origins of international students are diverse, representing virtually every country in the world, the destinations of international students are relatively small, with more than 90% of movements accounted for by less than five destinations (Australia, Canada, New Zealand, the United States, and the UK). The UK's international market share of international students stood at around 11% in 2004 (Vickers & Bekhradnia, 2007). The 2006/07 National Statistics on student enrolments on higher-education courses in England show that the number of all other European Union (EU) domiciled students increased by 6% (from 106,225 to 112,260) and the number of non-EU domiciled students increased by 7% (from 223,855 to 239,210) on the previous year (Higher Education Statistics Agency, 2008). In 2004/5, the annual value of international students in UK higher-education institutions in tuition fees alone was estimated to be in the region of £1.4 billion (see Vickers & Bekhradnia, 2007), with a further £2.35 billion estimated net injection into the UK economy resulting from expenditure by international students.

In this study, data were collected by interviewing recent immigrants who came for a medium-term educational stay. Respondents had been resident in the UK for less than three months and had moved beyond the 'honeymoon' period of travelling to a new country (Oberg, 1960). The data-collection phase was completed over a 12-week period between October and January. This was the first semester period of academic study for the respondents. An exploratory phase of focus groups was completed by week 4, and the questionnaire was administered during weeks 8–12. Six focus-group interviews were completed, involving between six and eight participants per group. The groups had a mixed composition in terms of gender and cultural background. The format of the focus-group discussions was structured around a series of questions relating to lifestyle, themes of acculturation, and possessions brought from home.

Data were collected in a face-to-face interview survey on a convenience sample of 576 international students. The interviews took place at the critical stage of negotiating or coping with the realities of their cultural fracture. There were slightly more women (60.1%) than men (39.9%), although both genders were represented across four age cohorts: 17–21 year olds (25.0%), 22–23 year olds (26.0%), 24–25 year olds (24.0%), and 26+ year olds (25.0%). The majority of respondents were single and unmarried (88.5%), did not have children (95.8%), and lived with their parents prior to arriving (72.0%). A significant minority (42.9%) had left full-time employment to study. In terms of nationality, just over half of the sample was from China or South East Asia (52.3%), and a quarter was from Western Europe or North America (24.5%). Other sample respondents had travelled from Central or Eastern Europe or Russia (11.2%). Respondents from the Indian subcontinent, the Middle East, Central or South America, and Africa constituted small minorities in the sample.

## Construct description and measurement

The survey captured four key constructs: cultural fracture experience, possession centrality, possessions brought from home and purchases made in UK stores, and lifestyle behaviours in the UK.

## Cultural fracture

Symbolic, emotional, and functional aspects of cultural fracture were measured on seven-point experiential-Likert scales. Seventeen items were developed from focus groups and captured in the questionnaire. A total of 66.1% of the sample indicated a strong expectation that they have to be more independent in the UK than they would at home, and 54.9% of the sample felt quite lonely in the UK. Feelings of frustration because it is difficult to follow usual patterns of behaviour (41.6%), finding it difficult to assess what people are thinking and feeling (39.4%), and feeling unsure of how to greet and behave in different social situations (38.0%) were also significant expressions of cultural fracture among the sample. Problems with using public transport were reported by a small proportion of the sample (24.7%). Overall, respondents reported higher levels of emotional fracture ($\mu = 3.9$) than symbolic ($\mu = 3.8$) and functional fracture ($\mu = 3.6$).

## Possession centrality

Possession centrality captures materialistic attitudes and, in the survey, it was measured using the six items from the scale developed by Ger and Belk (1990) and Belk (1984, 1985) and captured on seven-point Likert scales. A minority of respondents (13.1%) disagreed that having their own things around them was important or that they would feel part of them was missing if they did not have their possessions around them (29.1%). Respondents over the age of 26 reported marginally lower levels of possession centrality ($\mu = 4.8$) compared to other age groups ($\mu$ for 17–21 yrs = 5.1, 22–23 yrs = 5.0, and 24–25 yrs = 5.2; $F = 3.32, df = 3, p = .02$). This is consistent with Belk's (1985) findings that show materialist values decrease with age.

## Consumption-related behaviours (possessions and purchases)

Seven categories of popular possessions brought from home and 15 popular products purchased post-arrival in the host culture served to construct two summative indices: an index of possession brought from home and an index of purchases made in the UK (see Table 1). They are related but distinct aspects of possession ownership ($r = .14$, $p = .001$). Product and service items for both indices were developed from qualitative analysis of six focus groups. Questionnaire piloting and an open-ended survey

**Table 1** Measurement constructs.

| Composite variables | Items used to construct composite variables | Factor loadings | Alpha reliability | Mean inter-item correlation |
|---|---|---|---|---|
| Emotional fracture | I have found it frustrating because I can't do the things I normally like to do | .55 | .7 | .4 |
| | I have always felt comfortable and relaxed here (reversed) | .70 | | |
| | There are times I have felt quite lonely here | .71 | | |
| Symbolic fracture | It hard to know what people are thinking and feeling | .70 | .6 | .4 |
| | I have found it difficult to know what type of greetings are appropriate for different social situations | .58 | | |
| | I quickly run out of things to talk about in everyday conversations | .50 | | |
| Functional fracture | Setting up a bank account and organising my finances has been relatively easy to do (reversed) | . 56 | .5 | .3 |
| | Working out how to use the trains and buses has been straightforward (reversed) | .71 | | |
| Lifestyle behaviours | Attitudes about food preparation | .45 | .5 | .2 |
| | Attitudes about fashion and clothing | .48 | | |
| | Attitudes about leisure activities | .70 | | |
| | Attitudes about language preference | .46 | | |
| | Attitudes towards media and current affairs | .45 | | |
| | Comparative attitudes on UK and home culture | .62 | | |
| | Attitudes about grocery shopping | .75 | | |
| Possession C = centrality | Having my own things around me is important to me | .75 | .7 | .3 |
| | If I couldn't have my possessions with me, I would feel that part of me was missing | .69 | | |
| | The things I own and buy really say something about me | .61 | | |

*(Continued)*

**Table 1 (Continued).**

| Composite variables | Items used to construct composite variables | Factor loadings | Alpha reliability | Mean inter-item correlation |
|---|---|---|---|---|
| | You can tell a lot about a person by looking at the possessions they have around them | .63 | | |
| Possessions brought index | CDs and music (82.9%), photographs of family and friends (79.8%), warm clothing on the expectation that the weather in the UK would be cold (78.9%), cameras and photographic equipment (76.1%), clothes for formal occasions (66.1%), computer equipment (61.7%), food items that were expected to be unavailable in the UK (61.2%) | | | |
| Purchases in UK index | Personal hygiene products (77.1%), domestic cooking appliances and utensils (73.1%), food items that were typical of the UK (66.4%), home furnishings (55.7%), warm clothing (55.7%), pictures and posters (50.2%), mobile phone (46.3%), music (43.8%), computer equipment (37.1%), sport equipment (33.3%), formal clothes (30.6%), British clothing (28.6%), camera (23.4%), TV/Video (19.1%), clothes to show where I am from (12.0%) | | | |

question ensured that the products, services, and possessions measured were comprehensive and exhaustive, providing a measure of content validity.

### Lifestyle behaviours

Acculturation behaviours include assimilation, cultural negotiation, and cultural affirmation (Berry, 1997; Wallendorf & Reilly, 1983), and have principally been measured as the extent to which an immigrant's lifestyle adopts characteristics that show compatibility with and replication of the host culture. Lifestyle measures used in the survey measured respondent behavioural disposition towards cooking and food preparation, cultural fashion styles, grocery shopping, choice of leisure partners/ activities, language use, and use of UK media. A summative lifestyle acculturation index was developed, where low values identify respondents who have a greater tendency to enact a cultural affirmation lifestyle and high values identify individuals who have a greater tendency to assimilate into a UK lifestyle. The degree to which behavioural disposition towards a cross-section of lifestyle behaviours can explain the experiences of cultural fracture is examined in the analysis. This allows for the relative strength of possession ownership and purchase, possession centrality and lifestyles enacted when resident in the UK to be compared in their ability to explain reported cultural fracture experience. Visitors who were successfully assimilating to the host culture in their lifestyle were expected to report lower levels of cultural fracture than visitors who had not.

Prior to structural equation analysis, several complementary techniques were used to assess the psychometric properties of the measurement scales and refine the scale measures. Internal consistency was measured by alpha reliability (Churchill, 1979; Nunnally, 1978), mean inter-item correlations (Briggs & Cheek, 1986), and exploratory principal component analyses (Bagozzi, 1983; Briggs & Cheek, 1986).

Kaiser-Meyer-Olkin tests of sampling adequacy and Bartlett's test of sphericity indicated that the data were appropriate for principal component analysis. Confirmatory factor analysis was used as a further means to assess the scales. For cultural fracture, these procedures resulted in the deletion of nine items. Final scales for symbolic and emotional fracture are measured by three variables, and functional fracture is measured by two. For possession centrality, scale purification resulted in the deletion of two items. Churchill (1979) recommends that an alpha reliability of .6 would be desirable for exploratory studies. Briggs and Cheek identify problems associated with alpha reliability as a measure of scale homogeneity and recommend using mean inter-item correlation. A mean inter-item correlation of between .2 and .4 is considered optimal. See Table 1.

## Analytic method

Structural equation modelling techniques with asymptotic distribution free estimation is used in this study. It follows a two-stage approach (Anderson & Gerbing, 1988) to avoid interpretational confounding (Bagozzi, 1981) that can occur if the measurement and structural model are estimated simultaneously.

A series of confirmatory factor models were conducted representing stage one in two-stage structural modelling (Anderson & Gerbing, 1988). Cultural fracture, possession centrality, and lifestyle acculturation were subject to confirmatory factor analyses as a three-factor, one-factor, and one-factor models respectively. Initially, very strict models, where all observed items are seen as equal in their correlation with their respective latent constructs, are examined. Here, observed variables are conceived as parallel measures. Possession centrality is the only construct to fulfil this requirement $(x^2 = 18.95, df = 5, p = .01, RMSEA = .07)$. Models and the modification indices are examined, which lead to the requirements for equal correlation to be relaxed. Relaxing the requirement for equal correlation of items with latent constructs results in acceptable model fit for the three-factor cultural fracture scale $(x^2 = 43.42, df = 18, p = .001; RMSEA = .05)$, and one-factor lifestyle acculturation scale $(x^2 = 15.44, df = 14, p = .349; RMSEA = .01)$. The incremental measures of fit recommended by Bagozzi and Yi (1988) and Bagozzi and Kimmel (1995) are at or above the acceptable thresholds in all models: (three-factor cultural fracture: GFI $= .98$; CFI $= .90$; one-factor possession centrality GFI $= .98$, CFI $= .90$; and one-factor lifestyle acculturation: GFI $= .99$, CFI $= .97$).

To establish discriminant validity, pairwise correlations between latent constructs are assessed using nested models where the correlation between two constructs is restricted to 1.0. Goodness of fit statistics for the constrained and unconstrained models are compared, and discriminant validity is confirmed when there is a statistical difference in the chi-square for the unconstrained model when compared to the constrained model (Burnkrant & Page, 1982). Pairwise analysis is employed to establish discriminant validity between measurement constructs. Significant differences are observed for the 15 pairwise comparisons (see Table 2), confirming adequate discriminant validity between exogenous variables, and importantly this highlights that consumption-based activities and possession centrality are discrete and that both are distinct from lifestyle acculturation behaviours.

## Findings

The second-stage of the analysis procedure involved testing the key structural relationships, specifically to examine the relative impact of possession centrality, consumption activity, and lifestyle acculturation on the experience of cultural

**Table 2** Discriminant validity – Chi-square differences for nested model comparisons.

| | $x^2$ value for constrained model ($M_c$) | $x^2$ value for unconstrained model ($M_c$) |
|---|---|---|
| Symbolic cultural fracture and functional cultural fracture | 307.9 | 10.7* |
| Emotional cultural fracture and functional cultural fracture | 298.5 | 11.0* |
| Symbolic cultural fracture and emotional cultural fracture | 58.0 | 25.5* |
| Possession centrality and emotional cultural fracture | 153.5 | 39.6* |
| Possession centrality and symbolic cultural fracture | 165.8 | 41.5* |
| Possession centrality and functional cultural fracture | 247.7 | 17.5* |
| Possession centrality and consumption activity | 549.9 | 17.5* |
| Possession centrality and lifestyle acculturation | 5606.9 | 4.1* |
| Lifestyle acculturation and emotional cultural fracture | 677.6 | 68.4* |
| Lifestyle acculturation and symbolic cultural fracture | 803.9 | 71.3* |
| Lifestyle acculturation and functional cultural fracture | 910.5 | 33.3* |
| Lifestyle acculturation and consumption-based activity | 560.2 | 4.1* |
| Consumption activity and emotional cultural fracture | 4309.2 | 28.9* |
| Consumption activity and symbolic cultural fracture | 5249.5 | 26.5* |
| Consumption-based activity and functional cultural fracture | 1218.1 | 6.6* |

*$p < .001$.

fracture (see Figure 1). Initial model estimation identifies the model to approximate the data at an acceptable level ($x^2 = 24.01$, $df = 10$, $p = .01$, GFI = .99, CFI = .89, RMSEA = .05). An examination of the modification indices indicates that to allow one pair of residual errors to correlate would significantly improve model fit. This approximates a correction for effects like common method variance (Ryan, 1982). The resulting model had improved measures of incremental fit ($x^2 = 19.21$, $df = 9$, $p = .03$, GFI = .99; CFI = .92; RMSEA = .04).

Detailed examination of the structural model shows that the experiences of cultural fracture are significantly related to possession centrality ($B = -.60$, $p = .02$), consumption-based activity ($B = .54$, $p = .02$), and lifestyle acculturation ($B = -.26$, $p = .03$). Together, the degree of variance explained ($R^2$) in cultural fracture by possession centrality, market-based activity, and lifestyle acculturation was 38%, providing a moderate level of explanation. The model is focused on only three

**Figure 1** Structural model.

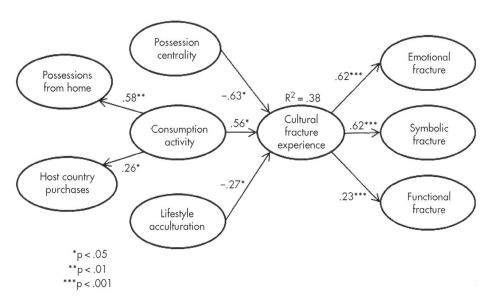

independent variables deemed the most relevant to pursue from the analysis of theory and literature concerning consumption, cultural transition, and acculturation. The structural relationships, their direction, and their relative strength are more important than the overall explained variance, showing that possession ownership and possession centrality have different impacts on cultural fracture.

These findings show that the greater the extent to which individuals assimilate with a host culture in terms of lifestyle behaviours, the smaller the reported incidence of cultural fracture. They also show possession centrality as able to help visitors cope with their experience of cultural fracture, and that possession centrality has the largest relative impact on cultural fracture experiences in our model. Individuals who claim to hold higher levels of possession centrality are shown to experience less cultural fracture. In contrast, the findings also show that possessions brought from home and items purchased in a host country are positively related to feelings of cultural fracture. These findings initially emphasise that ownership and purchase behaviour do not enable understanding and assimilation into new cultural contexts. Rather, these frustrate or anchor visitors at higher levels of fracture experience.

The study findings highlight the importance of possession centrality to understand how consumption is implicated in the experiences of cultural fracture. They reveal that consumption activity or the physical purchase and possession of consumption items have an impact on fracture but that this is distinct from possession centrality. Possession centrality is conceived of as a consumption-related skill and the study findings provide clear indication that it is this skill rather than purchase behaviour that is able to facilitate individuals in understanding and assimilation into a host culture.

## Conclusions and discussion

In common with the canon of research into consumer acculturation (Mehta & Belk, 1991; Ogden, Ogden, & Schau, 2004; Penaloza, 1989, 1994), this study shows that buyer behaviour and materialism are implicated in the experiences of cultural transition. The study findings presented here demonstrate that possession centrality (a consumption-related attitude) can facilitate the transition of moving to a new culture. Purchases and possession ownership have a separate and opposite impact.

The role of consumption activities and possession centrality in moderating cultural fracture is shown to be complex. Possession centrality reduces the degree of cultural fracture that is experienced. However, possession ownership and purchase activity does not guarantee or provide access to understanding and assimilation into a host culture. As such, this study begins to conclude that buying particular types of products or services once a visitor arrives in host cultural environments does not necessarily moderate cultural fracture and nor does successful transition require that certain consumption activities be embraced. This study demonstrates that cultural fracture is lower for those who have greater possession centrality. These people are better equipped to employ material possessions and categories as symbolic resources to represent themselves to others, read the host culture, and feel familiar with it. This highlights the importance of material culture in cultural identity and the role that markets and consumer behaviour have in orientating individuals to their cultural surroundings.

One reading of the data would be that possession centrality moderates what Winkelman (1994) terms role shock, which results from ambiguity about social position, and the loss of 'normal' social relations and roles consistent with a prior-held self-concept. When employed to maintain the self-concept (Belk, 1988), materialistic values and attitudes may be less vulnerable to cultural misrepresentation. Whereas meanings derived from social status and group membership may translate poorly between cultural spaces, meanings derived from beliefs about possessions may be more resistant. Individuals who live in consumer cultures and have therefore developed abilities to read, encode, and interpret consumption symbolism are likely also to be better able to cope with the transnational movement, and it also provides an explanation as to why nationality alone remains a weak predictor of the ability to cope in new cultural environments, since different national boundaries often contain pockets and regions of consumer culture that are absent elsewhere (Batra, 1997). Taken together, the study findings support the view that materialism is implicated in processes of globalisation, despite its numerous culturally specific manifestations. Recent research does, however, suggest that caution is needed to avoid simplistic conclusions on this point of materialism and standardisation. Dana, Steenkamp, and Batra (2006, p. 235) for instance find that 'globalization and cultural homogenization are not equivalent. Rather, consumers more often integrate local and global consumption symbols'. International visitors with higher possession centrality are perhaps better equipped to undertake this integrative activity than those with lower centrality.

### Future research

The study findings presented here can be used to develop further research in several ways. Student visitors were interviewed three months post arrival in a host culture. A longitudinal study would usefully examine the role of possession centrality at all stages of transnational experience. Such a study could assess whether an individual's disposition towards materialism consistently moderates aspects of cultural disorientation. It would, for example, be useful to examine whether possession centrality continues to moderate aspects of long-term cultural fracture, or whether other factors become more relevant. Ethnographic approaches could be usefully deployed to gather a deeper understanding of the biography of visitor's possessions (Shankar, Elliott, & Fitchett, 2009) and their relative importance in culture fracture experiences.

The complexities of research attending to the experiences of crossing culture make it impossible to identify a representative international consumer or a generic model of consumption in acculturation. The acculturation context of students must be recognised as different from longer-term immigration and short-stay vacation travel. International students may desire to try out and experience host UK culture, but there is no necessity to do so. They can, should they wish to do so, spend most of their time and build most of their friendships with others who are equally unfamiliar with UK culture. This may include people who share their own ethnic background, as well as other migrants who have different ethnicities to their own. An additional feature of the student acculturation context is based on the fact that the period of residence in the host culture is predetermined prior to moving, and all of the students we interviewed planned to return to their home cultures at a specified future date. Furthermore, the university environment is a particular type of host environment that is more cosmopolitan, culturally diverse, and ethnically tolerant than many other social contexts in the UK. The cross-cultural experience is also willingly entered into, rather than forced or coerced by, for example, economic or political factors. Finally, it is predicated, at least in part, on the idea of 'experiencing a new culture' and being away from home for a specified period (Gmelch, 1997; Jackson, 2009). The extent to which these findings, which is bound in the cultural context of UK higher education, can relate to other international visitors, travelling to other countries, and for other motivations, offers several sites for study replication and comparison (Chirkov, 2009).

The temporary and time-bound character of many transnational experiences for expatriate workers, students, and tourists means that a type of cultural fracture is also likely to be encountered when visitors return to their 'home' cultural environment (Y. Chang, 2009), and examining the role of possession centrality in moderating repatriation is a logical extension of this research.

# References

Anderson, J.C., & Gerbing, D.W. (1988). Structural equation modelling in practice: A review and recommended two-step approach. *Psychological Bulletin, 103*(3), 411–423.

Andreasen, A.R. (1990). Cultural interpenetration: A critical consumer research issue for the 1990s. In M.E. Goldberg, G. Gorn, & R.W. Pollay (Eds.), *Advances in Consumer Research, 17*, 847–849.

Askegaard, S., Arnould, E.J., & Kjeldgaard, D. (2005). Postassimilationist ethnic consumer research: Qualifications and extensions. *Journal of Consumer Research, 32*, 160–170.

Aycan, Z. (1997). Expatriate adjustment as a multifaceted phenomenon: Individual and organizational level predictors. *International Journal of Human Resource Management, 8*(4), 434–456.

Bagozzi, R.P. (1981). Evaluating structural equation models with unobservable variables and measurement error: A comment. *Journal of Marketing Research, 18*, 375–381.

Bagozzi, R.P. (1983). A holistic methodology for modeling consumer response to innovation. *Operations Research, 31*, 128–176.

Bagozzi, R.P., & Kimmel S.K. (1995). A comparison of leading theories for the prediction of goal-directed behaviours. *British Journal of Social Psychology, 34*, 437–461.

Bagozzi, R.P., & Yi, Y. (1988). On the evaluation of structural equation models. *Journal of the Academy of Marketing Science, 16*, 74–94.

Batra, R. (1997). Marketing issues and challenges in transitional economies. *Journal of International Marketing, 5*(4), 95–114.

Belk, R.W. (1984). Three scales to measure constructs related to materialism: Reliability, validity, and relationships to measures of happiness. In T. Kinnear (Ed.), *Advances in Consumer Research, 11*, 291–297.

Belk, R.W. (1985). Materialism: Trait aspects of living in the material world. *Journal of Consumer Research, 12*, 265–279.

Belk, R.W. (1988). Possessions and the extended self. *Journal of Consumer Research, 15*, 139–168.

Berry, J.W. (1997). Immigration, acculturation, and adaptation. *Applied Psychology: An International Review, 46*, 5–68.

Bhatia, S., & Ram, A. (2009). Theorizing identity in transnational and Diaspora cultures: A critical approach to acculturation. *International Journal of Intercultural Relations, 33*(2), 140–149.

Briggs, S.R., & Cheek, J.M. (1986). The role of factor analysis in the development and evaluation of personality scales. *Journal of Personality, 54*(1), 106–148.

Burnkrant, R.E., & Page, T.J. (1982). An examination of the convergent, discriminant, and predictive validity of Fishbein's behavioral intention model. *Journal of Marketing Research, 19*(4), 550–561.

Chang, L., & Arkin, R.M. (2002). Materialism as an attempt to cope with uncertainty. *Psychology and Marketing, 19*, 389–406.

Chang, Y. (2009). A qualitative study of temporary reentry from significant others' perspective. *International Journal of Intercultural Relations, 33*(3), 259–263.

Chataway, C.J., & Berry, J.W. (1989). Acculturation experiences, appraisal, coping, and adaptation: A comparison of Hong Kong Chinese, French, and English students in Canada. *Canadian Journal of Behavioral Science, 21*(3), 295–309.

Chirkov, V.I. (2009). Critical psychology of acculturation: What do we study and how do we study it, when we investigate acculturation? *International Journal of Intercultural Relations, 32*, 427–440.

Churchill, G.A. (1979). A paradigm for developing better measures of marketing constructs. *Journal of Marketing Research, 16*, 64–73.

Cleveland, M., & Laroche, M. (2006). Acculturation to the global consumer culture: Scale development and research paradigm. *Journal of Business Research, 60*, 249–259.

Cleveland, M., Laroche, M., & Papadopoulos, N. (2009). Cosmopolitanism, consumer ethnocentrism, and materialism: An eight-country study of antecedents and outcomes. *Journal of International Marketing, 17*(1), 116–146.

Cui, G. (2001). Marketing to ethic minority consumers: A historical journey (1932–1997). *Journal of Macromarketing, 21*(1), 23–31.

Dana, L.A., Steenkamp, J.E.M., & Batra, R. (2006). Consumer attitudes toward marketplace globalization: Structure, antecedents and consequences. *International Journal of Research in Marketing, 23*(3), 227–239.

Davies, A., & Fitchett, J.A. (2004). 'Crossing culture': A multi-method enquiry into consumer behaviour and the experience of cultural transition. *Journal of Consumer Behaviour, 3*(4), 315–330.

Doran, K.B. (1994). Exploring cultural differences in consumer decision making: Chinese consumers in Montréal. *Advances in Consumer Research, 21*, 318–322.

Douglas, M., & Isherwood, B. (1978). *The world of goods*. London: Allen Lane.

Elliott, R., & Wattanasuwan, K. (1998). Brands as symbolic resources for the construction of identity. *International Journal of Advertising, 17*, 131–144.

Escalas, J.E., & Bettman, J.R. (2005). Self-construal, reference groups, and brand meaning. *Journal of Consumer Research, 32*(3), 378–389.

Ethier, K., & Deaux, K. (1994). Negotiating social identity when contexts change: Maintaining identification and responding to threat. *Journal of Personality and Social Psychology, 67*(2), 247–251.

Fritz, M.V., Chin, D., & DeMarinis, V. (2008). Stresses, anxiety, acculturation and adjustment among international and North American students. *International Journal of Intercultural Relations, 32*(3), 244–259.

Furnham, A., & Bochner, S. (1986). *Culture shock: Psychological reactions to unfamiliar environments*. London: Methuen.

Ger, G., & Belk, R.W. (1990). Measuring and comparing materialism cross-culturally. *Advances in Consumer Research, 17,* 186–192.

Ger, G., & Belk, R.W. (1996). Cross-cultural differences in materialism. *Journal of Economic Psychology, 17,* 55–77.

Ger, G., & Belk, R.W. (1999). Accounting for materialism in four cultures. *Journal of Material Culture, 4*(2), 183–204.

Gmelch, G. (1997). Crossing cultures: Student travel and personal development. *International Journal of Intercultural Relations, 21,* 475–490.

Higher Education Statistics Agency (2008). *HESA SFR 117* [online]. Retrieved September 29, 2008, from http://www.hesa.ac.uk/index.php/content/view/1100/161/

Jackson, J. (2009). Globalization, internationalization, and short-term stays abroad. *International Journal of Intercultural Relations, 32,* 349–358.

Kilbourne, W., Grungahen, M., & Foley, J. (2005). A cross-cultural examination of the relationship between materialism and individual values. *Journal of Economic Psychology, 26,* 624–641.

Lerman, D., Maldonado, R., & Luna, D. (2008). A theory-based measure of acculturation: The shortened cultural life style inventory. *Journal of Business Research, 62*(4), 399–406.

Mehta, R., & Belk, R.W. (1991). Artifacts, identity and transition: Favorite possessions of Indians and Indian immigrants to the United States. *Journal of Consumer Research, 17,* 398–411.

Michon, R., & Chebat, J. (2004). Cross-cultural mall shopping values and habitats: A comparison between English and French speaking Canadians. *Journal of Business Research, 57*(8), 883–892.

Miller, D. (1995). Consumption as the vanguard of history. In D. Miller (Ed.), *Acknowledging consumption* (pp. 1–55). London: Routledge.

Nolan, R.W. (1990). Culture shock and cross-cultural adaptation or I was OK until I got here. *Practicing Anthropology, 12*(4), 2–20.

Nunnally, J.C. (1978). *Psychometric theory*. New York: McGraw-Hill.

Oberg, K. (1960). Cultural shock: Adjustment to new cultural environments. *Practical Anthropology, 7,* 177–182.

O'Guinn, T.C., & Faber, R.J. (1985). New perspectives on acculturation: The relationship of general and role specific acculturation with Hispanics' consumer attitudes. *Advances in Consumer Research, 12,* 113–117.

Ogden, D.T., Ogden, J.R., & Schau, H.J. (2004). Exploring the impact of culture and acculturation on consumer purchase decisions: Toward a microcultural perspective. *Academy of Marketing Science Review 3* Retrieved September 29, 2008, from http://www.amsreview.org/

Penaloza, L.N. (1989). Immigrant consumer acculturation. *Advances in Consumer Research, 16,* 110–118.

Penaloza, L.N. (1994). Atravesando fronteras/Border crossings: A critical ethnographic exploration of the consumer acculturation of Mexican immigrants. *Journal of Consumer Research, 21,* 289–294.

Penaloza, L.N., & Gilly, M.C. (1999). Marketer acculturation: The changer and the changed. *Journal of Marketing, 63*(3), 84–104.

Richins, M., & Dawson, S. (1992). A consumer values orientation for materialism and its measurement: Scale development and validation. *Journal of Consumer Research, 19,* 303–316.

Rudmin, F. (2009). Constructs, measurements and models of acculturation and acculturative stress. *International Journal of Intercultural Relations, 33*(2), 106–123.

Ryan, M.J. (1982). Behavioral intention formation: The interdependency of attitudinal and social influence variables. *Journal of Consumer Research, 9,* 263–278.

Shaffer, M.A., Harrison, D.A., & Gilley, K.M. (1999). Dimensions, determinants and differences in the expatriate adjustment process. *Journal of International Business Studies, 30*(3), 557–581.

Shankar, A., Elliott, R., & Fitchett, J.A. (2009). Identity, consumption and narratives of socialization. *Marketing Theory, 9*(1), 75–94.

Stroh, L.K., Dennis, L.E., & Cramer, T.C. (1994). Predictors of expatriate adjustment. *International Journal of Organizational Analysis, 2*(2), 176–192.

Triandis, H.C. (1989). The self and social behavior in differing cultural contexts. *Psychological Review, 96*(3), 506–520.

Üstüner, T., & Holt, D.B. (2007). Dominated consumer acculturation: The social construction of poor migrant women's consumer identity projects in a Turkish squatter. *Journal of Consumer Research, 34*, 41–56.

Vanitha, S., Page, K.L., & Gürhan-Canli, Z. (2007). 'My' brand or 'our' brand: The effects of brand relationship dimensions and self-construal on brand evaluations. *Journal of Consumer Research, 34*(2), 248–259.

Vickers, P., & Bekhradnia, B. (2007). *The economic costs and benefits of international students.* Oxford, England: Higher Education Policy Institute.

Wallendorf, M., Belk, R.W., & Heisley, D. (1988). Deep meanings in possessions. *Advances in Consumer Research, 15*, 528–530.

Wallendorf, M., & Reilly, M. (1983). Ethnic migration, assimilation, and consumption. *Journal of Consumer Research, 10*, 292–302.

Ward, C., & Kennedy, A. (1994). Acculturation strategies, psychological adjustment, and sociocultural competence during cross-cultural transitions. *International Journal of Intercultural Relations, 18*(3), 329–343.

Winkelman, M. (1994). Culture shock and adaptation. *Journal of Counselling and Development, 73*, 121–126.

Yavas, U., & Bodur, M. (1999). Correlates of adjustment: A study of expatriate managers in an emerging country. *Management Decision, 37*(3), 267–278.

# A comparative examination of consumer decision styles in Austria

Rudolf R. Sinkovics, *Manchester Business School, UK*
Kannika 'Mink' Leelapanyalert, *University of London, UK*
Mo Yamin, *Manchester Business School, UK*

**Abstract** Mental orientations characterising a consumer's approach to making choices – in short, consumer decision styles – have attracted considerable interest from researchers and practitioners for their value in predicting purchasing behaviour. As a result, they play a key role for marketing activities such as market segmentation, positioning, and tailoring marketing strategies. To contribute to an internationally valid and reliable research instrument, this paper tests a well-documented and accepted research instrument, the Consumer Styles Inventory in another country context and, for the first time, with a sample ($n = 225$) representative of the general population. Results indicate that some dimensions seem to be universal, while national idiosyncrasies emerged as well.

## Introduction

Globalisation drivers such as intensified levels of international exposure through international tourism, media coverage, and advanced technology have arguably contributed to homogenisation of consumer needs and wants (Levitt, 1983). From a company perspective, this trend has triggered an increasing number of product and store offerings, which in turn challenges marketers to become savvier in terms of understanding how consumers make decisions to buy products and which orientations they are taking when choosing among numerous options. The globalisation debate has not been uncontested, and thus the issue of cultural homogeneity versus cultural heterogeneity has come to the fore. Hence, it is questioned whether indeed consumers can be increasingly seen as a homogenous unit, transcending beyond cultural boundaries, or whether companies must learn to work with increasingly fragmented units of analysis (Firat, 1997; Firat & Shultz, 1997; Wickliffe, 2004), suggesting multitudes of products, lifestyles, and experiences.

In this context, the concept of consumer decision styles (CDS) and their measurement using the Consumer Styles Inventory (CSI) play a pivotal role. The CSI is a method for measuring the type of mental characteristics that are present when consumers make purchasing decisions. It is used in this study to examine its comparative usefulness and applicability in a country context, which has until now been unexplored. Thus this study contributes to the examination of the validity of the concept. We argue that issues observed in multicultural societies may not only reside within culturally diverse societies, but can also arise in cross-cultural communication and understanding activated within a culturally homogenous society and, as a result, globalisation triggers the cross-border mobility of products, brands, services, information, and consumers. To this end, the comparative examination of CDS in Austria is a meritorious contribution to the debate about the usefulness of the concept.

## Purpose of this research

For a number of years, the way in which consumers approach purchasing decisions has attracted considerable research attention (e.g. Bettman, 1979; G.B. Sproles, 1985; Thorelli, Becker, & Engeldow, 1975; Westbrook & Black, 1985). Findings show that consumers approach complex purchasing decisions by displaying particular information search, learning, and decision patterns (E.K. Sproles & Sproles, 1990). These 'mental orientations characterising a consumer's approach to making choices' (G.B. Sproles & Kendall, 1986) are crucial, as they are closely linked to the actual purchasing behaviour (Mitchell & Bates, 1998). A number of studies have investigated the decision-making styles in particular contexts, for example, the relationship between product involvement and decision-making styles (Bauer, Sauer, & Becker, 2006), whether the purchase is online (Cowart & Goldsmith, 2007), whether the purchase is of a domestic or foreign brand (Wang, Siu, & Hui, 2004), and shopping Mall consumer behaviour (Wesley, LeHew, & Woodside, 2006). To this end, their insights are relevant for both academics and managers, who may use this information for segmentation and targeting activities. This research on consumer decision making also touches on cultural dimensions and has implications for cross-cultural research (Hofstede, 1983).

Most of the previous CSI studies have looked at the United States (G.B. Sproles, 1985; G.B. Sproles & Kendall, 1986), with some studies providing evidence from the UK (Bakewell & Mitchell, 2006; Mitchell & Bates, 1998; Mitchell & Walsh, 2004), Germany (Mitchell & Walsh, 2004; Walsh, Mitchell, & Hennig-Thurau, 2001), South Korea (Hafstrom, Chae, & Chung, 1992), India, Greece, New Zealand (Lysonski, Durvasula, & Zotos, 1996), China (Fan & Xiao, 1998; Wang et al., 2004), Taiwan (Yang & Wu, 2007), and Iran (Hanzaee & Aghasibeig, 2008). These cross-national applications of CSI have been highly meritorious in terms of establishing the usefulness of the concept in the respective country and cultural contexts. However, following Durvasula, Lysonski, and Andrews (1993), it is important to establish the applicability of consumer research measures to further contexts and societies. There is also a danger of simply using 'borrowed scales' (Douglas & Nijssen, 2003) in cross-national research, and further replication and extension studies are thus strongly recommended to minimise the detrimental effects of wrong conceptualisation and operationalisation. Specifically, cross-national consumer-research instruments are sensitive to the nature of the attitudinal constructs, the nationality of the respondents, and the country-of-origin effects examined in the research. The instrument is also sensitive to lower-order interactions between these factors. Parameswaran and Yaprak (1987) encourage cross-national work and discuss ways to facilitate more rigorous comparative work.

Unfortunately, replications – while from an epistemological perspective an important part of research and vital to scientific progress (Collins, 1985; Easley, Madden, & Dunn, 2000; Evanschitzky, Baumgarth, Hubbard, & Armstrong, 2007; Hubbard & Armstrong, 1994) – are not very popular, especially in marketing, consumer behaviour, and advertising research (Hubbard & Armstrong, 1994; Madden, Easley, & Dunn, 1995). Hubbard and Armstrong (1994, p. 236) define replication as 'duplication of a previously published empirical study that is concerned with assessing whether similar findings can be obtained upon repeating the study'.

The specific contribution of our work to cross-national research and the consumer behaviour literature is thus on an epistemological ground, in that we test a well-documented and accepted research instrument, the CSI (G.B. Sproles & Kendall, 1986), in another country context (Berry, 1980; Douglas, Morrin, & Craig, 1994; Hui & Triandis, 1985). Particularly in the context of multicultural research, replications make an important contribution to the advancement and generalisation of marketing results (Koçak, Abimbola, & Özer, 2007), and this paper takes the CSI forward and examines it in the Austrian consumer context. Furthermore, results are compared with previous studies from Germany, the UK, the United States, South Korea, China, and so on. It is interesting to compare the mental characteristics of CSI across countries, as it will be beneficial for MNEs to understand local consumers' decision-making behaviour and help them to identify target customers and segment them. Based on a sample of 225 Austrian consumers, representative of the general population, the instrument is probed for its validity beyond student samples. Next, an overview of the existing literature, methodology, and outcome of the empirical work are presented. The findings are discussed in the light of results previously obtained with the CSI and are followed by recommendations for future research.

## Background

From a managerial perspective, CDS lend themselves extremely well to key marketing activities such as market segmentation and positioning or tailoring marketing strategies. What applies in the domestic context is even more vital in an international setting. The international marketing mix either allows standardisation or requires differentiation, depending on the variations in CDS across borders. However, this calls for an 'internationalisation' of marketing research tools, such as psychographic scales, as well. As Theodosiou and Leonidou (2003) observe, customer preferences is one of the antecedent factors that determines whether a company would use standardisation or follow the adaptation approach. It follows that a research instrument to profile CDS needs to produce valid and reliable results across consumer populations and independent of national contexts.

In contrast to this demand, empirical research on decision-making styles to date has concentrated primarily on US consumers. Only a few studies have extended their focus beyond the US context (Durvasula, Lysonski et al., 1993; Fan & Xiao, 1998; Mitchell & Bates, 1998; Walsh, Hennig-Thurau, Wayne-Mitchell, & Wiedmann, 2001), and even fewer have engaged in multi-country comparisons (e.g. Kaynak & Kucukemiroglu, 2001; Lysonski et al., 1996). Therefore, an internationally valid and reliable research instrument is not yet in place. In addition to the limited geographical reach, previous studies have all been based on student samples. Although we do agree with Campbell (1986, p. 276) that 'college students really are people' and do not want to 'throw out the baby with the bath water' (Dobbins, Lane, & Steiner, 1988; Slade, Gordon, Dobbins, Lane, & Steiner, 1988), we feel that using student samples clearly limits the research instrument's generalisability across consumer populations.

Starting in the 1950s, the concept of CDS became popular and has been used in numerous studies (e.g. Darden & Reynolds, 1971; Moschis, 1976, 1977; Stone, 1954; Thorelli et al., 1975; Wells, 1975). However, it was not until the late 1980s that cross-country comparisons were undertaken (e.g. Durvasula, Lysonski et al., 1993; Fan & Xiao, 1998; Hafstrom et al., 1992; Lysonski et al., 1996; Mitchell & Bates, 1998; G.B. Sproles, 1985; G.B. Sproles & Kendall, 1986). Despite some overlaps in the scale content, most studies pertain to different areas, resulting in different research instruments. In their article, Lysonski et al. (1996) provide a valuable categorisation of the existing research in this area. They distinguish three different approaches: (1) the consumer typology approach (Darden & Reynolds, 1974; Moschis, 1976); (2) the psychographics/lifestyle approach (Lastovicka, 1982; Wells, 1975); and (3) the consumer characteristics approach (E.K. Sproles & Sproles, 1990; G.B. Sproles, 1985; G.B. Sproles & Kendall, 1986). In general, these approaches revolve around the several dimensions a consumer has to consider simultaneously when making a decision. Specifically, issues such as the right time for deciding, the amount of information to be collected, the time spent on searching, the amount to be paid, as well as the importance of brands and product quality, are included. The consumer characteristics approach was attributed the highest explanatory power, as it maps consumers' affective and cognitive orientation within the decision-making process (Lysonski et al., 1996).

Among the research work pertaining to the consumer characteristics approach, G. B. Sproles and Kendall's (1986) CSI received the most attention. For two reasons, the CSI was judged particularly qualified for comparative work: (1) the existence of a robust questionnaire and (2) the availability of prior research for comparison (Durvasula, Lysonski et al., 1993; Hafstrom et al., 1992; Lysonski et al., 1996; G.B. Sproles & Kendall, 1986). Therefore, based on our research intentions, we have used the CSI for the underlying contribution. Table 1 gives an overview of earlier CDS studies and the CSI traits identified in these. Based initially on six traits, G.B. Sproles and Kendall (1986) developed a more parsimonious version resulting in eight dimensions mapping consumer decision making. This eight-factor structure has been replicated in most other studies so far. Some studies have deviated slightly on the dimensions of the decision-making styles. For example, Hafstrom et al. (1992) and Fan and Xiao (1998) identified a 'Time–Energy Conservation' dimension. However, this trait seemed to be specific to the particular cultural setting from which these studies originating (Korea and China). Walsh Hennig-Thurau et al. (2001) found seven characteristics in the German case and, in particular, identified 'variety seeking' as one of the CSI dimensions in Germany. Thus, according to this study, Germans are particularly prone to look for more product variety. Later studies look at CSI in different genders (Bakewell & Mitchell, 2004, 2006; Mitchell & Walsh, 2004). Bakewell and Mitchell (2004) found 'recreation shopping consciousness' in male shopping behaviour in the UK, and emphasise the importance of the 'efficiency shopping process' for male consumers. They also found 'store-loyalty/low-price seeking' in male shopping behaviour, and thus identified an opportunity to maintain loyalty by using loyalty cards and price-related activities (Bakewell & Mitchell, 2004, 2006). Mitchell and Walsh (2004) found that the seven characteristics that they had previously found in their CSI research in Germany (Walsh, Mitchell et al., 2001) were valid for females. Only four could be confirmed in the male German case.

**Table 1** Studies using the Consumer Styles Inventory (CSI) and traits identified.

| G.B. Sproles (1985) | G.B. Sproles and Kendall (1986) | Hafstrom, Chae, and Chung (1992) | Durvasula, Lysonski, and Andrews (1993) | Lysonski, Durvasula, and Zotos (1996) | Mitchell and Bates (1998) | Fan and Xiao (1998) | Siu, Wang, Chang, and Hui (2001) |
|---|---|---|---|---|---|---|---|
| United States | United States | South Korea | United States | Greece, India, New Zealand, United States | UK | China | China |
| Perfectionism | Perfectionism | Perfectionism | Perfectionism | Perfectionism | Perfectionism | Quality Oriented | Perfectionism |
| Value Consciousness | Price-Value Consciousness | Price-Value Consciousness | Price-Value Consciousness | | Price-Value Consciousness | Price-Value Consciousness | |
| Brand Consciousness | Brand Consciousness | Brand Consciousness | Brand Consciousness | Brand Consciousness | Brand Consciousness | Brand Consciousness | Brand Consciousness |
| Novelty-Fashion Consciousness | Novelty-Fashion Consciousness | | Novelty-Fashion Consciousness | Novelty-Fashion Consciousness | | | Novelty-Fashion Consciousness |
| Shopping Avoidance | | | | | | | |
| Confused by Over-choice | Confused by Over-choice | Confused by Over-choice | Confused by Over-choice | Confused by Over-choice | Confused by Over-choice | Information Seekers | |
| | Recreational Shopping Consciousness | Recreational Shopping Consciousness | Recreational Shopping Consciousness | Recreational Shopping Consciousness | Recreational Shopping Consciousness | | Recreational Shopping |
| | Impulsiveness | Impulsiveness | Impulsiveness | Impulsiveness | Impulsiveness | | |
| | Habitual, Brand Loyalty | Habitual, Brand Loyalty | Habitual, Brand Loyalty | Habitual, Brand Loyalty | Habitual, Brand Loyalty | | |
| | | Time-Energy Conserving | | | | Time-Energy Conserving | |

*(Continued)*

**Table 1 (Continued).**

| Walsh, Mitchell, and Henning-Thurau (2001) | Wesley, LeHew, and Woodside (2006) | Yang and Wu (2007) | Cowart and Goldsmith (2007) | Hanzaee and Aghasibeig (2008) | Zhou, Arnold, Pereira, and Yu (2010) |
|---|---|---|---|---|---|
| Germany | United States | Taiwan | United States | Iran | China |
| Perfectionism | Perfectionism | Perfectionism | Quality Consciousness | Perfectionism | Perfectionism |
| | Price-Value Consciousness | | | | Price-Value Consciousness |
| Brand Consciousness | Brand Consciousness | Brand Consciousness | Brand Consciousness | Brand Consciousness | Brand Consciousness |
| Novelty-Fashion Consciousness | Novelty-Fashion Consciousness | Novelty-Fashion Consciousness | Fashion Consciousness | Fashion Consciousness | Novelty-Fashion Consciousness |
| Confused by Over-choice | Confused by Over-choice | Confused by Over-choice | | Confused by Over-choice | Confused by Over-choice |
| Recreational/Hedonism | Recreational Shopping Consciousness | | Hedonistic shopping | Recreational Shopping Consciousness | Recreational Shopping Consciousness |
| Impulsiveness | | Impulsiveness | Impulsiveness | Impulsiveness | Impulsiveness |
| Time-Energy Conserving | Habitual, Brand Loyalty | Brand Loyalty | Brand Loyalty | Habitual, Brand Loyalty | Habitual, Brand Loyalty |
| | | | Time-Energy Conserving | | |
| Variety Seeking | | | | Low-Price Seekers | |
| | | | | Non-Perfectionist/ Brand Indifference | |

Furthermore, the Internet has strongly contributed to the development of online consumer purchasing. Yang and Wu (2007) found six characteristics in CSI of Taiwanese online shoppers. They found that impulsive shopping still occurred in online shopping, which means that consumers still buy products online without an initial intention to purchase. In online consumer research, male and female shopping behaviours are different. The online male consumer has a strong brand consciousness. The search for novel fashion occurs with online female consumers (Yang & Wu, 2007).

## Methodology

### Questionnaire design

Following the methodology of related studies, a questionnaire was designed, comprising 54 questions and incorporating suggestions from the most recent study in the area of CDS (Mitchell & Bates, 1998). Three native English speakers were involved in the questionnaire development, and two academics moderated the process of developing items, following Brislin's (1970) back-translation approach (see the Appendix for the items used in the questionnaire). For the purposes of evaluating validity, six additional questions from the 'domain specific innovativeness' (DSI) scale were added (Gatignon & Robertson, 1985; Goldsmith & Hofacker, 1991; Price & Ridgeway, 1983). Following the theory, the characteristics of CDS are linked to the mental orientation of the consumer when they make their purchasing decision (G.B. Sproles & Kendall, 1986). The items were varied based on three different products (toothpaste, a vacuum cleaner, and a computer) to measure the consistency of responses, therefore adding up to 18 additional questions.[1] Items were anchored on a five-point Likert scale, where 1 = 'strongly agree', 2 = 'agree', 3 = 'neither agree nor disagree', 4 = 'disagree', and 5 = 'strongly disagree'.

### Sampling and data collection

Most of the earlier CSI studies are limited in that they used student samples. Walsh et al. (2001) collected information from shoppers of both genders in Germany. In this paper, a quota sample representative of the general Austrian population based on age, gender, and level of education was applied. A total of 1200 questionnaires were distributed nationwide by means of the 'questionnaire-drop-in' technique. In this case, interviewers were involved in distributing the questionnaires to potential interview partners with matching characteristics. Specifically, a team of 50 interviewers was advised to distribute the questionnaires to interviewees with predefined demographics, following a quota-sample design (age, gender, and education characteristics). The sample was designed to mirror closely the Austrian population, and was therefore deemed to overcome the generalisability problems that were associated with earlier studies. The returned questionnaires were handled anonymously, so a follow up of non-respondents was not possible.

The questionnaires were completed in the absence of the interviewer and collected after successful completion. While this procedure incurred increased time and costs, it helped to safeguard against self-selection bias and to deliver high-quality data with a pleasingly high response rate.

---

[1] As indicated, DSI items referred to a different domain, were included for subsequent validation purposes only, and were therefore not included in the factor analysis.

In total, 225 usable questionnaires were returned, which equals a response rate of 19%. Due to the specifics of the sampling and data-collection procedure, non-response bias (Armstrong & Overton, 1977; Lambert & Harrington, 1990) was not an issue and thus was not tested for. Table 1 provides an overview of the sample characteristics.

## Analysis

Descriptive analyses indicate that the sample reflects the Austrian population very well. To determine whether the factors identified by G.B. Sproles and Kendall (1986) are relevant to the Austrian data set, a factor analysis (principal components, varimax rotation) was conducted. Except for two items, which were subsequently deleted, all the items produced acceptable loadings. Next, Cronbach's alpha coefficients were computed to assess the scale reliabilities of the factors identified and to make comparisons with G.B. Sproles and Kendall's (1986) findings. In cross-cultural research, such an approach is commonly the first step in determining the generalisability of a model or scale to another cultural context (Irvine & Carroll, 1980).[2] For all but two factors, acceptable Cronbach's alpha coefficients between .63 and .78 were obtained (Nunnally, 1964). The factors 'Time–Energy Conserving' and 'Brand-Store Loyalty', however, displayed little internal consistency, with alphas of .40 and .34. Even when correcting for alpha's tendency to underestimate factor reliabilities and calculating unbiased coefficient thetas from the factor analysis, the reliability scores did not improve significantly. Therefore, the 'Time–Energy Conserving' and 'Brand-Store Loyalty' items cannot be perceived to be reliable measures of the dimensions in the Austrian context. While this is surprising at first sight, it does provide something of a pattern with the other studies. It was only in the UK, South Korean, and Chinese studies that 'Time–Energy Conserving' was identified, and only in the UK study that 'Brand-Store Loyalty' played a role. For the purposes of testing concurrent validity, a score for the positively anchored DSI items was calculated and correlated with the six CSI dimensions. In line with the hypothesised directions, 'Perfectionist', 'Novelty-Fashion Conscious', and 'Brand-Store Loyalty' factors showed significant positive correlations with the DSI scores, therefore confirming concurrent validity.

Table 2 gives a simplified overview of the Austrian findings and contrasts them with previous results using CSI in different country contexts. In addition to the findings obtained, demographic/economic indicators have been included to complement the interpretation.

The six factors derived from the Austrian samples correspond well to the factors already explored in previous studies. When looking at the CSI results across studies, there are some patterns that are particularly interesting. 'Perfectionist', 'Brand Conscious', 'Confused by Over-choice' occurred in most countries, including the Austrian case. This research confirms Mitchell and Bates's (1998) finding that 'Confused by Over-choice' occurs in most countries, as consumers become overloaded with information and face too many product choices (Klausegger, Sinkovics, & Zou, 2007). This research also found the 'Recreational Shoppers' characteristic, which appears in most countries studied, apart from China, and in the

---

[2]While we are aware that additional confirmatory approaches to data analysis will help to generalize our findings further, we did not aim at addressing more rigid equivalence tests (Steenkamp & Baumgartner, 1998) at this stage in our research. By applying the aforementioned exploratory analysis technique, we did, however, test for configural invariance (Douglas et al., 1994) and furthermore stay in line with earlier research in this area.

**Table 2** Country comparison of CSI results.

| Country | Austria | UK | United States | United States | United States | S. Korea | India | Greece | New Zealand | China | China | China | Germany | Taiwan | Iran |
|---|---|---|---|---|---|---|---|---|---|---|---|---|---|---|
| Authors/Year |  | Mitchell and Bates [1998] | G.B. Sproles and Kendall [1986] | Wesley, LeHew, and Woodside [2006] | Cowart and Goldsmith [2007] | Hafstrom, Chae, and Chung [1992] | Lysonski, Durvasula, and Zotos [1996] | Lysonski, Durvasula, and Zotos [1996] | Durvasula, Lysonski, and Andrews [1993] | Fan and Xiao [1998] | Zhou, Arnold, Pereira, and Yu [2010] | Siu, Wang, Chang, and Hui [2001] | Walsh, Mitchell, and Henning-Thurau [2001] | Yang and Wu [2007] | Hanzaee and Aghasibeig [2008] |
| Sample size[a] | 225 | 401 | 482 | 527 | 357 | 310 | 73 | 96 | 210 | 271 | 440 | 744 | 455 | 472 | 692 |
| Number of factors explored | 6 | 8 | 8 | 7 | 6 | 8 | 7 | 7 | 7 | 5 | 8 | 4 | 7 | 6 | 10 |
| Perfectionist | X | X | X | X |  | X | X | X | X |  | X | X | X | X | X |
| Brand Conscious | X | X | X | X | X | X | X | X | X | X | X | X | X | X | X |
| Confused by Over-choice | X | X | X | X |  | X | X | X | X |  | X |  | X | X | X |
| Time-Energy Conserving |  | X |  |  |  | X |  |  |  | X |  |  |  |  | X |
| Novelty-Fashion Conscious | X | X | X | X | X |  | X | X | X |  | X | X | X | X | X |
| Price-Value Conscious | X | X | X | X |  | X |  |  |  | X | X |  |  |  |  |
| Recreational Shoppers | X | X | X | X | X | X | X | X | X |  | X | X | X |  | X |
| Brand-Store Loyalty |  |  |  |  | X |  |  |  |  |  |  |  |  | X |  |
| Impulsiveness |  | X | X |  | X | X | X | X | X |  | X |  | X | X | X |
| Habitual Brand-Loyal |  |  | X | X |  | X | X | X | X |  | X |  |  |  | X |
| Quality Conscious |  |  |  |  | X |  |  |  |  | X |  |  |  |  |  |
| Information Seekers |  |  |  |  |  |  |  |  |  | X |  |  |  |  |  |
| Variety Seekers |  |  |  |  |  |  |  |  |  |  |  |  | X |  |  |
| Low-Price Seekers |  |  |  |  |  |  |  |  |  |  |  |  |  |  | X |
| Non-perfectionist/Brand Indifference |  |  |  |  |  |  |  |  |  |  |  |  |  |  | X |

[a] Valid sample size used in the study.

online Taiwanese study (Yang & Wu, 2007). As reported earlier, 'Time–Energy Conserving' and 'Brand-Store Loyalty' could not be identified in the Austrian context. While the latter only showed up in the UK study, the first dimension was also reported in two additional countries (South Korea and China). It has been found that neither 'Brand-Store Loyalty' nor 'Habitual Brand-Loyal' appear in either Austria or Germany. This shows that Austrian and German consumers' attitudes towards brand loyalty and brand-store loyalty are different from those of consumers in other countries. On top of that, there are similar CSI patterns between Austria and the United States, except that the 'Impulsiveness' and 'Habitual Brand-Loyal' dimensions did not show up in the Austrian study (as in the Chinese study). Although the latter finding is in line with the suggestion that Austrians are generally rather 'motionless' and 'traditional' people (Bernhard, 1974), we do not have a conceptually sound explanation for this finding. To some extent, the differing results may arise from the exploratory rather than confirmatory approach used by the studies outlined (except for Durvasula, Lysonski et al., 1993). However, these differences may also be attributed to more substantial cross-border differences. To provide additional insight into the country differences observed, demographic and economic key indicators were introduced. To date, the CSI has been tested in three different groups of countries: (1) economically well-developed countries such as Austria, Germany, the UK, and the United States; (2) emerging markets, such as China, Taiwan, South Korea, and India; and (3) countries in between, such as Greece and New Zealand, with modest or low annual GDP growth rates ranking in the upper middle with regards to living standards (New Zealand ranks at 27; Greece ranks at 35). A closer look from this perspective reveals some more detail: there is some evidence that the stage of economic development may impact the CSI's dimensionality.

Another objective of this research work was to test the CSI's explanatory power in a sample drawn from the general population. As Table 2 shows, the results from Austria are highly congruent with findings from previous studies using student samples. Therefore, the CSI may be deemed robust under a different sampling frame. While these results appear promising and support the cross-national applicability of the CDS construct to a considerable extent, they are to be considered – as was mentioned earlier – exploratory at this stage. Further analysis, following confirmatory model testing techniques is needed to establish fully credibility in terms of the generalisability of the results.

## Conclusion, limitations, and future research

This paper attempts to test a well-established tool for measuring CDS in a different cultural context. This research thus contributes to cross-culture research by comparing the CSI of Austrian consumers with those from other countries. While previous studies have mainly drawn on samples from students, this paper draws its results from a more general sample of Austrians, which makes the findings inherently better suited to be generalised for the population as a whole. As the results indicate, the factors initially explored by G.B. Sproles and Kendall and refined during later studies seem to explain CDS to a large extent. This is an important contribution, which rests on the understanding that replications in marketing and consumer behaviour are not only useful but an important component of scientific inquiry (Evanschitzky et al., 2007; Hubbard & Armstrong, 1994). Our approach was also pursued with reference to previous work that dealt specifically with consumer behaviour research and its cross-national applicability in particular (Douglas & Nijssen, 2003; Durvasula, Andrews,

Lysonski, & Netemeyer, 1993). Hence, the findings strengthen an epistemological perspective, which suggests that replications are an important component of scientific progress (Collins, 1985).

Nonetheless, the results have to be interpreted with caution. The time span between the early studies (1986) and this particular research project (2002) is quite considerable and may thus distort the findings. Also there are demographic differences between this and the earlier studies, which were largely drawn from student samples. To the extent that our study draws on the general Austrian population, earlier generalisations may have returned higher levels of homogeneity. Finally, the question may be raised whether the similarities or differences observed are in fact real, with reference to measurement equivalence (Berry, 1969; Cavusgil & Das, 1997; Ewing, Salzberger, & Sinkovics, 2005; Salzberger, 2009; Sinkovics & Salzberger, 2006).

Therefore, we see three different avenues for future research. First, based on the experience of the studies already available, the CSI could be re-evaluated and adapted. In our view, it makes sense to review the items used so far critically, replace some, and add new items. Also, the scale should be designed in a way that is applicable to new sales channels such as the Internet. A redesigned scale could then be developed in different languages simultaneously and tested within a short period concurrently to increase comparability. Second, to be considered a useful tool, the samples used should mirror the overall population's demographics in each country. We therefore strongly advocate testing the scale on the entire population. Third, and most crucial in our view, is to address measurement equivalence, which has been criticised in cross-cultural research for quite some time (Albaum & Peterson, 1984; Aulakh & Kotabe, 1993; Davis, Douglas, & Silk, 1981; Salzberger, Sinkovics, & Schlegelmilch, 1999). The following diagnostic techniques for evaluating measurement equivalence in cross-national research may be used: first, alternating least squares optimal scaling (optimal scaling), which allows the estimation and comparison, item by item, of the underlying metrics of the ordinal measures across countries; and second, the analysis of multiple group structural equation measurement models (Mullen, 1995). The emerging perspective of Rasch modelling may offer further promising avenues for establishing equivalence in research results (Ewing et al., 2005; Salzberger & Sinkovics, 2006).

Given the critical importance of identifying CDS, and the extensive data available already, we strongly advocate the continuation of research using CSI. The suggestions for future research may contribute, in our view, to considerable improvements and the cross-national usability of the scale. Eventually, the CSI will become a powerful tool for marketing practitioners to improve their segmenting and targeting across borders.

## Acknowledgements

The authors gratefully acknowledge the constructive comments of Barbara Stöttinger on an earlier version of this paper. We also appreciate the support and encouragement of Maria Piacentini and Charles C. Cui and two anonymous reviewers in developing this paper further.

## References

Albaum, G., & Peterson, R.A. (1984). Empirical research in international marketing, 1976–1982. *Journal of International Business Studies*, 15(1), 161–173.

Armstrong, J.S., & Overton, T.S. (1977). Estimating nonresponse bias in mail surveys. *Journal of Marketing Research*, *14*(3), 396–402.

Aulakh, P.S., & Kotabe, M. (1993). An assessment of theoretical and methodological development in international marketing: 1980–1990. *Journal of International Marketing*, *1*(2), 5–28.

Bakewell, C., & Mitchell, V.-W. (2004). Male consumer decision-making styles. *International Review of Retail, Distribution and Consumer Research*, *14*(2), 223–240.

Bakewell, C., & Mitchell, V.-W. (2006). Male versus female consumer decision making styles. *Journal of Business Research*, *59*(12), 1297–1300.

Bauer, H.H., Sauer, N.E., & Becker, C. (2006). Investigating the relationship between product involvement and consumer decision-making styles. *Journal of Consumer Behaviour*, *5*(4), 342–354.

Bernhard, T. (1974). *Die Macht der Gewohnheit*. Frankfurt am Main, Germany: Suhrkamp.

Berry, J.W. (1969). On cross-cultural comparability. *International Journal of Psychology*, *4*(2), 119–128.

Berry, J.W. (1980). Introduction to methodology. In H.C. Triandis & J.W. Berry (Eds.), *Handbook of cross cultural psychology* (Vol. 2, pp. 1–29). Boston: Allyn & Bacon.

Bettman, J.R. (1979). *An information processing theory of consumer choice*. Reading, MA: Addison-Wesley.

Brislin, R.W. (1970). Back translation for cross-cultural research. *Journal of Cross-Cultural Psychology*, *1*(3), 185–216.

Campbell, J.P. (1986). Labs, fields, and straw issues. In E.A. Locke (Ed.), *Generalizing from laboratory to field settings: Research findings from industrial-organizational psychology, organizational behavior, and human resource management* (pp. 269–279). Lexington, MA: Lexington Books.

Cavusgil, S.T., & Das, A. (1997). Methodological issues in empirical cross-cultural research: A survey of the management literature and a framework. *Management International Review*, *37*(1), 71–96.

Collins, H.M. (1985). *Changing order: Replication and induction in scientific practice*. Beverly Hills, CA: Sage.

Cowart, K.O., & Goldsmith, R.E. (2007). The influence of consumer decision-making styles on online apparel consumption by college students. *International Journal of Consumer Studies*, *31*(6), 639–647.

Darden, W.R., & Reynolds, F.D. (1971). Shopping orientations and product usage rates. *Journal of Marketing Research*, *8*, 505–508.

Darden, W.R., & Reynolds, F.D. (1974). Backward profiling of male innovators. *Journal of Marketing Research*, *11*(1), 79–85.

Davis, H.L., Douglas, S.P., & Silk, A.J. (1981). Measure unreliability: A hidden threat to cross-national marketing? *Journal of Marketing*, *45*(2), 98–109.

Dobbins, G.H., Lane, I.M., & Steiner, D.D. (1988). A note on the role of laboratory methodologies in applied behavioural research: Don't throw out the baby with the bath water. *Journal of Organizational Behavior*, *9*(3), 281–286.

Douglas, S.P., Morrin, M.A., & Craig, S.C. (1994). Cross-national consumer research traditions. In G. Laurent, G. Lilien, & B. Pras (Eds.), *Research traditions in marketing* (pp. 289–306). Dordrecht, Germany: Kluwer Academic.

Douglas, S.P., & Nijssen, E.J. (2003). On the use of 'borrowed' scales in cross-national research: A cautionary note. *International Marketing Review*, *20*(6), 621–642.

Durvasula, S., Andrews, C.J., Lysonski, S., & Netemeyer, R.G. (1993). Assessing the cross-national applicability of consumer behavior models: A model of attitude toward advertising in general. *Journal of Consumer Research*, *19*(4), 626–636.

Durvasula, S., Lysonski, S., & Andrews, C.J. (1993). Cross-cultural generalizability of a scale for profiling consumers' decision making styles. *The Journal of Consumer Affairs*, *27*(1), 55–65.

Easley, R.W., Madden, C.S., & Dunn, M.G. (2000). Conducting marketing science: The role of replication in the research process. *Cross-Cultural Consumer and Business Research*, 48(1), 83–92.

Evanschitzky, H., Baumgarth, C., Hubbard, R., & Armstrong, J.S. (2007). Replication research's disturbing trend. *Journal of Business Research*, 60(4), 411–415.

Ewing, M.T., Salzberger, T., & Sinkovics, R.R. (2005). An alternate approach to assessing cross-cultural measurement equivalence in advertising research. *Journal of Advertising*, 34(1), 17–36.

Fan, J.X., & Xiao, J.J. (1998). Consumer decision-making styles of young-adult Chinese. *Journal of Consumer Affairs*, 32(2), 275–295.

Firat, A.F. (1997). Educator insights: Globalization of fragmentation – A framework for understanding contemporary global markets. *Journal of International Marketing*, 5(2), 77–86.

Firat, A.F., & Shultz, C.J., II. (1997). From segmentation to fragmentation: Markets and marketing strategy in the postmodern era. *European Journal of Marketing*, 31(3), 183–207.

Gatignon, H., & Robertson, T.R. (1985). A propositional inventory for new diffusion research. *Journal of Consumer Research*, 11, 849–867.

Goldsmith, R.E., & Hofacker, C. (1991). Measuring consumer innovativeness. *Journal of the Academy of Marketing Science*, 19(3), 209–221.

Hafstrom, L.J., Chae, J.S., & Chung, Y.S. (1992). Consumer decision making styles: Comparison between United States and Korean young consumers. *The Journal of Consumer Affairs*, 26(1), 146–158.

Hanzaee, K.H., & Aghasibeig, S. (2008). Generation Y female and male decision-making styles in Iran: Are they different? *The International Review of Retail, Distribution and Consumer Research*, 18(5), 521–537.

Hofstede, G. (1983). The cultural relativity of organisational practices and theories. *Journal of International Business Studies*, 14(2), 75–89.

Hubbard, R., & Armstrong, J.S. (1994). Replications and extensions in marketing: Rarely published but quite contrary. *International Journal of Research in Marketing*, 11(3), 233–248.

Hui, H.C., & Triandis, H.C. (1985). Measurement in cross-cultural psychology: A review and comparison of strategies. *Journal of Cross-Cultural Psychology*, 16(2), 131–152.

Irvine, S.H., & Carroll, W.K. (1980). Testing and assessment across cultures: Issues in methodology and theory. In H.C. Triandis & J.W. Berry (Eds.), *The Handbook of Cross-Cultural Psychology* (pp. 127–180). Boston: Allyn & Bacon.

Kaynak, E., & Kucukemiroglu, O. (2001). A comparative study of family decision making in US and Turkish households by correspondence analysis. *Journal of Targeting, Measurement and Analysis for Marketing*, 9(3), 254–269.

Klausegger, C., Sinkovics, R.R., & Zou, H.J. (2007). Information overload: A cross-national investigation of influence factors and effects. *Marketing Intelligence and Planning*, 25(7), 691–718.

Koçak, A., Abimbola, T., & Özer, A. (2007). Consumer brand equity in a cross-cultural replication: An evaluation of a scale. *Journal of Marketing Management*, 23(1/2), 157–173.

Lambert, D.M., & Harrington, T.C. (1990). Measuring nonresponse bias in customer service mail surveys. *Journal of Business Logistics*, 11(2), 5.

Lastovicka, J.L. (1982). On the validation of lifestyle traits: A review and illustration. *Journal of Marketing Research*, 19(1), 126–138.

Levitt, T. (1983). The globalization of markets. *Harvard Business Review*, 61(3), 92–102.

Lysonski, S., Durvasula, S., & Zotos, Y. (1996). Consumer decision making style: A multi-country investigation. *European Journal of Marketing*, 22(12), 10–21.

Madden, C.S., Easley, R.W., & Dunn, M.G. (1995). How journal editors view replication research. *Journal of Advertising*, 24(4), 77–87.

Mitchell, V.-W., & Bates, L. (1998). UK consumer decision-making styles. *Journal of Marketing Management, 14*(1/3), 199–225.

Mitchell, V.-W., & Walsh, G. (2004). Gender differences in German consumer decision-making styles. *Journal of Consumer Behaviour, 3*(4), 331–346.

Moschis, G.P. (1976). Shopping orientations and consumer uses of information. *Journal of Retailing, 52*(2), 61–70.

Moschis, G.P. (1977). Purchasing pattens of adolescent consumers. *Journal of Retailing, 53*(1), 17–26.

Mullen, M.R. (1995). Diagnosing measurement equivalence in cross-national research. *Journal of International Business Studies, 26*(3), 573–596.

Nunnally, J.C. (1964). *Educational measurement and evaluation.* New York: McGraw-Hill.

Parameswaran, R., & Yaprak, A. (1987). A cross-national comparison of consumer research measures. *Journal of International Business Studies, 18*(1), 35–49.

Price, L.L., & Ridgeway, N.M. (1983). Development of a scale to measure use innovativeness. In R.P. Bagozzi & A.M. Tybout (Eds.), *Advances in consumer research* (Vol. 10, pp. 679–684). Ann Arbor, MI: Association for Consumer Research.

Salzberger, T. (2009). *Measurement in marketing research – An alternative framework.* Cheltenham, England: Edward Elgar.

Salzberger, T., & Sinkovics, R.R. (2006). Reconsidering the problem of data equivalence in international marketing research: Contrasting approaches based on CFA and the Rasch model for measurement. *International Marketing Review, 23*(4), 390–417.

Salzberger, T., Sinkovics, R.R., & Schlegelmilch, B.B. (1999). Data equivalence in cross-cultural research: A comparison of classical test theory and latent trait theory based approaches. *Australasian Marketing Journal, 7*(2), 23–38.

Sinkovics, R.R., & Salzberger, T. (2006). Introduction to the special issue on 'Issues and advances in international marketing research'. *International Marketing Review, 23*(4), 349–352.

Siu, N.Y.M., Wang, C.C.L., Chang, L.M.K., & Hui, A.S.Y. (2001). Adapting consumer style inventory to Chinese consumers: A confirmatory factor analysis approach. *Journal of International Consumer Marketing, 13*(2), 29.

Slade, L.A., Gordon, M.E., Dobbins, G.H., Lane, I.M., & Steiner, D.D. (1988). On the virtues of laboratory babies and student bath water: A reply to Dobbins, Lane, and Steiner; A further examination of student babies and laboratory bath water: A response to Slade and Gordon. *Journal of Organizational Behavior, 9*(4), 373–378.

Sproles, E.K., & Sproles, G.B. (1990). Consumer decision-making styles as a function of individual learning styles. *Journal of Consumer Affairs, 24*(1), 134–147.

Sproles, G.B. (1985). *From perfectionism to fadism: Measuring consumers' decision making styles.* Paper presented at the 30th Annual Meeting, American Council on Consumer Interest Conference, Columbia.

Sproles, G.B., & Kendall, E.L. (1986). A methodology for profiling consumers' decision making styles. *Journal of Consumers Affairs, 20*(2), 267–279.

Steenkamp, J.-B.EM., & Baumgartner, H. (1998). Assessing measurement invariance in cross-national consumer research. *Journal of Consumer Research, 25*(1), 78–90.

Stone, G.P. (1954). City shoppers and urban identification: Observations on the social psychology of city life. *American Journal of Sociology, 60*, 36–45.

Theodosiou, M., & Leonidou, L.C. (2003). Standardization versus adaptation of international marketing strategy: An integrative assessment of the empirical research. *International Business Review, 12*(2), 141–171.

Thorelli, H.B., Becker, H., & Engeldow, J. (1975). *The information seekers: An international study of consumer information and advertising image.* Cambridge, MA: Ballinger.

Walsh, G., Hennig-Thurau, T., Wayne-Mitchell, V., & Wiedmann, K.-P. (2001). Consumers' decision-making style as a basis for market segmentation. *Journal of Targeting, Measurement and Analysis for Marketing, 10*(2), 117–131.

Walsh, G., Mitchell, V.-W., & Hennig-Thurau, T. (2001). German consumer decision-making styles. *Journal of Consumer Affairs*, 35(1), 73–95.

Wang, C.-L., Siu, N.Y.M., & Hui, A.S.Y. (2004). Consumer decision-making styles on domestic and imported brand clothing. *European Journal of Marketing*, 38(1/2), 239–252.

Wells, W.D. (1975). Psychographics: A critical review. *Journal of Marketing Research*, 12(2), 196–213.

Wesley, S., LeHew, M., & Woodside, A.G. (2006). Consumer decision-making styles and mall shopping behavior: Building theory using exploratory data analysis and the comparative method. *Cross-Cultural Consumer and Business Research*, 59(5), 535–548.

Westbrook, R.A., & Black, W.C. (1985). A motivation-based shopper typology. *Journal of Retailing*, 61, 78–103.

Wickliffe, V.P. (2004). Refinement and re-assessment of the consumer decision-making style instrument. *Journal of Retailing and Consumer Services*, 11(1), 9–17.

Yang, C., & Wu, C.-C. (2007). Gender and Internet consumers' decision-making. *CyberPsychology and Behavior*, 10(1), 86–91.

Zhou, J.X., Arnold, M.J., Pereira, A., & Yu, J. (2010). Chinese consumer decision-making styles: A comparison between the coastal and inland regions. *Cross-Cultural Consumer and Business Research*, 63(1), 45–51.

# Appendix

## *Questionnaire – Instructions*

Please indicate to what extent the following statements apply to you. Tick a number to indicate your likely cause of action. Circle '1' if you strongly agree with this statement or '5' if you strongly disagree with this statement. [1 = 'strongly agree', 2 = 'agree', 3 = 'neither agree nor disagree', 4 = 'disagree', 5 = 'strongly disagree'.]

## *Questionnaire items for consumer decision styles*

I spend little time deciding on the products and brands I buy. / Shopping in different stores is a waste of time. / Shopping is very enjoyable to me. / I enjoy shopping, just for fun. / Shopping is not a pleasant activity to me. / I only shop stores that are close and convenient to me. / I spend little time deciding on the products I buy. / I usually compare at least three brands before choosing. / Getting good quality is very important to me. / I have very high standards and expectations for products I buy. / I really don't give my purchases much thought or care. / In general, I usually try to buy the best overall quality. / I make a special effort to choose the very best quality products. / I normally shop quickly, buying the first product I find that seems good enough. / I shop quickly, buying the first product or brand I find that seems good enough. / When it comes to purchasing products, I try to get the very best, or perfect choice. / A brand recommended in a consumer magazine is an excellent choice for me. / I usually compare advertisements to buy fashionable products. / To get variety, I shop in different stores and buy different brands. / It's fun to buy something new and exciting. / I keep my wardrobe up to date with the changing fashions. / There are so many brands to choose from that I often feel confused. / I usually have at least one outfit of the newest style. / Fashionable, attractive styling is very important to me. / I usually buy the very newest style. / I get confused by all the information on different products. / The more I learn about products, the harder it seems to choose the best. / Sometimes it's hard to decide in which stores to shop. / All brands are the same in overall quality. / I consider price first. / I cannot choose products by myself. / I prefer buying the best-selling brands. / I have favourite brands that I buy every time. / Once I find a product I like, I buy it regularly. / The higher the price of the product, the better its quality. / I usually buy well-known brands. / A product doesn't have to be exactly what I want, or the best on the market, to satisfy me. / I regularly change the brands I buy. / I go to the same store each time I shop. / I usually buy the more expensive brands. / Good quality department and speciality stores offer the best products / The most advertised brands are usually good choices. / Expensive brands are usually the best. / Once I find a product or brand I like, I buy it over and over. / The well-known national brands are best for me. / I buy as much as possible at sale price. / I usually buy the lower-price products. / I look very carefully to find the best value for the money. / I look carefully to find the best value for money. / I carefully watch how much I spend. / I should spend more time deciding on the products I buy. / I often make purchases I later wish I had not. / I frequently purchase on impulse. / I take the time to shop carefully for best buys.

# Do brand names in a foreign language lead to different brand perceptions?

Laura Salciuviene, *Lancaster University, UK*
Pervez N. Ghauri, *Kings College London, UK*
Ruth Salomea Streder, *Lewis-Global Public Relations, UK*
Claudio De Mattos, *Manchester Business School, UK*

**Abstract** This study examines the effects of brand names in a foreign language, country of origin, and the incongruence between the two on brand perceptions of services. Employing congruity and categorisation theory as a theoretical foundation, this study empirically tests a number of hypotheses. The findings suggest that services with a French brand name are perceived as more hedonic. In the context of hedonic services, the incongruence between brand names in a foreign language and country of origin leads to increased perceptions of services as more hedonic. In the context of utilitarian services, the same incongruence leads to higher perceived suitability and preference for brand names in a foreign language. The paper concludes with research and managerial implications for brand managers and further research directions.

## Introduction

Prior research in the domain of brand management suggests that brand names are key indicators of the products that have become an imperative asset that influences consumer brand perceptions in today's highly competitive environment (Ailawadi & Keller, 2004). Brand names simplify consumer choices by helping them to recognise products more easily (Friedman, 1985). Well-chosen brand names contribute to the strength of the product. Brand names that are associated with positive attributes score higher on overall liking (Kohli & Harich, 2005). Moreover, sounds (phonetic structure) of brand names may affect consumer attitudes (Yorkston & Menon, 2004). Although companies tend to use 'brand names that suggest language origins different from the brands' true country-of-origin' (Samiee, Shimp, & Sharma 2005, p. 391), evidence of consumer preferences for foreign brand names is limited and 'the literature on branding in an international context is somewhat sparse' (Alashban, Hayes, Zinkhan, & Balazs, 2002, p. 38).

Country of origin is another important concept in international marketing that has been documented to affect consumer perceptions (e.g. Lotz & Hu, 2001; for a good overview, see Balabinis & Diamontopoulos, 2008; Bhaskaran & Sukumaran, 2007; Leonidou, Palihawadana, & Talias, 2007; Usunier, 1994, 2006) and has connotations with foreign brand names (Kinra, 2006). The extant literature on country-of-origin effects suggests that, due to the rise in multinational production, international companies are increasingly paying less attention to the importance of country of origin as a source of competitive advantage and as a driver of customer preferences (Baker & Ballington, 2002; Jo, Nakamoto, & Nelson, 2003; Kinra, 2006). Yet, this area remains important for both academics and practitioners for reasons related to consumer preferences for brands in relation to country of origin and international marketing gaps in existing knowledge (Balabanis & Diamantopoulos, 2008; Samiee et al., 2005; Schuiling & Kapferer, 2004; Steenkamp, Batra, & Alden, 2003). Thus calls have been made that 'further examination is required of the relationship between brand management and country-of-origin' (Dinnie, 2004, p. 199).

This study, a response to previous literature, increases our understanding of the effectiveness of brand names in a foreign language and incongruence with country of origin to generate preferred perceptions. By combining the concepts of brand names in a foreign language and country of origin, and examining the effects of incongruity between the two on the preference for brand names in respect to hedonic versus utilitarian perceptions, the study aims to make a contribution towards theory development in this field. This study also details the concept of foreign branding. A further contribution of this study is to investigate these concepts and their incongruence in the services sector, as most of the previous studies on brands and country of origin were conducted in the context of consumer products. Methodologically, the study contributes towards a better understanding of actual consumers (rather than students) of specific services. It provides more accurate insights into the effects of a brand name in a foreign language and country of origin, and their incongruence, on consumer perceptions.

## Background and hypotheses

### Congruity and categorisation theory

The researchers apply congruity and categorisation theory (Osgood & Tannenbaum, 1955) to understand how to enhance brand perceptions of consumers. The congruity perspective enlightens how congruent versus incongruent information changes consumer attitudes (Osgood & Tannenbaum, 1955). In other words, congruity explains 'the attitude change that occurs when a source is connected to a particular attitude object' (Jagre, Watson, & Watson, 2001, p. 439). In this study, 'congruity' refers to the condition in which the language of a brand name matches the country of origin of the language (i.e. German brand name and Germany as country of origin), while 'incongruity' refers to the state in which the language of a brand name is different from the country of origin (i.e. German brand name and France as a country of origin).

Previous studies suggest that the influence of congruity on enhanced consumer attitudes is not unambiguous and provide mixed results in the context of product branding or country-of-origin effects. For instance, some studies suggest a link between congruity and higher product-purchase intentions (Chao, Wuhrer, & Werani, 2005) and positive product quality judgements (Häubl & Elrod, 1999). Yet, other studies call this assumption into question, suggesting that the effect of congruity is not so clear under certain conditions. Partial or no support was found suggesting that congruity does not always generate more positive product or brand evaluations (Leclerc, Schmitt, & Dubé, 1994) or has no effects on product perceptions (Hui & Zhou, 2003; Thakor & Pacheco, 1997).

In addition, consumers may have categorically different attitudes based on their prior expectations and knowledge about brands. Therefore, categorisation theory is used as a theoretical basis for this study, as it has been applied to similar studies in the context of product branding (Samiee et al., 2005). Categorisation theory also takes into account incongruity or mismatch perceived by consumers. Categorisation theory suggests that if information is new, it is likely to be linked with existing knowledge (Cohen & Basu, 1997). 'If a new stimulus can be categorised as an example of a previously defined category, then the affect associated with the category can be quickly retrieved and applied to the stimulus' (Sujan, 1985, p. 31). Therefore, consumers are likely to link language and new sounds of a 'foreign brand' to prior information on country of origin. Such information generates positive consumer attitudes and enables individuals to categorise products according to their relative hedonic/utilitarian nature (Batra & Ahtola, 1990; Dhar & Wertenbroch, 2000; Hirschman & Holbrook, 1982; Mano & Oliver, 1993).

In the context of this study, the category refers to a brand name in a foreign language of services. The authors define 'a brand name in a foreign language' as a name that reads or sounds as originating from a foreign language and not from the consumer's native language (based on Leclerc et al., 1994; Li & Murray, 1998; Samiee et al., 2005). This study posits that services with brand names in a foreign language may be perceived to be somewhat unique and categorically different from services with local brand names. Thus 'incongruence' between a brand name and country of origin should lead to increased hedonic perceptions, higher suitability, and preferences for brand names in a foreign language.

## Foreign brand names and brand perceptions

Research in international branding reports that limited attention has been given to brand names (Alashban et al., 2002), in particular to foreign brand names. Previous studies in this area can be divided into a few groups. One group of researchers examines brand-name origin perceptions (e.g. Balabanis & Diamantopoulos, 2008; Eckhardt, 2005; Samiee et al., 2005). For instance, Samiee et al. (2005) indicate that consumers recognise brands on the basis of brand-name associations with languages that refer to the brand origin. Another group of researchers highlights that products can be consumed because of evaluations of products as hedonic/utilitarian and thus influence consumer evaluations (e.g. Gürhan-Canli & Maheswaran, 2000; Nebenzahl, Jaffé, & Usunier, 2003; Thakor & Lavack, 2003). Leclerc et al. (1994) suggest that foreign brand names have positive effects on hedonic product evaluations. Harris, Garner-Earl, Sprick, and Carroll (1994) examine consumer preferences for brand names in different languages when evaluating advertisements. Thakor and Pacheco (1997) report no significant differences with regard to foreign brand names and their effects on perceptions of hedonic products. Thakor and Kohli (1996) suggest that products with French brand names lead to significant differences in product ratings than products with brands in another language. Leclerc, Schmitt, and Dubè-Rioux (1989) demonstrate that a French pronunciation highlights the hedonic characteristics of the product. Thus, based on the above evidence:

*H1: Services branded with brand names in a French language are perceived as more hedonic.*

### Country-of-origin effects

The starting point of foreign branding emerged in the research stream provided by country-of-origin studies. It is generally acknowledged that country of origin affects consumers' evaluations (see Bhaskaran & Sukumaran, 2007). Country of origin in this study refers to the country from where services originate.

The importance of country of origin, however, has changed in the last 35 years, since Schooler (1965) introduced the country-of-origin concept, as a consequence of major evolution in sourcing and branding policies of multinational corporations (Nebenzahl et al., 2003). The Internet, without country boundaries acceptance (Pharr, 2005), also blurs the validity of country of origin (Samiee et al., 2005). Thus companies increasingly focus on brands in order to hide the country of origin of products due to a more difficult identification of country of origin, as more products are designed in one country and manufactured in another (Usunier, 2006).

In evaluating products, customers not only rely on specific product information (Leonidou et al., 2007), but also use their expertise to develop notions about the products of a particular country (Chattalas, Kramer, & Takada, 2008; Lin & Chen, 2006), using country's image to ease their choices. Research points out that consumer perceptions of country image form their positive or negative attitudes towards products that were made in that country (Ahmed, Johnson, Fang, & Hui, 2002; Hongzhi & Knight, 2007; Vida & Reardon, 2008). Country image refers to the stereotypes that consumers hold about a particular country in terms of economic development, political stability, and cultural environment. Country image is particularly important when consumers are not familiar with the brand names; its influence is therefore higher than that of a brand (Nebenzahl & Jaffé, 1996). Products from a country that has a more hedonic image (e.g. France) are perceived as more hedonic than those from a country that has no perceptions of a hedonic image (e.g. the United States) (Leclerc et al., 1994). Thus:

> H2: Services associated with a country that has a hedonic image (France) are perceived as more hedonic.

### Incongruence between a brand name in a foreign language and country of origin

Similar to previous country-of-origin studies, studies on product branding produced equivocal results on the effects of incongruence/congruity on attitude formation. Regarding congruity, Chao et al. (2005) indicate that consumers prefer factors to be congruent. Yet, Leclerc et al. (1994) suggest that congruity is not an advantage, as it does not lead to more positive hedonic perceptions of ads, while incongruent associations lead to less positive evaluations. Hui and Zhou (2003) point out that country-of-origin information and brand name, when they are congruent, are likely to have no effects on product perceptions. Similarly, Thakor and Pacheco (1997) find no significant effects of congruity between a brand and country of origin on perceptions.

The literature on incongruence suggests that consumers memorise expectancy-incongruent information and recall it better (Stangor & McMillan, 1992). In the context of a sponsor and its associated event, 'the tendency to sponsor events that provide a consistent "fit" with a company may not be an effective way to enhance company's image' (Jagre et al., 2001, p. 444). Drawing on categorisation theory, when consumers are presented with new brand-name country-of-origin information that does not match their existing experience, the likelihood of enhanced favourability for incongruence increases. Moreover, the novelty of incongruence boosts excitement (Mandler, 1982). In our study, we posit that incongruity evokes interesting associations and is well accepted by consumers. Thus:

> H3a: In the context of utilitarian services, incongruence between the language of the brand name and the country of origin elicits consumers' preference for those services.

> H3b: In the context of utilitarian services, incongruence between the language of the brand name and the country of origin strengthens the perceived suitability of those brand names for the services.

### Role of gender in favouring foreign brand names

Despite the extant research in demographics and their moderating role in consumer attitudes (e.g. Devlin, 2007; Schaefer, 1997), there is disagreement on perceptions caused by gender differences. Earlier country-of-origin studies have attempted to link gender and behavioural outcomes but have produced somewhat mixed results. One group of studies reports that females rate foreign products higher than males (e.g. Wall & Heslop, 1986), while men are more responsive than women to 'buy national' campaigns (Ettenson, Wagner, & Gaeth, 1988). A second group of previous studies suggests that female consumers have more favourable views than males of domestic products (e.g. Good & Huddleston, 1995; Sharma Shimp, & Shin, 1995; Vida & Fairhurst, 1999). Females tend to choose ads (Harris et al., 1994) and sunglasses (Thakor & Pacheco, 1997) with foreign brand names compared to males. Thus:

> H4: Contrary to males, females favour foreign brand names rather than local ones.

Figure 1 depicts a detailed contextualised model of the hypothesised relationships. It incorporates concepts of a brand name in a foreign language, country of origin, the incongruence between the two, and gender effects on hedonic/utilitarian perceptions, preference for brand names, and perceived suitability. Previous studies have yielded somewhat controversial findings on the effects of incongruence between a brand name and country of origin. The research hypotheses in this study are proposed in line with this framework.

## Method

### Pretest and research setting

As a large body of research provides strong evidence of product country oforigin (see Usunier, 2006) and branding for consumer goods (Ailawadi & Keller, 2004), the literature demands further investigation into these concepts in the services field (Berry, 2000; De Chernatony & Segal-Horn, 2001, 2003; O'Cass & Grace, 2003; O'Loughlin & Szmigin, 2007; Roth, 1995). Thus, answering to the call for more branding and country-of-origin studies in services field, this study focuses on the services industry, specifically two leisure services: all-inclusive hotels and insurance. Hotels are associated with pleasure, fun, and other hedonic perceptions. Insurance services are associated with functional and other utilitarian perceptions. These services therefore were deemed as representing both ends of hedonic/utilitarian dimensions (Dhar & Wertenbroch, 2000; Hirschman & Holbrook, 1982) and thus are appropriate for this study.

**Figure 1** A detailed contextualized model of the hypothesised relationships.

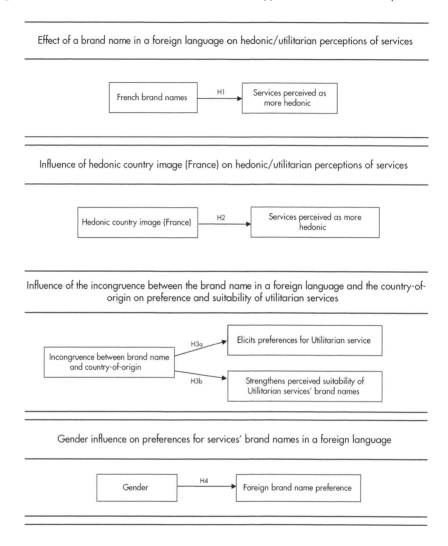

A pretest of four phases was conducted with leisure travellers to create stimuli for the study. During the first phase, participants were asked to rate the services on a seven-point Likert scale (Ghauri & Gronhaug, 2005) across two dimensions: utilitarian and hedonic (Hirschman & Holbrook, 1982). Overall, travel insurance scored the lowest and the all-inclusive hotel the highest. Thus they were chosen for further investigation.

The objective of the second phase was to generate a list of countries that had perceptions of a hedonic country image. Participants were asked to prepare a list with the countries and to rank them accordingly (from 1 = 'lowest' to 5 = 'highest'). France scored highest on having a hedonic country image, while Germany and the UK scored lower on this dimension.

During the third phase, brand-name stimuli were chosen for the current study. Fictitious brand names were employed with the purpose of eliminating the effects of consumers' prior knowledge and experiences with the brands (Keller, 1993). None of these fictitious brand names has a meaning in any of these languages. The fictitious German brand names (Dapöhn and Rimöhr) accompanied the made-up French (Dapōne and Rimoré) and English (Dapon and Rimor) brand names and were adopted from Leclerc et al. (1994) to ensure associations with French and English languages.

During the final phase, an instrument with a sample size of 24 respondents was pretested in each location. This number of respondents meets the requirement of the minimum number of 10 (Fink, 1985) and ensures the instrument be pretested at least twice. Minor modifications were made before distributing the final versions (Saunders, Lewis, & Thornhill, 2003).

## Research design and procedures

In the context of this study, the dependent variables include perceptions of services as hedonic/utilitarian, preference for brand names, and perceived suitability of services brand names. The study followed a factorial design resulting in pairing every level of country of origin with every level of brand name. The first factor was country of origin and the second factor was brand name.

Subjects were 240 leisure travellers waiting to board aircrafts at international airports, as in previous similar studies conducted in services settings (e.g. Bitner, 1990). Thus the researchers hold that this setting diminished any time pressures, allowing respondents to involve themselves with the questions and provide their best responses. Respondents usually took between 20 and 30 minutes to complete the questionnaire. A total of 46% of the travellers approached agreed to participate in the study. After the initial screening and agreement to take part in the study, respondents were randomly assigned to one of 12 experimental treatments (size of cells = 20). This sample size and size of cells is similar to previous studies (e.g. Leclerc et al., 1994) and is as per the recommendations of Hair, Anderson, Tatham, and Black (1998) and Tabachnick and Fidell (2001).

This study employed an experimental design that considers the impact of several independent variables simultaneously on related metric dependent variables utilising multivariate analysis of variance (MANOVA) (Hair et al., 1998). This technique employs sums-of-squares and cross-products matrices (SSCP) to test for differences among groups (Diamantopoulos & Schlegelmich, 2002). The variance between groups is determined by partioning the total SSCP matrix and testing for significance. The statistical Box's test was also used. This test is sensitive to departures from the assumption of normality and examines whether the observed covariance matrices of the dependent variables are equal across the groups (Hair et al., 1998).

## Sampling and data collection

Previous studies have been criticised for researching students because of biased responses (Liefeld, 1993). In an attempt to overcome this criticism and to strengthen the external validity (Ghauri & Gronhaug, 2005), the current study focuses on actual consumers. Respondents were screened prior to the start of the survey. They had to be leisure travellers with previous leisure travel experience in order to ensure their familiarity with tourism-related services (Johansson, Douglas, & Nonaka, 1985; Quer, Claver, & Andreu, 2007).

A survey was conducted at airports in the UK (Manchester and Stansted) and Germany (Hamburg and Munich). The UK and Germany were chosen as locations for the current study due to the high volume of flights and leisure travellers (IATA, 2007). These airports were also used because they are (a) major airports for holidaymakers, maximising sample representativeness of the leisure travel population (Piron, 2000); (b) not major airports in those countries and so are used by budget airlines targeting leisure travellers; and (c) of similar size, allowing for equivalence of samples.

### Respondents' profile

Data were collected at different gates within the respective international airports at various times of the day (e.g. Bitner, 1990) to minimise the potential bias that could have occurred had data been collected at a single time on a single day (Ghauri & Gronhaug, 2005). Table 1 depicts demographic characteristics of the sample.

Of a total of 240 subjects, 46% were females and 54% were males. Subjects were distributed similarly among age groups. Additionally, 50% were British and 50% were German respondents with a wide range of income. As these demographic characteristics did not have significant effects on dependent variables, they were excluded from further data analysis.

### Measures

Twelve different treatments demanded two different versions of the questionnaire. Depending on the treatment (brand name [English, German, or French] and country of origin provided [UK, France, or Germany]), respondents were presented either with the longer or the shorter version of the questionnaire (brand name [English, German, or French] and no country-of-origin information provided). A sample questionnaire with country-of-origin information is presented in Appendix 1. The explanation of the terms 'hedonic' and 'utilitarian' services was provided in the questionnaire, and

**Table 1** Sample demographic characteristics.

| Item | Frequency | Percentage |
|---|---|---|
| *Gender* | | |
| Male | 130 | 54% |
| Female | 110 | 46% |
| *Age Group* | | |
| 25–30 | 64 | 26.7% |
| 31–35 | 55 | 22.9% |
| 36–40 | 57 | 23.8% |
| 41–45 | 64 | 26.7% |
| *Nationality* | | |
| British | 120 | 50% |
| German | 120 | 50% |
| *Income* | | |
| Under £20,000 | 7 | 2.9% |
| £20,001–£30,000 | 53 | 22.1% |
| £30,001–£40,000 | 75 | 31.3% |
| £40,001–£50,000 | 68 | 28.3% |
| Above £50,001 | 37 | 15.4% |

examples of these concepts were presented alongside with an explanation of the term 'country of origin'. 'Hedonic services' refer to services that provide experiential consumption in terms of pleasure, fun, and excitement (Holbrook, 1986), while 'utilitarian services' refer to services that provide rational (instrumental) usage in terms of functionality of services (Hirshman, 1980).

Respondents were asked to evaluate the services (insurance and hotel) based on their preferences for brand names, suitability of services' brand names, and perceptions of services as utilitarian/hedonic on a seven-point Likert scale (Ghauri & Gronhaug, 2005). The measurement scales were adopted from Harris et al. (1994), Leclerc et al. (1994), Papadopoulos, Heslop, and Bamossy (1990), Peabody (1985), and Thakor and Pacheco (1997).

The questionnaires refer to service companies (e.g. insurance) operating in the home country of the respondent. Those service companies held brand names associated with different languages (i.e. German, French, and British). There are mechanisms for ensuring quality of services; for instance in the UK, there is the Insurance Ombudsman Bureau (e.g. Rawlings & Willett, 1994; Tyldesley, 1998). The implicit assumption is that the general perception of the consumers regarding the companies operating in a certain sector in their home country applies to all companies. The researchers interpret the study's findings in the light of positive associations with brand names in different languages.

### Analysis plan and procedures

The data were checked, the assumptions of MANOVA were satisfied in all cases, and the requirement for a cell size of 20 was achieved, as recommended by Hair et al. (1998). First, to test H1, one independent variable (brand name) was run against the dependent variable (hedonic/utilitarian perceptions). Then H2 was tested regarding effects of the independent variable (county of origin) on the dependent variable (hedonic/utilitarian perceptions). Next, H3a and H3b were tested with regard to effects of incongruence (e.g. services branded in French that originate from UK or Germany) on dependent variables. The independent variables (brand name in French, German, and English, and country-of-origin – UK, France, and Germany) were run against all our dependent variables. Finally, H4 was tested by running the independent variable (gender) against the dependent variable (preference for a brand name).

# Analysis and findings

### Brand names and perceptions of services as hedonic

The results suggest that, for utilitarian services, a brand name in the French language induces a perception of services as more hedonic than other two languages (English and German), $F = 9.95$, $p = .000$; the homogeneity assumption is supported, Box's $M = 17.66$, $F = 2.80$, $p = .010$ (Hair et al., 1998; Tabachnick & Fidell, 2001). This means that individuals perceive insurance services branded with French names as offering higher perceived hedonic value than services branded with German or English brand names (see Figure 2). Thus H1 is supported.

**Figure 2** Perception of services with French brand names as more hedonic.

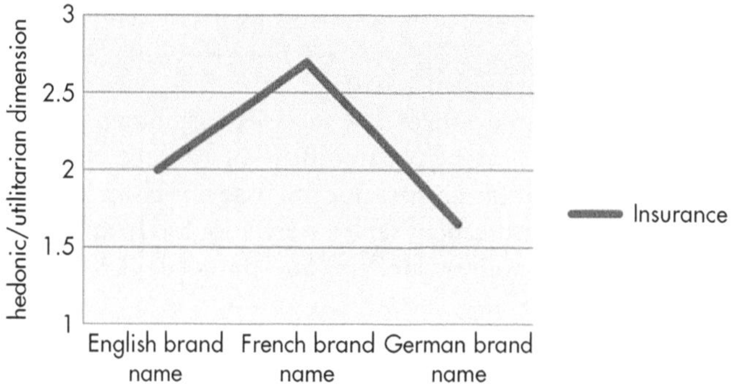

## Country-of-origin image and perceptions of services as hedonic

The results suggest that, in case of incongruence and in the context of hedonic services, H2 is supported, $F = 4.38$, $p = .002$; the homogeneity assumption is also satisfactory, Box's $M = 21.05$, $F = .84$, $p = .69$. This confirms that hedonic services are seen as more hedonic when the country of origin has a hedonic image. In this specific case, hotel services associated with France are perceived as more hedonic (see Table 2).

## Incongruence between a brand name in a foreign language and country of origin

The results suggest that, for utilitarian services, incongruence between the language of the brand name and the country of origin elicits consumers' preference for those services, $F = 12.24$, $p = .001$; the homogeneity assumption is satisfactory, Box's $M = 6.43$, $F = 2.11$, $p = .96$. The hypothesis H3a is supported. This means that, for insurance services, brand names in languages other than the language of the country of origin (incongruence) increase consumer preferences for those services (see Figure 3).

The results suggest that, for utilitarian services, incongruence between the language of a brand name and country of origin leads to a stronger perception of the suitability of those brand names, $F = 52.77$, $p = .000$; the homogeneity assumption is satisfactory, Box's $M = 2.04$, $F = .67$, $p = .57$. The hypothesis H3b is supported, meaning consumers perceive a brand name as more suitable for utilitarian services when the language of the brand name is different from the language associated with the country of origin (i.e. incongruence between those two) (see Figure 4).

**Table 2** MANOVA results: Means of hotel services in each of the experimental conditions.

| Hedonic services | Country of origin | Brand name | | | |
| | | English | French | German | Total |
| --- | --- | --- | --- | --- | --- |
| Hotel | UK | 4.50 | 4.95 | 5.20 | 4.88 |
| | France | 5.45 | 4.75 | 5.65 | 5.28 |
| | Germany | 5.00 | 5.50 | 4.75 | 5.08 |

$1 =$ 'definitely utilitarian', $7 =$ 'definitely hedonic'.

**Figure 3** Incongruence and consumer preferences for utilitarian services.

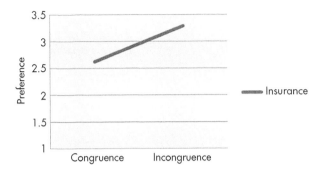

**Figure 4** Incongruence and perceived suitability for utilitarian services.

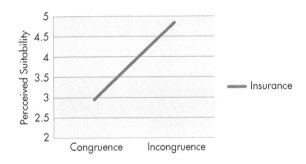

### Gender and foreign brand-name preferences

The results for the final hypothesis, H4, that 'contrary to males, females favour foreign brand names rather than local ones' are not significant, $p > .05$.

## Discussion of findings

This study contributes to the literature by increasing our understanding of how country of origin and brand names in a foreign language, independently or combined (e.g. incongruently), may generate preferred consumer perceptions. This study makes additional contributions by clarifying the conceptualisation of 'foreign branding' through a derived concept, which is 'a brand name in a foreign language' that was tested in the context of services. Methodologically, the country-of-origin and brand-name connection was tested with actual consumers of the services under investigation.

The results of this study suggest that: (1) consumers prefer brand names in the French language, with such brand names leading to more hedonic perceptions of utilitarian services; (2) France as the country of origin strengthens the perception of services as hedonic; (3) incongruence between the language of the brand name and the country of origin increases the perceived suitability and preferences for utilitarian services (see Figure 5 and Table 3). Thus the findings expand on the conclusions of previous studies in the literature.

**Figure 5** Integrated model for the supported hypotheses.

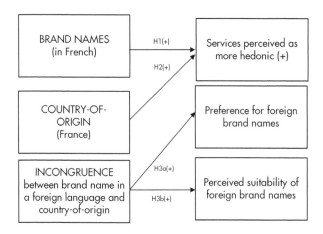

**Table 3** Hypotheses overview.

| | Hypothesis | Result |
|---|---|---|
| H1 | In the context of utilitarian services, services branded with brand names in a French language are perceived as more hedonic. | Supported |
| H2 | In case of incongruence and in the context of hedonic services, services associated with a country that has a hedonic image (France) are perceived as more hedonic. | Supported |
| H3a | In the context of utilitarian services, incongruence between the language of the brand name and the country of origin elicits consumers' preference for those services. | Supported |
| H3b | In the context of utilitarian services, incongruence between the language of the brand name and the country of origin strengthens the perceived suitability of those brand names for the services. | Supported |
| H4 | Contrary to males, females favour foreign brand names rather than local ones. | Not supported |

First, it emerged from the results that brand names in the French language lead to more hedonic perceptions of utilitarian services. The results of this study are in line with Thakor and Kohli (1996), who suggest that French brand names highlight hedonic characteristics and English and German brand names draw attention to utilitarian characteristics in the context of products. However, the outcome of this study is in opposition to the results of Leclerc et al. (1994) in the context of utilitarian products, in which they found a weak effect on attitudes toward the brand names in French. A possible explanation might be due to focus on products rather than services (as in the context of this study).

Observing these results, unanswered questions emerge and solicit further research. Why does the French language, compared to other languages, lead to more positive perceptions for services? Does the French language sound more pleasant for respondents? Categorisation theory indicates one possible explanation, that is, brands in French are categorised as more enjoyable due to the past (enjoyable) experience associated with French names. Thus individuals perceive services branded in French as more pleasurable.

Examining the relationship between perceptions of services as hedonic and country image, the second finding of this study suggests that services are perceived as more hedonic if they have associations with France, a country that has a hedonic country image. This finding is in line with previous studies on country images (Ahmed et al., 2002). However, this is in contrast with the previous brand studies in the context of product (e.g. Leclerc et al., 1994). A possible explanation is our services context. Large French players dominate the tourism industry. For example, there exist several famous French hotel chains across Europe (e.g. Novotel, Ibis). Because of this French dominance, consumers' French brand-name recall and recognition are relatively high and therefore might have an indirect influence on attitudes toward hotel services. Associations with sophistication, pleasure, fun, and elegance lead to perceptions of services as hedonic, eliciting positive associations with France as a country image.

Our next finding relates to 'incongruence/congruity'. Contrary to previous studies, we find that incongruence between a brand name and the country of origin leads to more positive brand perceptions (i.e. stronger perceived suitability and preference for brands). This finding is observed only in the case of utilitarian services. In other words, individuals prefer utilitarian services branded with brand names that are incongruent with the country of origin (i.e. a mismatch between the language of a brand name and country of origin). This opposes the results of some previous studies carried out in the context of products. Those studies suggest that congruence (rather than the incongruence seen in this study) between a product brand name and country of origin has a positive influence on purchase intentions (Cho, Wuhrer, & Werani, 2005; Pecotich & Ward, 2007). In contrast, other studies report no significant results (Thakor & Pacheco, 1997) or no relationships (Hui & Zhou, 2003) with regard to congruence. One possible explanation for the significant results in this study regarding incongruence is that leisure travellers going on holiday in a foreign country may be expecting to encounter foreign brands and might thus be more open to foreign brand names. This may create an atmosphere of unfulfilled hedonic experiences. In addition, the incongruence between a brand name and country of origin strengthens the perceived suitability of brand names for utilitarian services. Another explanation is related to the perception of local services as low in quality. Assuming the overall perceptions of quality in a certain service sector (e.g. insurance) are higher in one country (e.g. Germany) than in another country (e.g. UK), these different perceptions could generate a response associated with negative rather than positive associations. For instance, respondents from the country in which insurance services are perceived as having low quality may tend to prefer French names because the alternative, that is, companies with English brand names, are associated with the provision of services of poor quality, and not because of any positive association that respondents may have with French company names.

Finally, the results of gender and its effects on preferences for foreign brand names were not significant. Therefore, the role of gender in choices of services branded in foreign languages is inconclusive and warrants further investigation.

Brand names in the French language increase hedonic consumer perceptions of utilitarian services. A country hedonic image (France) also increases hedonic consumer perceptions for hedonic services. Incongruence between a brand name in a foreign language and the country of origin strengthens perceived suitability and increases preference for brand names in the context of utilitarian services. Further, consumer characteristics (i.e. gender) did not seem to influence consumer preferences for foreign brand names of services. However, with the exception of effects of country image, consumer perceptions of hedonic services remain unclear and call for additional examination.

## Managerial implications and future research

The results of this study are of interest to practitioners, as timely and up-to-date knowledge on the effectiveness of brand names in a foreign language in the context of services can facilitate service branding strategies. Considering the broad range of services and the different ways of strategy implementation in services as compared to those in products (De Chernatony & Seagal-Horn, 2003), practitioners should start their strategies of services branding by analysing how consumers perceive specific characteristics (utilitarian/hedonic) of services. As the findings suggest that French enhances hedonic perceptions of utilitarian (i.e. insurance) services, a French brand name for services originating from the UK or Germany may have a positive effect on consumer perceptions. Practitioners can therefore use brands in a foreign language to enhance more favourable consumer attitudes towards their utilitarian services, as the creation of positive and relevant brand associations is essential to consumer-based brand equity management (Romaniuk & Gaillard, 2007). This is especially important for utilitarian services that are more difficult to differentiate due to their lack of perceived enjoyment and fun that are characteristics of hedonic services. Moreover, as emerged in this study, for utilitarian services, incongruence between a brand name and the country of origin increases consumer preference, as well as perceived suitability of brand names in a foreign language. The question arises 'is it simple to implement that'? Practitioners might strengthen their brand communication strategies by clearly differentiating between the language of a brand name and the country of origin. In addition, this study also identified that services are perceived as more hedonic when they have associations with France. Thus practitioners could underline positive associations when designing their brand communication strategy. Furthermore, associations may evolve in space and time and vary among groups with different demographic characteristics. Thus a positive association with France (French) may vary among groups (e.g. generations) of consumers, as well as differing justifications.

These results warrant further investigation, and this study has limitations. As international services encompass such a diverse range of activities, they seem to defy the possibility of generalisation about them (Clark, 1990). Thus the application of the results to other service sectors would need to be made tentatively. Given that consumers may be psychologically attached to specific brands and/or any country of origin due to various reasons, including consumer ethnocentrism (Vida & Reardon, 2008), status enhancement, and authenticity (Batra, Ramaswamy, Alden, Steenkamp, & Ramchander, 2000), the results may also be applied to other services with caution.

Another limitation concerns perceptions regarding service quality and its effects on services preference. If the overall perceptions of quality in a certain service sector (e.g. insurance) is higher in one country (e.g. Germany) than in another country (e.g. UK), these different perceptions regarding quality level could generate a response associated with negative associations rather than positive associations. For instance, respondents from the country in which insurance services are perceived as having low quality may tend to prefer French names because the alternative, companies with English brand names, are associated with the provision of services of poor quality, and not because of any positive association that respondents may have with French company names. It can be expected that different justifications for services preferences will be pursued in further research.

A convenient sampling (Kerlinger, 1992) was utilised in this study. Thus the results should be interpreted with caution. This topic requires further investigation when controlling for consumers' levels of experience with leisure services. For instance, two groups of leisure travellers (with and without previous experience with leisure products) could be compared regarding the effects of brand names in a foreign language on consumer perceptions. Future research needs to be extended to assess the effects of incongruence between foreign brand names and country of origin on bilingual consumers' perceptions in the context of services. Future investigation is needed to examine services that are branded in foreign languages in both developed and emerging economies.

## Acknowledgements

The authors would like to thank the guest editors, Dr Charles Cui and Dr Maria Piacentini, and two anonymous reviewers for their helpful comments in relation to the revision of the manuscript.

## References

Ahmed, Z.U., Johnson, J.P., Fang, T.W., & Hui, A.K. (2002). Country-of-origin and brand effects on consumers' evaluations of cruise lines. *International Marketing Review, 19*(3), 279–302.

Ailawadi, K.L., & Keller, K.L. (2004). Understanding retail branding: Conceptual insights and research priorities. *Journal of Retailing, 80*(4), 331–342.

Alashban, A.A., Hayes, L.A., Zinkhan, G.M., & Balazs, A.L. (2002). International brand-name standardization/adaptation: Antecedents and consequences. *Journal of International Marketing, 10*(3), 22–48.

Baker, M.J., & Ballington, L. (2002). Country of origin as a source of competitive advantage. *Journal of Strategic Marketing, 10*(2), 157–168.

Balabanis, G., & Diamantopoulos, A. (2004). Domestic country bias, country-of-origin effects, and consumer ethnocentrism: A multidimensional unfolding approach. *Journal of the Academy of Marketing Science, 32*(1), 80–95.

Balabanis, G., & Diamantopoulos, A. (2008). Brand origin identification by consumers: A classification perspective. *Journal of International Marketing, 16*(1), 39–71.

Batra, R., & Ahtola, O.T. (1990). Measuring the hedonic and utilitarian sources of consumer attitudes. *Marketing Letters, 2*(2), 159–170.

Batra, R., Ramaswamy, V., Alden, D.L., Steenkamp, J.B., & Ramchander, S. (2000). Effects of brand local/non-local origin on consumer attitudes in developing countries. *Journal of Consumer Psychology, 9*(2), 83–95.

Berry, L.L. (2000). Cultivating service brand equity. *Journal of Academy of Marketing Science, 28*(1), 128–137.

Bhaskaran, S., & Sukumaran, N. (2007). Contextual and methodological issues in COO studies. *Marketing Intelligence and Planning, 25*(1), 66–80.

Bitner, M.J. (1990). Evaluating service encounters: The effects of physical surroundings and employee responses. *Journal of Marketing, 54*(2), 69–82.

Chao, P., Wuhrer, G., & Werani, T. (2005). Celebrity and foreign brand name as moderators of country-of-origin effects. *International Journal of Advertising, 24*(2), 173–192.

Chattalas, M., Kramer, T., & Takada, H. (2008). The impact of national stereotypes on the country of origin effect: A conceptual framework. *International Marketing Review, 25*(1), 54–74.

Cho, P., Wuhrer, G., & Werani, T. (2005). Celebrity and foreign brand name as moderators of country-of-origin effects. *International Journal of Advertising, 24*(2), 173–192.

Clark, T. (1990). International marketing and national character: A review and proposal for an integrative theory. *Journal of Marketing, 54*(4), 66–79.

Cohen, J.B., & Basu, K. (1997). Alternative models of categorization: Toward a contingent processing framework. *Journal of Consumer Research, 13*, 445–472.

De Chernatony, L., & Segal-Horn, S. (2001). Building on services' characteristics to develop successful services brands. *Journal of Marketing Management, 17*(7–8), 645–669.

De Chernatony, L., & Segal-Horn, S. (2003). The criteria for successful services brands. *European Journal of Marketing, 37*(7/8), 1095–1118.

Devlin, J.F. (2007). Complex services and choice criteria: An example from the life assurance market. *Journal of Marketing Management, 23*(7–8), 631–650.

Dhar, R., & Wertenbroch, K. (2000). Consumer choice between hedonic and utilitarian goods. *Journal of Marketing Research, 37*(1), 60–71.

Diamantopoulos, A., & Schlegelmilch, B.B. (2002). *Taking the fear out of data analysis*. London: Thomson.

Dinnie, K. (2004). Country-of-origin 1965–2004: A literature review. *Journal of Customer Behaviour, 3*, 165–213.

Eckhardt, G.M. (2005). Local branding in a foreign product category in an emerging market. *Journal of International Marketing, 13*(4), 57–79.

Ettenson, R., Wagner, J., & Gaeth, G. (1988). Evaluating the effect of country-of-origin and the 'Made in the USA' campaign: A conjoint approach. *Journal of Retailing, 64*(1), 85–100.

Fink, A. (1985). *The survey handbook*. Thousand Oaks, CA: Sage.

Friedman, M. (1985). The changing language of a consumer society: Brand name usage in popular american novels in the postwar era. *Journal of Consumer Research, 11*, 927–938.

Ghauri, P.N., & Gronhaug, K. (2005). *Research methods in business studies: A practical guide*. London: Pearson.

Good, L.K., & Huddleston, P.T. (1995). Ethnocentrism and the Eastern European consumer: Are feelings and intentions related? *International Marketing Review, 12*(15), 35–48.

Gürhan-Canli, Z., & Maheswaran, D. (2000). Cultural variations in country of origin effect. *Journal of Marketing Research, 37*(3), 309–317.

Hair, J.F., Anderson, R.E., Tatham, R.L., & Black, W.C. (1998). *Multivariate data analysis*. London: Prentice Hall.

Harris, R.J., Garner-Earl, B., Sprick, S., & Carroll, C. (1994). Effects of foreign product names and country-of-origin attributions on advertisement evaluations. *Psychology and Marketing, 11*(2), 129–143.

Häubl, G., & Elrod, T. (1999). The impact of congruity between brand name and country of production on consumers' product quality judgements. *International Journal of Research in Marketing, 16*, 199–215.

Hirschman, E.C., & Holbrook, M. (1982). Hedonic consumption: Emerging concepts, methods and propositions. *Journal of Marketing, 46*(3), 92–101.

Hirshman, E.C. (1980). The effect of verbal and pictorial advertising stimuli on aesthetic, utilitarian and familiarity perceptions. *Journal of Advertising, 15*, 27–34.

Holbrook, M.B. (1986). Emotion in the consumption experience: Towards a new model of the human consumer. In R.A. Peterson, W.H. Hoye, & W.R. Wilson (Eds.), *The role of affect in consumer behaviour: Emerging theories and applications* (pp. 17–52). Lanham, MD: Lexington Books.

Hui, M.K., & Zhou, L. (2003). Country-of-manufacture effects for known brands. *European Journal of Marketing, 37*(1/2), 133–153.

Hongzhi, G., & Knight, J. (2007). Pioneering advantage and product-country image: Evidence from and exploratory study in China. *Journal of Marketing Management, 23*(3–4), 367–385.

IATA (2007) accessed online via http://www.iata.org/Pages/default.aspx

Jagre, E., Watson, J.J., & Watson, J.G. (2001). Sponsorship and congruity theory: A theoretical framework for explaining consumer attitude and recall of event sponsorship. *Advances in Consumer Research, 28,* 439–445.

Jo, M.-S., Nakamoto, K., & Nelson, J.E. (2003). The shielding effects of brand image against lower quality countries-of-origin in global manufacturing. *Journal of Business Research, 56,* 637–646.

Johansson, J.K., Douglas, S.P., & Nonaka, I. (1985). Assessing the impact of country of origin on product evaluations: A new methodological perspective. *Journal of Marketing Research, 22*(4), 388–396.

Keller, K.L. (1993). Conceptualizing, measuring and managing customer based brand equity. *Journal of Marketing, 57*(1), 1–22.

Kerlinger, R.N. (1992). *Foundations of behavioral research.* Fort Worth, TX: Harcourt Brace College.

Kinra, N. (2006). The effect of country-of-origin on foreign brand names in the Indian market. *Marketing Intelligence and Planning, 24*(1), 15–31.

Kohli, C.S., & Harich, L.L. (2005). Creating brand identity: A study of evaluation of new brand names. *Journal of Business Research, 58,* 1506–1515.

Leclerc, F., Schmitt, B., & Dubé-Rioux, L. (1994). Foreign branding and its effects on product perceptions and attitudes. *Journal of Marketing Research, 31*(2), 263–269.

Leclerc, F., Schmitt, B., & Dubè-Rioux, L. (1989). Brand name a la française? Oui, but for the right product. *Advances in Consumer Research, 16*(1), 253–257.

Leonidou, L., Palihawadana, D., & Talias, M.A. (2007). British consumers' evaluations of US versus Chinese goods: A multi-level and multi-cue comparison. *European Journal of Marketing, 41*(7/8), 786–820.

Li, Z.G., & Murray, W.L. (1998). Should you use foreign branding in China? An exploratory study. *AMA Conference Proceedings, 9,* 233–241.

Liefeld, J.P. (1993). Consumer use of country-of-origin information in product evaluations: Evidence from experiments. In N. Papadopoulos & L. Heslop (Eds.), *Product and country image: Concepts, practices and implications* (pp. 117–156). Binghamton, NY: Haworth Press.

Lin, L.-Y., & Chen, C.-S. (2006). The influence of the country-of-origin image, product knowledge and product involvement on consumer purchase decisions: An empirical study of insurance and catering services in Taiwan. *Journal of Consumer Marketing, 23*(5), 248–265.

Lotz, S.L., & Hu, M.Y. (2001). Diluting negative country of origin stereotypes: A social stereotype approach. *Journal of Marketing Management, 17,* 105–135.

Mandler, G. (1982). The structure of value: Accounting for taste. In M. Clark & S. Friske (Eds.), *The 17th Annual Carnegie Symposium on Cognition* (pp. 3–36). Hillsdale, NJ: Lawrence Erlbaum.

Mano, H., & Oliver, R.L. (1993). Assessing the dimensionality and structure of the consumption experience: Evaluation, feeling and satisfaction. *Journal of Consumer Research, 20,* 451–466.

Nebenzahl, I.D., & Jaffé, E.D. (1996). Measuring the joint effect of brand and country image in consumer evaluation of global products. *International Marketing Review, 13*(4), 5–22.

Nebenzahl, I.D., Jaffé, E.D., & Usunier, J.-C. (2003). Personifying country of origin research. *Management International Review, 43*(4), 383–406.

O'Cass, A., & Grace, D. (2003). An exploratory perspective of service brand associations. *Journal of Services Marketing, 17*(5), 452–475.

O'Loughlin, D., & Szmigin, I. (2007). Services branding: Revealing the rhetoric within retail banking. *The Service Industries Journal, 27*(4), 435–452.

Osgood, C.E., & Tannenbaum, P.H. (1955). The principle of congruity in the prediction of attitude change. *Psychological Review, 62*(1), 42–55.

Papadopoulos, N., Heslop, L.A., & Bamossy, G. (1990). A comparative analysis of domestic versus imported products. *International Journal of Research in Marketing, 7*(4), 283–294.

Peabody, D. (1985). *National characteristics*. Cambridge, England: Cambridge University Press.

Pecotich, A., & Ward, S. (2007). Global branding, country of origin and expertise. *International Marketing Review, 24*(3), 271–296.

Pharr, J.M. (2005). Synthesizing country of origin research from the last decade: Is the concept still salient in an era of global brands? *Journal of Marketing Theory and Practice, 13*(4), 34–45.

Piron, F. (2000). Consumers' perceptions of the country-of-origin effect in purchasing intentions of (in)conspicuous products. *Journal of Consumer Marketing, 17*(4), 308–321.

Quer, D., Claver, E., & Andreu, R. (2007). Foreign market entry model in the hotel industry: The impact of country- and form-specific factors. *International Business Review, 16*(3), 362–376.

Rawlings, P., & Willett, Ch. (1994). Ombudsman schemes in the United Kingdom's financial sector: The insurance ombudsman, the banking ombudsman, and the building societies ombudsman. *Journal of Consumer Policy, 17*(3), 307–333.

Romaniuk, J., & Gaillard, E. (2007). The relationship between unique brand associations, brand usage and brand performance: Analysis across eight categories. *Journal of Marketing Management, 23*(3–4), pp. 267–284.

Roth, M.S. (1995). Effects of global market conditions on brand image customization and brand performance. *Journal of Advertising, 24*(4), 55–75.

Samiee, S., Shimp, T., & Sharma, S. (2005). Brand origin recognition accuracy: Its antecedents and consumers' cognitive limitations. *Journal of International Business Studies, 36*, 379–397.

Saunders, M., Lewis, P., & Thornhill, A. (2003). *Research methods*. Harlow, England: Pearson Education.

Schooler, R.D. (1965). Product bias in the Central American common market. *Journal of Marketing Research, 2*(4), 394–397.

Schuiling, I., & Kapferer, J.-N. (2004). Real differences between local and international brands: Strategic implications for international marketers. *Journal of International Marketing, 12*(4), 97–112.

Schaefer, A. (1997). Do demographics have an impact on country of origin effects. *Journal of Marketing Management, 13*(8), 813–834.

Sharma, S., Shimp, T.A., & Shin, J. (1995). Consumer ethnocentrism: A test of antecedents and moderators. *Journal of the Academy of Marketing Science, 23*(1), 26–37.

Stangor, Ch., & McMillan, D. (1992). Memory for expectancy-congruent and expectancy-incongruent information: A review of the social and social developmental literatures. *Psychological Bulletin, 3*(1), 42–61.

Steenkamp, J.-B., Batra, R., & Alden, D. (2003). How perceived brand globalness creates brand value. *Journal of International Business Studies, 34*(1), 53–65.

Sujan, M. (1985). Consumer knowledge: Effects on evaluation strategies mediating consumer judgements. *Journal of Consumer Research, 12*(3), 31–46.

Tabachnick, B.G., & Fidell, L.S. (2001). *Using multivariate statistics*. Boston: Allyn and Bacon.

Thakor, M.V., & Kohli, C.S. (1996). Brand origin: Conceptualization and review. *The Journal of Consumer Marketing, 13*(3), 27–42.

Thakor, M.V., & Lavack, A.M. (2003). Effect of perceived brand origin associations on consumer perceptions of quality. *Journal of Product and Brand Management, 12*(6), 394–407.

Thakor, M.V., & Pacheco, B.G. (1997). Foreign branding and its effects on product perceptions and attitudes: A replication and extension in a multicultural setting. *Journal of Marketing Theory and Practice*, 5(1), 15–30.

Tyldesley, P.J. (1998). The insurance ombudsman bureau – The early history. *Analysis – The insurance ombudsman bureau*, pp. 34–43. Available at http://www.peterjtyldesley.com/files/2003%20The-Insurance-Ombudsman-Bureau-the-early-history.pdf

Usunier, J.-C. (1994). Social status and country-of-origin preferences. *Journal of Marketing Management*, 10(8), 765–783.

Usunier, J.-C. (2006). Relevance in business research: The case of country of origin research in marketing. *European Management Review*, 3, 60–73.

Vida, I., & Fairhurst, A. (1999). Factors underlying the phenomenon of consumer ethnocentricity: Evidence from four Central European countries. *The International Review of Retail, Distribution and Consumer Research*, 9(4), 321–337.

Vida, I., & Reardon, J. (2008). Domestic consumption: Rational, affective or normative choice? *Journal of Consumer Marketing*, 25(1), 34–44.

Wall, M., & Heslop, L. (1986). Consumer attitudes toward Canadian-made versus imported products. *Journal of the Academy of Marketing Science*, 14(2), 27–36.

Yorkston, E., & Menon, G. (2004). A sound idea: Phonetic effects of brand names on consumer judgements. *Journal of Consumer Research*, 31, 43–45.

# Appendix. Sample outline of the questionnaire

Section A: General information:

> Age, gender, nationality, and annual income

Brief purpose of the study
Definitions (explanations) of:

> utilitarian services,
>
> hedonic services, and
>
> country of origin

Section B1:

> Type of service: Travel insurance
>
> Specification: worldwide cover, refund of cancelation cost, insurance of all baggage, emergency evacuation
>
> Brand name: Dapône
>
> Country-of-origin: Germany
>
> Question (a) services perceptions as hedonic versus utilitarian (on a seven-point Likert scale)
>
> Question (b) brand name preference (using a seven-point Likert scale)
>
> Question (c) brand name suitability (using a seven-point Likert scale)

Section B2:

> Type of service: All-inclusive hotel
>
> Specification: three-star hotel, 200 bungalows along a palm fringed beach, pool and sports facilities, accommodation, meals and entertainment included

Brand name: Rimoré

Country of origin: Germany

Question (a) services perceptions as hedonic versus utilitarian (on a seven-point Likert scale)

Question (b) brand name preference (using a seven-point Likert scale)

Question (c) brand name suitability (using a seven-point Likert scale)

# Consuming Bollywood: Young Sikhs social comparisons with heroes and heroines in Indian films

Amandeep Takhar, *Keele University, UK*
Pauline Maclaran, *University of London, UK*
Elizabeth Parsons, *Keele University, UK*
Anne Broderick, *De Montfort University, UK*

**Abstract** This interpretivist study uses social comparison and social identity theory to consider how members of the British Sikh community are consuming Bollywood films (the Indian movie industry). In applying social comparison theory to this ethnic context, we seek to extend knowledge of how this theory relates to cultural identity construction. In terms of social identity and acculturation, the social function of Bollywood films and their popular consumption provide a valuable narrative space to negotiate and 'remoor' ethnic identity. Three key themes emerged to illustrate the ways in which the social comparisons that Bollywood encourages are influencing the identities of third generation British Sikhs: (1) social comparison and ideals of romance; (2) gender differences: making comparisons to heroes and heroines; and (3) British versus Indian self: Bollywood as a medium for identity reconstruction.

## Introduction

Social comparison theory has been used by consumer researchers in a variety of ways to understand the effects of comparisons that consumers make between themselves and others. It has been found particularly useful to explore the influence of idealised images in advertisements (Lin & Tsai, 2006; Richins, 1991, 1992; Stewart & Clark, 2007), but also in relation to possessions (Ackerman, MacInnis, & Folkes, 2000; Belk & Pollay, 1985) and physical attractiveness (Martin & Kennedy, 1993, 1994). Recent studies have also explored individuals' inclination to compare themselves to others of their own gender (Knobloch-Westerwick & Hastall, 2006), as well as the inclination to self-monitor (Harnish & Bridges, 2006).

Where social comparison theory can be powerful is in its capacity to incorporate cultural and ethnic self-categorisation. Arguing that a system of social categorisations 'creates and defines an individual's own place in society', Tajfel (1972, p. 293) posits that social identity is motivated by an underlying need for self-esteem. The current study uses social comparison theory and self-categorisation constructs to understand better how members of the third-generation British Sikh community are consuming Bollywood films (the Indian movie industry), and how this may link to ethnic identity maintenance.

In applying social comparison theory and self-categorisation constructs (Dakin & Arrowood, 1981; Hogg & Terry, 2000; Laverie & McDonald, 2007) in this very specific and dynamic cultural context, we hope to extend our knowledge of social comparison theory, exploring in particular how it relates to identity construction. In considering this cinema genre as a consumption context that encourages a 'cultural remooring' (as in Ethier & Deaux, 1994) of Sikh identity for some young British Asians, the more general aim of the paper is to contribute to debates surrounding the consumption of cinema and its relations with culture. By choosing to explore Bollywood, the paper focuses on the ways in which the wider processes of globalisation and acculturation play out through this medium and how, in turn, this may impact on the identities of its young audience at the local level.

## Social identity, self-categorisation, and how they inform social comparison theory

Tajfel (1972, p. 292) defined social identity as 'the individual's knowledge that he belongs to certain social groups together with some emotional and value significance to him of this group membership'. In the same vein, Ashforth and Mael (1989, p. 21) see identity as 'a perceptual cognitive construct', in which members need only perceive themselves as psychologically belonging to a group, and intertwined with its fate. Essentially, social identities emerge from the various social roles that individuals assume (Laverie & McDonald, 2007). Social identity may consist of several 'loosely coupled' identities, in which previous identities are revisited, or new identities are predicted, as noted by Haslam (2000, p. 236): 'We organize and construe the world in a way prescribed by the groups to which we belong, ... our social histories lend stability and predictability to experience'.

The focus on Bollywood films in this study is potentially fruitful as explanatory of one shared element of social history that young British Sikhs experience and the construction they may place on the content and actors in such films as a part of their social identity formation as romantic selves.

Hogg and Terry (2000, p. 123) regard self-categorisation theory as a 'powerful new conceptual component of an extended social identity theory'. Social categorisation of self, in the words of Hogg and Terry, 'cognitively assimilates self to the ingroup stereotype and thus, depersonalizes self-conception'. This transformation of the self, according to Hogg and Terry, can produce normative behaviour, ethnocentrism, positive group cohesion, shared norms, and mutual influence; behaviours that are characteristic of the British Sikh ethnic identity.

For social identity theorists, self-categorisation is motivated by a need for self-esteem (Abrams & Hogg, 1988; Rubin & Hewstone, 2004) and uncertainty reduction (Hogg & Turner, 1985). This, according to Hogg and Terry (2000), may take the form of uncertainty about one's perceptions, one's self-concept, and place in the social world. Acknowledged uncertainty within third-generation British Sikh identity is a powerful, relevant aspect of the consumption context in the study.

## Social comparison theory and consumer research

Social comparison theory helps us understand an important element of the processes that underpin self-categorisation. The theory maintains that individuals compare themselves to others to evaluate their ability level and suitability of their opinions (Festinger, 1954). Consumer researchers using social comparison theory have often focused on advertising to understand how consumers compare themselves with persons portrayed in advertisements (Ackerman et al., 2000). Like film images, advertising images are frequently not realistic and are designed to evoke fantasising. Though consumers may seek out some of these images, other media, such as advertising on buses or magazines at grocery checkout stands, are unsought and, therefore, infringe on our senses (Richins, 1992). Although the levels of beauty and physical attractiveness possessed by nearly all the actors and models (especially females) are only available to an extremely small segment of the population (Ackerman et al., 2000; Richins, 1991), consumers nevertheless aspire to replicate this level of beauty within the reality of their lives. These media images operate at both conscious and subconscious levels, suggesting to consumers 'what ought to be in their lives' (Richins, 1992, p. 205). While Festinger (1954) identified the original motive for social comparison as 'self-evaluation', Martin and Kennedy (1994) identified two additional motives: self-improvement and self-enhancement.

More recent consumer research (Heaney & Goldsmith, 2005) has concluded that consumers who socially compare adopt a status consumption mindset, which leads them to consume materially in search of status. Other studies confirm this theory, as, for example, in Chan and Zhang's (2007) examination of the influence of peers and media celebrities on young people. These authors found that peer communication and susceptibility to media influence were positively related to social comparison. Increasing numbers of consumers are influenced to consume in order to emulate their preferred celebrity. It is well documented that celebrity endorsements of advertised products influence consumers to purchase products in an effort to imitate the behaviour or lifestyle of preferred celebrities (Chan & Zhang, 2007).

Within social comparison theory, gender has also become a topic of increasing interest, and some researchers suggest that there may be a gender-based preference for comparison contexts, as both males and females prefer to compare to individuals of their own sex (Knobloch-Westerwick & Hastall, 2006). In addition, females are inclined to be more susceptible than males to social comparison, although males are not entirely unaffected by social comparisons. The gender aspects of social comparison are important for the present study, as the Sikh community still maintains very clearly defined gender role expectations. Moreover, in relation to ethnic minorities such as the Sikh community, Bristow and Kleindl (1997) have illustrated how lower levels of acculturation can impact on self-esteem, making consumers more susceptible to social comparisons with their host country.

## Sikh culture, Bollywood, and social comparison

The Sikh community exists primarily within India, although, with migration, significant communities have been founded in Canada, the UK, and the United States. The 2001 UK census (HMSO, 2003) indicated that just over one million people claimed to be descended from India, with 13% of these stating their religion as 'Sikh' (Jacob, Bhudra, Lloyd, & Mann, 1998). The first Sikh families came to Britain in the 1950s. At an early age, Sikh children are socialised into Indian collectivist cultural values of co-operation, duty, favouritism, interdependence, nurturing, obedience, and reliability (Triandis, Chen, & Chan, 1998). Within both the Asian and British Sikh family unit, family loyalty is regarded as 'dharma' or sacred duty (Lindridge, Hogg, & Shah, 2004). The individualism that is typical of Western society is perceived in a negative manner by the older generations of the British Sikh community who often actively resist being fully acculturated into a British way of life.

For the third generation of British Sikhs, who are currently living within the dominant Westernised culture but have been exposed to a powerful socialisation through Sikh cultural values, this can generate uncertainty in social identity, which fundamentally influences their self-esteem. What the adoption of a social-identity lens offers in this study is a focus on the uncertainty reduction motivations that may be operative when ethnic identities feel under threat from a more dominant culture (as is arguably the case for young British Sikhs in the UK, who can feel threatened by Westernised consumption values).

Bollywood, the moniker for the popular Hindi cinema from Mumbai, India, has become an important catchword vocabulary of global Asian popular culture (Mishra, 2002; Virdi, 2003). Bollywood signifies the large number of films made and viewed in the city of Mumbai (estimated at around 200 films annually). Although Bollywood films maintain no sense of reality, millions of Indians, including the British Sikh community, derive pleasure from and construct social meanings around this genre of films. Bollywood encourages the pursuit of romance with heroes and heroines that seek 'true love' outside the Indian tradition of arranged marriages. Bollywood films are often referred to as 'unrealistic, emotional and over the top', and the Indian cinema has a reputation in the West as being founded more on myth than reality (Johnson, 1987).

Many of the younger generation of the British Sikh community experience a cultural struggle that impacts deeply on their sense of social identity. They turn to Bollywood to reinforce their Indian identity because it is encouraged and approved of by the older generations. This identity can come together on the big screen to offer an intended message of identification (of race, gender, class, and nation) that has been handcrafted (Dudrah, 2006). Part of that handcrafting is a conscious self-categorisation that embodies distinctive elements of Indian culture.

For this third generation of British Sikhs, Bollywood heroes and heroines may seem more acceptable than Western actors or actresses, making them more accessible candidates for social comparison. Tajfel (1972) suggests that social categorisation consists of intergroup social comparisons that seek to confirm or establish what he terms 'evaluative distinctiveness between ingroup and outgroup'. In terms of social comparison, in the case of young British Sikhs in this study, the 'evaluative distinctiveness' to which Tajfel (1972) refers, is problematic and gives rise to re-evaluation and renegotiation of their identity.

## The research site

Shaadi.com is a globalised website catering to the Indian community. It was founded in 1997 with the explicit aim of providing Indians with a superior matchmaking service. They claim to have over five million members worldwide and over 500,000 success stories. It aims to give customers control over the selection process with easy function that allows members to identify, filter, and contact potential partners. Shaadi.com has gained acceptance in the Sikh community amongst both parents and children as a way to find a marriage partner. Part of this acceptance is due to the fact that arranged marriages are still commonplace – when a Sikh son or daughter reaches a marriageable age, parents tell family and friends who then actively search for and suggest potential candidates. The traditional matchmaking process is dominated by classic patterns of social identification, illustrated in societal norms and the values of intergroup behaviour (Rubin & Hewstone, 2004; Tajfel, 1972). Matching education, occupation, religious affiliation, ethnic background, and caste are all extremely important. When a candidate is put forward, the two families involved usually request photos, and if these are acceptable to both sides, the couple will meet up in the presence of the middle person, often termed the 'middle agent', who presides over the occasion and acts as a go-between for developing the relationship or not. Notwithstanding the continuity of courtship patterns across successive Sikh generations, within this process, significant tensions are now emerging between parents and their more Westernised children. These tensions are evidenced by a subtle change in the middleman role – through the Internet dating site of Shaadi.com, young British Sikhs now seek a more cogent sense of *contemporary* social identification, reflective of the complex and evolving nature of social self-esteem (Hogg & Terry, 2000; Rubin & Hewstone, 2004). Relative to the courtship rituals of their parents, their virtual self-presentation exhibits a greater focus on self-distinctiveness rather than self-continuity (in line with the key motivations for social identification in Chattopadhyay, Tluchowska, & George, 2004). In contemporary Sikh communities, Shaadi.com is frequently regarded by Sikh parents as an efficient way to replace the middle person. Multiple potential partners can be screened, with extensive background information readily available and, thus, they see it as assisting them in their parental duties.

## Methodology

The data for this paper was gathered as part of a larger study into the use of Internet dating by the Sikh community. All the interviews were conducted with informants from the British Sikh community, these being the sons and daughters of the second generation of Sikhs that migrated to Britain from India. The overall approach was interpretivist, and data collection followed a multi-method design that combined netnography (online interviews) (Kozinets, 2002) with offline semi-structured interviews. Consistent with a netnographic research approach, which requires an immersive combination of participation and observation, one of the authors of this study, herself a third-generation British Sikh, participated in the Shaadi.com community for a two-and-half-year period (see Kozinets, 1997, 2002; Maclaran & Catterall, 2002) as she too searched for a marital partner through Shaadi.com. In keeping with recommended research ethics for online research (Sharf, 1999) and the ESOMAR code of conduct, she announced her presence prior to any direct interaction and guaranteed to protect the anonymity of all informants. The netnography resulted in field notes that documented interactions between members on the site and the researcher's own thoughts and feelings about the processes taking place, in line with Maxwell (2005). Table 1 gives further details of the phases of primary research and multi-method approach adopted.

This study was carried out longitudinally over a period of two and a half years, and the final data set included transcripts from 15 online interviews, 15 offline interviews, and copious field notes from the participant observations. The study adopted a

**Table 1** Process of data collection.

| Time period | Research phase | Research methods |
|---|---|---|
| October 2004 –March 2005 | Exploratory phase | – Observations of shaadi.com<br>– Observation of competitors websites<br>– Online participant observation<br>– Full experience of the online dating and transition to the offline experience |
| April 2005 –December 2005 | Phase 1: Development of emergent themes Access to parents and young adults | – Online participant observation<br>– Online interviews (4)<br>– In-depth interview with users (2)<br>– Autoethnographic accounts |
| January 2006 –June 2006 | Phase 2: Development of core constructs | – Online participant observation<br>– Offline observations<br>– Online interviews (8)<br>– In-depth interviews (6)<br>– Autoethnographic accounts |
| July 2006 –December 2006 | Phase 3 | – Online interviews (3)<br>– In-depth interviews (7)<br>– Autoethnographic accounts |

theoretical sampling approach, which involves continually comparing and contrasting the data being collected and seeking informants on the basis of the emergent constructs, in line with Cresswell (2007). For example, having talked online to several young Sikh users, in-depth interviews were conducted offline with young adults in the British Sikh community to explore in detail their 'lived' experience of using the site. Interviews sought to gain in-depth insight into the motivations behind the social comparison patterns and to encourage informants to explore for themselves their experience of identity maintenance. The informants for the online interviews were recruited through the website's online community. However, the informants for the offline interviews were recruited through interaction within the Sikh community and networking at the Sikh temple (Gurdwara) to find users of Shaadi.com. The third-generation participants were all single and aged between 22 and 35, that being the age group with potentially high engagement in acculturation issues and currently facing considerable pressure to marry.

During the early online interviews, a major factor to emerge was the influence of Bollywood as an important cultural reference point (a) for the acculturation issues that were reflective of conflicted Sikh social identity; (b) for the significant degree of social comparison with Bollywood heroines and heroes; and (c) for their exposure, through Bollywood, to distinctive Sikh courtship rituals. The core research question for the present study, as reported here, was twofold: (1) in what way do the third generation of British Sikhs make social comparisons to the heroes and heroines of Bollywood movies; and (2) how does their consumption of this medium relate to their own Sikh identity maintenance? Three key themes emerged as significant in answering this question: (1) social comparisons and ideals of romance; (2) gender differences: making comparisons with heroes and heroines; and (3) the British versus Indian self: Bollywood as a medium for identity reconstruction.

# Findings

## *Social comparison and ideals of romance*

Bollywood is a key medium through which the ideals of love and romance are formed and circulate within the Sikh community (Dudrah, 2006). These ideals are particularly attractive for the group of third-generation Sikhs who are experiencing a particularly challenging phase of acculturation as they grapple with their identities. Shabs spoke excitedly of how she felt about Bollywood movies:

> I am mad about Bollywood, and it's because it's all about romance and happiness. People believe in love and romance and that helps them get through everything. I think at my low points, it's the Bollywood films that helped me get through. Anytime I was miserable, I would just pray my prince would come along and save me. (Shabs, Sikh Female, Offline)

To Shabs, Bollywood films represent the good life (Belk & Pollay, 1985); for her, the films are all about 'romance and happiness'. When life disappoints her, dreams of Bollywood ideal love and life support her through these difficult times. However, for some, these ideals are a source of frustration rather than inspiration, as they compare them negatively to their own life experiences, as Sundeep illustrates:

> That's where I get my romance and love ideas from. Every time I watch a film, I get depressed, because none of that stuff happens to me. It's always to someone else, which is so irritating and unfair. I watch these films and how much they love each other and that makes me yearn for the same thing. I want someone that will shower me with love and romantic gestures everyday, and I know that no one really does that openly in Indian society, but to some extent I don't care, I want that, and when I get it, I ain't letting go of it. (Sundeep, Sikh Female, Online)

Sundeep differs from Shabs. Shabs only dreams about Bollywood ideal love, whereas Sundeep believes these ideals are achievable in reality. However, the social comparison she makes between her own life and the films leaves her in a state of frustration as she 'yearns for the same thing'. As Richins (1991, 1995) found, exposure to idealised images (in her case advertising images) often has the effect of generating dissatisfaction, particularly in setting notions of what 'ought to be' but is not (Richins, 1992). Additionally Sundeep's frustrations stem from the restrictions she perceives in Indian society, as she says 'no one really does that openly in Indian society'. Torn between the ideals of the Sikh culture, British culture, and Bollywood, perhaps the easy option is to immerse herself in the world of Bollywood. Undoubtedly, Bollywood films do facilitate a degree of escapism for this group (Johnson, 1987). As Amar explains:

> Its just escapism I think, it's nice to escape into this fantasy world where there is no stress and everything ends happily. Every Hindi film is a love story and they will do anything for each other and everyone wants that. But mum says it's stupid because life's not all about romance and love. That's what Bollywood leads the younger generation to believe. (Amar, Sikh Male, Offline)

Like many third-generation Sikhs, Amar believes that Bollywood is an influential factor in setting his ideals of love and romance. However, Amar demonstrates a degree of reflexivity; he does not unquestioningly accept these ideals, readily acknowledging that they are really a fantasy. The power of the Bollywood film genre is apparent in not only influencing ideals but playing a key role in setting aspirations and thus changing behaviours amongst this group. The third generation of British Sikhs are now challenging the views and authority of their parents – Bollywood is a key resource for these new ideals, acting as a catalyst for developing the romantic visions and aspirations of the younger generation of Sikhs. This group are experiencing a significant period of acculturation. As they absorb elements of British culture, yet maintain elements of what it means to be Sikh, the Bollywood filmic medium both reflects and facilitates this process. This genre can be seen as a context that serves to 'culturally remoor' (Ethier & Deaux, 1994) their ethnic identity. Yet, it is an intermediate context – neither fully reflective of the powerful ethnic identity or value congruence that has traditionally characterised first- and second-generation British Sikh culture, nor fully contemporary in terms of individualised male–female courtship rituals. For many young Sikhs, these films represent the zeitgeist of contemporary life.

### Gender differences: Making comparisons to heroes and heroines

Both male and female informants cherish the role of Bollywood films in their lives and constantly make comparisons between their own situations and those of the heroes and heroines portrayed in the films. Consistent with the findings of Knobloch-Westerwick and Hastall (2006), the young women in our study tended to compare themselves to heroines, whereas the young men tended to compare themselves to heroes. For example, the females referred to Bollywood heroines such as 'Rani Mukherjee' or 'Aishwarya Rai', and the males talked of heroes such as 'Vivek Oberoi'. But it was not just the celebrity status that influenced them, or the idealised lifestyles with which they made comparisons; it was also the traditional Indian roles that these heroes and heroines enacted.

Although Jaya, a third-generation British Sikh female, complained vociferously during her interview about what she perceives to be the gender-based double standards operating within the Sikh community, she still admits to being influenced by the traditional daughter-in-law role as depicted in Bollywood films. In fact, Jaya is a young female that conforms to Lindridge et al.'s (2004) notion of how 'women negotiate their transactions between two contrasting cultures by projecting multiple identities' (p. 212). Jaya uses Bollywood and Shaadi.com to navigate the border crossings between societal contexts:

> I think the biggest influence – this is really sad – but, you know, when you see the Naw [daughter-in-law]. She manages the whole house. And everyone's proud of her, and wherever she goes, everyone's like, 'oh you're so lucky to have a daughter-in-law like that'. I see myself like that. (Jaya, Sikh Female, Offline)

Despite reflecting on her social comparisons and aspirations as 'sad', Jaya cannot stop herself from wishing to be the perfect daughter-in-law so admired by the Sikh community. Yet, in reality, she resents the pressures and demands that she believes are placed upon her by her parents and the Sikh community in general. The comparisons made with her Bollywood heroines are likely to produce feelings of inadequacy (Festinger, 1954; Richins, 1995). This in turn may encourage the low self-esteem that makes social comparison more likely (Bristow & Kleindl, 1997). In this way, Bollywood films may act like a vicious circle fuelling a constant cycle of social comparisons.

Likewise, Honey refers to the role of the Indian wife that she aspires to be as she compares herself to the gendered images in Bollywood films:

> When I'm married I want to look like a good, sexy Indian wife. Bollywood is just good to watch because I love the culture, I love the clothes, the music and, yes, the romance. (Honey, Sikh Female, Offline)

As Honey discusses her aspirations, we can see that the roles of wife and daughter-in-law are enacted as part of an overall glamorised lifestyle with unquestioned underpinning gendered assumptions. The world of Bollywood carries young Sikh females into a fantasy world and their dreams impact on not only how they perceive their own roles, but also how they perceive the role of their prospective partner. Sunny illustrates this vividly when she asserts: 'I want my prince, I want romance, I want to be showered with love. I live my own little heer ranjha [Bollywood film] fairy tale'.

Bollywood films reflect the consumption of a cultural prototype, a cognitive representation that defines the stereotypical attributes of a group (i.e. the Sikh family) in accord with social identity theory. For Hogg and Terry (2000), prototypes embody all critical attributes that characterise an (ethnic) group, including beliefs, attitudes, feelings, and behaviours, and they may, 'maximise similarities within and differences between groups, thus defining groups as distinct entities' (p. 124). Bollywood films, with their protypical heroines, represent a contemporary consumption context in which stereotypical attributes can become a form of self-categorisation through social comparison.

The third generation of British Sikh males were similarly influenced and stimulated by Bollywood portrayals of heroes. Like their female counterparts, this extended to their role expectations of the opposite sex. Baz speaks of a particular film that he idolises; we can see the longings engendered by the social comparisons he is making:

> You know that film Kabhi Khushi Kabhi Gham and there's that scene where he sees that girl dancing and totally falls in love with her. I watch that over and over and wish that would happen to me. But the thing is though, I kind of wonder whether it really does happen in real life. I really do want it so badly. I do love Bollywood films because I grew up with that and that's what I expected from my marriage. It's like – have you seen Dosti [film] and when they sing 'Aur Tum Aaye' [song] and realise they are right for each other? I love stuff like that – it makes my heart melt, but then I get all like why can't I get that? I want to sing in the fields with my soul mate. (Baz, Sikh Male, Online)

Again, the potentially negative aspects of these longings are also evident; Baz questions why his own life does not match that of his Bollywood role model. Conversely, although like Baz, Sarvjit wants 'to be like the guy in the films', he sees this identification as a very positive aspect in his life:

> I tend to get carried away because without a doubt Bollywood does influence me. I watch these films and think I wish this could happen to me. I do get all my ideals of how marriage, love, romance and me should be from Bollywood. That's not a bad thing I just think I want something different to previous generations. I want that attraction, that passion, the butterflies. I want it all and to be like the guy in the films. (Sarvjit, Sikh Male, Offline)

Across male and female informants, Bollywood film is an intermediate consumption context in which non-Western ideals of male and female courtship can be accessed, consumed, and taken on board, with a powerful value congruence among young Sikhs in the UK. In that consumption, culturally shared with their peers, is a self-defining capacity that emerges through social comparison with the Bollywood male prototype.

However, this is also a problematic social comparison. For male respondents, the self-definition or self-enhancement that seems relevant in the intermediate context of Bollywood appears less satisfying in their actual relationship development. Thus their consumption of the genre exhibits a more evaluative social identification (Chattopadhyay et al., 2004; van Dick & Wagner, 2002) than some of the female respondents, evident in their acknowledgement that in terms of actual relationship development, Bollywood prototypes are romanticised and unreal.

For instance, despite Sarvjit's positive assertions above, there is no doubt that more male than female informants were apologetic for making what they perceived to be unrealistic comparisons, and they frequently described themselves in pejorative terms for having these romantic longings. Like young Sikh females, males also engaged in forms of social comparisons:

> How many girls do I have to meet and make small talk with before I get to the one for me? I feel hopeless, but a good old romantic movie gives me the hope back, like the Indian *Sleepless in Seattle*. (Baz, Sikh Male, Online)

### British vs Indian self: Bollywood as a medium for identity reconstruction

The term 'British Sikh' in itself refers to two cultures, and existing in two cultures may generate both congruence and conflict in social identification. Social comparisons that are made with the Bollywood concept strongly reflect this:

> I was talking to my mum the other day about Bollywood and how it has changed me, because, before I was so white, if someone put on a film I would scream. I thought it was really sad and all my friends were white so they definitely wouldn't have thought it was cool but now I realise how stupid I was. Bollywood has helped me to get back in touch with my culture and who I am. I have learnt so much about being Indian and my culture through Bollywood and now Bollywood is more a part of my life than Hollywood, which is a total reversal. I'm Indian, and Bollywood is a part of being Indian and I'm proud of that. (Simran, Sikh Female, Online)

Through her interpretation of, and engagement with, Bollywood films, Simran has been able to reconnect with aspects of her Indian identity. The wording used by Simran also indicates a discernible change in social identification (Ashforth & Mael, 1989; van Dick & Wagner, 2002). She appears to be aligning herself not only with a desirable cultural product (Bollywood 'concept'), she is also identifying herself with what she perceives to be a currently attractive social group (Indian ethnic group). This is in line with work on motivations for social identification (Abrams & Hogg, 1988; Dutton, Dukerich, & Harquail, 1994). She mentions previously screaming when someone put on a Bollywood film, in part because of the lack of congruence between watching such films and her affiliation with her 'then' prestigious social group – her 'white friends'. She now acknowledges a 'total reversal' in her estimation of Bollywood – which may be seen as a self-attribution of the qualities that now appear to be attractive in Indian culture, thus corresponding to self-categorisation (Turner, 1987). She interprets this as a greater awareness of her Indian culture; she seems to be socially comparing herself to the concept of being Indian now accessible through Bollywood films (Dakin & Arrowood, 1981). This is in line with the group self-esteem associated with self-categorisation theory (Turner & Reynolds, 2004).

It is easier for young Sikhs to compare themselves socially to heroes and heroines in Bollywood films because, arguably, they imitate Indian cultural customs and rituals, thus offering congruence with their own lives (as noted above by Simran). On the other hand, Bollywood films, as noted in the discussion of ideals of romance, do not reflect the reality of what is culturally expected or anticipated in Sikh relationships. They are a good space of identification for reconnecting with aspects of Indian identity, but they also give rise to a conflicted self (Baumeister, 1999; Travers, 1994), as noted below by Jinder:

> Sikh marriage is based on materialistic and status factors, and Western society does the opposite. So the younger generation of Sikhs today are somewhere in the middle but I want love and romance, I want the butterflies, excitement, anxiety, all of it. That's what is fun about relationships and that's what I like. I can romance and fall for someone like in the Hindi films. (Jinder, Sikh Male, Online)

Jinder here is expressing frustration with the traditional model of Sikh marriage and sees his age group in a cultural juxtaposition between two expectations; that of making a good marriage economically (congruent with the traditions of Sikh social structure) and experiencing a loving romantic relationship (less congruent with Sikh values). Clearly experiencing a state of 'the torn self', as Jafari and Goulding (2008) proposed, Jinder now sees his own generation as 'somewhere in the middle'. Nonetheless, he firmly articulates his desire for the emotional fulfilment that Bollywood films appear to offer. In this expression of inner desires, in contrast to Simran, he is acknowledging a 'possible' self, as noted by Markus and Kitayama (1986), in their argument that we all inhabit multiple selves. He is seeking to inhabit this possible self, and feels conflicted because it is out of reach within his primary cultural identification. For Jinder, a coherent self-categorisation (Turner, 1987) by aligning towards his Indian ethnic group is not definitive; it entails conflict. Jinder is exemplary of how 'identities are subject to new determinations and forces' (Bhatia, 2002). Bollywood is clearly one of these forces. His 'dialogical voices' Bhatia (2002) encourage him to constantly negotiate his multiple and often conflicting identities in an attempt to self-categorise.

First- and second-generation Sikhs share a deep similarity through socialisation processes that involve close family ties, specific family rituals, normative role behaviours (related to social role, Popitz, 1967; Raffel, 1999), and a range of dominant ethnic group customs that were largely unchallenged. Third-generation British Sikhs, in contrast, have been exposed to less bounded socialisation processes, to many alternative Western customs, less specific rituals, less normative behaviours through their college reference groups, and wider friendship and social-networking groups. Social bonds to their primary ethnic group are therefore more diffused than those of their parents. Yet it appears from the findings that Bollywood movies are assisting some re-acculturation to the Indian culture for British Sikhs. Bollywood films represent the British Sikh ethnic identity as less uncertain, and unconsciously define salient characteristics of their ingroup (ideal Sikh females).

## Discussion

This study extends previous research in two ways: on the one hand, by capturing the value in social comparison theory when examining consumption and acculturation; and on the other, by identifying this unique genre of cinema as a valuable yet under-researched consumption context of identity renegotiation.

### The value of social comparison and social categorisation theory

Social comparison and social categorisation theory offer a powerful lens of analysis to understand cultural consumption (for high-involvement concepts). First, in terms of consumer affiliation to cultural role models, the study extends the aspirational dimension in previous studies of social comparison theory on consumption of advertising and celebrity endorsement (Lin & Tsai, 2006; Stewart & Clark, 2007). The research findings have, in particular, confirmed gender patterns as noted in Knobloch-Westerwick and Hastall (2006) and the link between social comparison in consumption and the potential for lower self-esteem (noted in Allen & Wilder, 1977; Wood, 1989). Furthermore, the majority of past research has examined social comparison in Western communities – this study has focused on social comparisons within an ethnic group with dual east–west cultural associations (British Sikhs).

Second, much previous research has focused on social comparisons in relation to media images or advertisements (Richins, 1995) or social comparisons to peers (Festinger, 1954). In this study, the value of social comparison theory to understand more high-involvement cultural consumption (in this case social films) is clearly articulated. Invoking emotion and social consciousness in their audiences, social films address themselves to cultural changes through the interplay of personal identity, love, human relationships, and family (Dudrah, 2006). In this regard, they are strongly socially embedded cultural products. Limited past research has addressed social comparison within such consumption categories.

These findings illustrate clearly that social comparison and social categorisation represent a valuable lens that can offer a useful distinction between personal and social identity, when applied to cultural consumption. Rather than being unidimensional, in social categorisation theory, there is a continuum ranging from 'acting in terms of self' to 'acting in terms of the group', according to Turner and Reynolds (2004, p. 261). In their engagement with Bollywood, respondents are constantly shifting along this continuum, thus reflecting a strong identity maintenance element in their consumption patterns.

Findings have also demonstrated that social comparison in consumption of socially embedded cultural concepts (such as Bollywood films represent) may generate more than low self-esteem – it may bring to the surface significant difficulties in achieving self-congruence for the consumer. For young Sikh women, where there is significant buy-in to the heroine roles and storylines as epitomising the ideal Indian relationship pattern, the discrepancy between their aspirational role (denoted in Bollywood) and their expected social role (within Sikh marriage traditions) is painfully felt. As noted above, when social comparison with a desirable 'concept' or outcome occurs in a socially embedded context, the discrepancy arising in the social comparison can powerfully influence social identity (Sierra & McQuitty, 2007; van Dick & Wagner, 2002).

Third, the social comparison perspective highlights the specific nature of the conflicted self (Taylor, 1989) in this context of high-involvement cultural consumption. Findings above demonstrate that social comparison articulates the areas of disconnection between the acculturation to Western 'individuated' ideals of romance and the striving to adhere to the essential Sikh traditions of courtship. Exposure to two conflicting communities leaves young British Sikhs in a state where they need to negotiate the demands that are placed on them – scenes in Bollywood films may mirror these pressures, and are thus a means of engaging dialogue about the issues.

### Engagement with the Bollywood film genre as an act of self-definition and identity renegotiation

Ethier and Deaux (1994) outlined two distinct paths to identity renegotiation. First, where there is initially strong ethnic identity, individuals may seek to deepen this through engagement in cultural activities (a form of social anchorage). In contrast, individuals with a weaker ethnic identity may perceive more threat and show decreases in self-esteem associated with group membership, thus lowering their identification with their ethnic group. In the Bollywood consumption context, there is, for young Sikhs who experience a weaker ethnic identity than first- and second-generation UK Sikh community members, as noted by Bristow and Kleindl (1997), an opportunity to deepen their ethnic identity (Padilla & Perez, 2003; Rubin & Hewstone, 2004). In contextual terms, findings in this study of British Sikhs show, on the one hand, some conflict in terms of self-esteem, but also highlight a greater engagement with and articulation of Sikh values. At the same time, any increased self-esteem is not necessarily from traditional Sikh community ties but from their own contemporary understanding, in part informed by the handcrafted Bollywood cultural phenomena (Dudrah, 2006). Bollywood films act as a form of social anchorage – thus encouraging a greater level of identification, but not necessarily an internalisation (Kelman, 1961).

Taking a social identity perspective, respondents' engagement with the Bollywood film genre can be interpreted as an act of self-definition. Hogg and Terry (2000) trace a direct link between self-categorisation theory (which reflects prototype-based characterisation) and self-enhancement, echoing Kelman's (1961, p. 62) view of social influence and identification:

> Identification can be said to occur when an individual adopts behaviour derived from another person or group because this behaviour is associated with a satisfying self-defining relationship to this person or group.

In relating to Bollywood films through social comparison with heroes and heroines, third-generation Sikhs can pursue a self-categorisation that is associated with an attractive social group (Ashforth & Mael, 1989). Attributing some of the prestige of the Bollywood concept to your own self is perhaps another dimension of the contemporary Indian self – one that permits self-distinctiveness (Dutton et al., 1994). The consumption of the Bollywood concept acknowledges self-distinctiveness within the Indian culture, whether it is largely through conscious role adoption patterned on the films (as with Shabs), through experimentation with a 'provisional' self (Ibarra, 1999), or through some recognition of the younger generation's need for self-determinism in relationships.

The third generation of British Sikhs exhibit multiple selves arising from their dual cultural identification and their need to reconcile different facets of each. The Indian self that is emerging in current British Sikh culture (third generation) with regard to relationships and marriage is multifaceted. It combines the 'possible' self (Markus & Kitayama, 1986) that desires the individual experience of romance, excitement, and 'falling in love' with a more 'defined' self (Taylor, 1989) that hankers after the strong social identification that derives from learning and knowing your own customs, valuing your own Indian rituals, and experiencing a self-congruence with your primary culture.

In terms of social identity and acculturation (Padilla & Perez, 2003), the subtle social function of Bollywood films and their popular consumption may be as an intermediate context, albeit complicated and problematic, which represents a valuable narrative space of negotiation in which young British Sikhs can 'remoor' their ethnic identity. Bollywood offers a third space where 'possible' selves and potential identities can be explored. For some commentators, these films are seen as being located between and beyond Hollywood and Bollywood (Desai, 2004). Bollywood films may encourage a conflicted sense of self and a social identity that is difficult to inhabit, but they also represent a powerful space for 'remooring' aspects of identity – a space that is currently shaping critical dialogues on identity among young British Sikhs.

## References

Abrams, D., & Hogg, M. (1988). Comments on the motivational status of self-esteem in social identity and intergroup discrimination. *European Journal of Social Psychology, 18*, 317–332.

Ackerman, D., MacInnis, D., & Folkes, V. (2000). Social comparisons of possessions: When it feels good and when it feels bad. *Advances in Consumer Research, 27*, 173–178.

Allen, V., & Wilder, D.A. (1977). Social comparison, self-evaluation and conformity to the group. In J.M. Suls & R.L. Miller (Eds.), *Social comparison processes: Theoretical and empirical perspectives* (pp. 187–208). Washington, DC: Hemisphere.

Ashforth, B., & Mael, F. (1989). Social identity theory and the organisation. *Academy of Management Review, 14*(1), 20–30.

Baumeister, R. (1999). The nature and structure of the self: An overview. In R. Baumeister (Ed.), *The self in social psychology*. Hove, England: Psychology Press.

Belk, R.W., & Pollay, R.W. (1985). Images of ourselves: The good life in twentieth century advertising. *Journal of Consumer Research, 11*, 887–897.

Bhatia, S. (2002). Acculturation, dialogical voices and the construction of the diasporic self. *Theory and Psychology, 12*(1), 55–77.

Bristow, D.N., & Kleindl, B. (1997). Consumer self-esteem and susceptibility to social influence: A cross-cultural comparison and investigation of advertising implications. *Cross Cultural Management: An International Journal, 4*(1), 7–17.

Chan, K., & Zhang, C. (2007). Living in a celebrity-mediated social world: The Chinese experience. *Young Consumers, 8*(2), 139–152.

Chattopadhyay, P., Tluchowska, M., & George, E. (2004). Identifying the in-group: A closer look at the influence of demographic dissimilarity on employee social identity. *Academy of Management Review, 29*(2), 180–202.

Cresswell, J. (2007). *Qualitative inquiry and research design: Choosing among five approaches.* Thousand Oaks, CA: Sage.

Dakin, S., & Arrowood, J.A. (1981). The social comparison of ability. *Human Relations, 34*, 89–109.

Desai, J. (2004). *Beyond Hollywood: The cultural politics of South Asian diasporic film.* New York: Routledge.

Dudrah, R.K. (2006). *Bollywood: Sociology goes to the movies.* New Delhi, India: Sage.

Dutton, J., Dukerich, J., & Harquail, C. (1994). Organizational images and member identification. *Administrative Science Quarterly, 39*, 239–263.

Ethier, K.A., & Deaux, K. (1994). Negotiating social identity when contexts change: Maintaining identification and responding to threat. *Journal of Personality and Social Psychology, 67*, 243–251.

Festinger, L. (1954). A theory of social comparison processes. *Human Relations, 7*, 117–140.

Harnish, R.J., & Bridges, R.K. (2006). Social influence: The role of self-monitoring when making social comparisons. *Psychology and Marketing, 23*(11), 961–973.

Haslam, S. (2000). *Psychology in organizations: The social identity approach.* Thousand Oaks, CA: Sage.

Heaney, J.G., & Goldsmith, R.E. (2005). Status consumption among Malaysian consumers: Exploring its relationships with materialism and attention-to-social-comparison-information. *Journal of International Consumer Marketing*, *17*(4), 81–96.

HMSO (2003). 2001 Census. Home Office for National Statistics [Online]. Retrieved January 27, 2008, from http://www.statistics.gov.uk/census2001/

Hogg, M., & Terry, D. (2000). Social identity and self-categorization process in organizational contexts. *Academy of Management Review*, *25*, 121–140.

Hogg, M., & Turner, J.C. (1985). Interpersonal attraction, social identification and psychological group formation. *European Journal of Social Psychology*, *15*, 51–66.

Ibarra, H. (1999). Provisional selves: Experimenting with image and identity in professional adaptation. *Administrative Science Quarterly*, *44*, 764–791.

Jacob, K.S., Bhugra, D., Lloyd, K., & Mann, A. (1998). Common mental disorders, explanatory models and consultation behaviour among Indian women living in the UK. *Journal of Royal Society of Medicine*, *91*(2), 66–71.

Jafari, A., & Goulding, C. (2008). We are not terrorists! UK-based Iranians, consumption practices and the 'torn self'. *Consumption, Markets and Culture*, *11*(2), 73–91.

Johnson, E. (1987). *Bombay talkies: Posters of the Indian cinema*. West Midlands Area Museum Service Travelling Exhibition: Birmingham Central Library.

Kelman, H. (1961). Process of opinion change. *Public Opinion Quarterly*, *25*(1), 57–78.

Kozinets, R.V. (1997). I want to believe: A netnography of the x-philes subculture of consumption. *Advances in Consumer Research*, *24*, 470–475.

Kozinets, R.V. (2002). The field behind the screen: Using netnography for marketing research in online communities. *Journal of Marketing Research*, *39*, 61–72.

Knobloch-Westerwick, S., & Hastall, M.R. (2006). Social comparisons with news personae: Selective exposure to news portrayals of same-sex and same-age characters. *Communication Research*, *33*(4), 262–284.

Laverie, D., & MacDonald, R. (2007). Volunteer dedication: Understanding the role of identity importance on participation frequency. *Journal of Macromarketing*, *27*(1), 274–289.

Lindridge, A.M., Hogg, M.K., & Shah, M. (2004). Identity, self and consumption: How British Asian women negotiate the border crossings between household and societal context. *Journal of Consumption, Markets and Culture*, *7*(3), 211–238.

Lin, C.H., & Tsai, C. (2006). Comparisons and advertising: The route from comparisons to effective advertising. *Journal of Business and Psychology*, *21*, 23–44.

Maclaran, P., & Catterall, M. (2002). Researching the social web: Marketing information from virtual communities. *Marketing Intelligence and Planning*, *20*(6), 319–326.

Markus, H. and Nurius, P. (1986) Possible Selves. American Psychologist, Vol 41, No. 9, pp. 954–969.

Martin, M.C., & Kennedy, P. (1993). Advertising and social comparison: Consequences for female preadolescents and adolescents. *Psychology and Marketing*, *10*(6), 513–530.

Martin, M.C., & Kennedy, P. (1994). Social comparison and the beauty of advertising models: The role of motives for comparison. *Advances in Consumer Research*, *21*, 365–371.

Maxwell, J. (2005). *Qualitative research design: An interactive approach* (2nd ed.). Thousand Oaks, CA: Sage.

Mishra, V. (2002). *Bollywood cinema: Temples of desire*. New York: Routledge.

Padilla, A., & Perez, W. (2003). Acculturation, social identity and social cognition: A new perspective. *Hispanic Journal of Behavioural Sciences*, *25*(1), 35–55.

Popitz, H. (1967). The concept of social role as an element of sociological theory. In J. Jackson (Ed.), *Role*. Cambridge, England: Cambridge University Press.

Raffel, S. (1999). Revisiting role theory: Roles and the problem of the self [online]. *Sociological Research Online*, *4*(2) http://www.socresonline.org.uk/socresonline/4/2

Richins, M.L. (1991). Social comparison ad the idealized images of advertising. *Journal of Consumer Research*, *18*, pp. 71–83.

Richins, M.L. (1992). Media images, materialism, and what ought to be: The role of social comparison. In F. Rudmin & M. Richins (Ed.), *Meaning, measure, and morality of materialism* (pp. 202–206). Kingston, Canada: Research Workshop on Materialism and Other Consumption Orientations.

Richins, M.L. (1995). Social comparison, advertising, and consumer discontent. *American Behavioural Scientist*, *38*(4), 593–607.

Rubin, M., & Hewstone, M. (2004). Social identity, system justification and social dominance: A commentary on Reicher, Jost et al. and Sidanius et al. *Political Psychology*, *25*(6), 823–844.

Shaadi.com (2008). Retrieved October 11, 2008, from http://www.Shaadi.com

Sharf, B. (1999). Beyond Netquette: The Ethics of Doing Naturalistic Discourse Research on the Internet, in S. Jones (Ed.), *Doing Internet Research: Critical Issues and Methods for Examining the Net*. Thousand Oates, CA: Sage, pp. 243–256.

Sierra, J., & McQuitty, S. (2007). Attitudes and determinants of nostalgia purchases: An application of social identity theory. *Journal of Marketing Theory and Practice*, *15*(2), 99–112.

Stewart, J.M., & Clark, M.K. (2007). The effect of syntactic complexity, social comparison and relationship theory on advertising slogans. *The Business Review*, *7*(1), p. 113.

Strauss, A., & Corbin, J. (1990). *Basics of qualitative research: Grounded theory procedures and techniques*. London: Sage.

Tajifel, H. (1972). La categorisation sociale. In S. Moscovici (Ed.), *Introduction à la psychologie sociale* (Vol. 1, pp. 272–302). Paris: Larousse.

Taylor, C. (1989). *Sources of the self: The making of the modern identity*. Cambridge, MA: Harvard University Press.

Travers, A. (1994). The unrequited self. *History of the Human Sciences*, *7*(2), 121–140.

Triandis, H.C., Chen, X.P., & Chan, D.K.-S. (1998). Scenarios for the measurement of collectivism and individualism. *Journal of Cross-Cultural Psychology*, *29*, 275–289.

Turner, J.C. (1987). A self-categorization theory. In M. Hogg, P. Oakes, S. Reicher, & M. Wetherell (Ed.), *Rediscovering the social group: A self-categorization theory* (pp. 42–67). Oxford, England: Blackwell.

Turner, J.C., & Reynolds, K.J. (2004). The social identity perspective in intergroup relations; Theories, themes and controversies. In M. Hewstone & M.B. Brewer (Eds.), *Self and social identity* (pp. 259–277). Malden, MA: Blackwell.

van Dick, R., & Wagner, U. (2002). Social identification among school teachers, dimensions, foci and correlates. *European Journal of Work and Organization Psychology*, *11*(2), 129–149.

Virdi, J. (2003). *The cinematic imagination: Indian popular films as social history*. New Brunswick, NJ: Rutgers University Press.

Wood, J.V. (1989). Theory and research concerning social comparisons of personal attributes. *Psychological Bulletin*, *106*, 231–248.

# Exploring appropriation of global cultural rituals

Julie Tinson, *University of Stirling, UK*
Peter Nuttall, *University of Bath, UK*

**Abstract** Adolescents, as a consequence of identification with popular culture, have been described as having homogenous consumption patterns. More recently, however, it has been recognised that 'glocalisation' (global practices reworked to fit local contexts) affords an opportunity for differentiation. This paper considers a recent UK phenomenon, namely that of the US high-school prom, and seeks to explore the ways in which this ritual has been adopted or adapted as part of youth culture. The method employed here was mixed methods, and included in-depth interviews with those who attended a prom in the last three years, as well as a questionnaire distributed amongst high-school pupils who were anticipating a high-school prom. The findings illustrate that the high-school prom in the UK is becoming increasingly integrated into the fabric of youth culture, although, depending on the agentic abilities employed by the emerging adults in the sample, there is differing appropriation of this ritual event, particularly in relation to attitudes towards and motivations for attending the prom. A typology of prom attendees is posited. This paper contributes to our understanding of this practice in a local context.

## Introduction

Ritualised activities and events that symbolise important and meaningful life experiences are regularly practised by consumers (Ruth, 1995). Interest in such events has led consumer researchers to explore the role of rituals by considering, amongst others: special holidays such as Halloween, Christmas, Valentine's Day (see Belk, 1990; Close & Zinkhan, 2006; Pollay, 1987); life-changing events such as marriage, divorce, birth, death (see Bonsu, 2001; McAlexander, 1991; Otnes & Lowrey, 1993; Ozanne, 1992); personal experiences such as body art, grooming, and car consumption (Belk, 2004; Rook & Levy, 1983; Watson, 1998); and shared occasions such as gift giving, sporting events, and food consumption (see, e.g., Chun, Gentry, & McGinnis, 2005; Fischer & Gainer, 1993). Curiosity in ritual behaviour is also global (see Chun, Gentry, & McGinnis, 2004; Fernandez & Veer, 2004), and in recent years, rituals practised in the United States have been embraced more fully in the UK (e.g. Halloween) with the ensuing commercialisation and consumption behaviour associated with such practices becoming increasingly apparent (Jeffries,

2004). However, the extent to which these rituals are being adapted, as well as adopted, is less well documented and needs further exploration.

## Globalisation and glocalisation

Before considering the appropriation of rituals (in this particular case the high-school prom), it is important to note that globalisation and its affects are vigorously debated and that there are 'many divergent views on the various aspects of globalisation such as who the main players are, what it's manifestations are and whether this phenomenon is good or bad, culturally or economically and for whom' (Eckhardt & Mahi, 2004, p. 136). Multinational corporations and governments are, in the context of business, identified as the key players when considering economic policy and resource allocation (Prakash & Hart, 2000), and in the discipline of marketing, consumers and their role in and relationship with globalisation have been of increasing interest. In 1993, Ritzer suggested that global consumer brands would change the culture in developing countries, consumers would be passive, and that brands, products, and the experiences of these would be homogenous. Ever since, the role of the consumer in globalisation has been contested, with Arnould and Thompson (2005) suggesting consumers are interpretive agents rather than 'passive dupes'; supporting Ger and Belk's (1996) definition of consumer agency as the ability of individuals and groups to transform and play with meaning.

Although it has been argued that cultural messages are differentially received and interpreted (Tomlinson, 1991) these local versions are still constrained within the boundaries of 'global structural commonalities' (Kjeldgaard & Askegaard, 2006, p. 245). That is, consumers are not entirely free agents nor are they completely bound by social structures. If, as suggested, homogenisation and heterogenisation are commonly interconnected processes (Robertson, 1994; Robertson & White, 2005), then local interpretation is not without the influence of the global. Local cultures and the influences of globalisation are 'co-shaping' (Thompson & Arsel, 2004) in this way, and it is this that is at the core of glocalisation (see Robertson, 1995). Furthermore, Giulianotti and Robertson (2007, p. 134) suggest that 'glocalisation both highlights how local cultures may critically adapt or resist "global" phenomena and reveals the way in which the very creation of localities is a standard component of globalisation'.

## Appropriation

Mere exposure to global cultural practice does not constitute appropriation (Rogers, 2006). Whilst appropriation can be described as a group borrowing or imitating the design or practices of another to call them their own (Ostergaard, Fitchett, & Jantzen, 1999; Shugart, 1997), this is not to say the appropriation of the design or practice is to distort or deconstruct its previous meaning and associated experiences. However, the appropriations process, 'incorporates everything done to the product from the time of acquisition until it is no longer owned by the consumer' (Ostergaard et al., 1999, p. 406). In doing so, the product, brand, or ritual is either adopted or adapted, but is subsequently transformed to reflect its owner(s) where consumption can meet the needs of both social engagement and distinction. An aspect of this transformation will also involve negotiating authenticity (Arthur, 2006). As a consequence of glocalisation, each culture has to define what is genuine, real, or trustworthy.

## Youth culture, glocalisation, and appropriation

Technology and media revolutions have transformed the lifestyles of young people on an international scale (Bynner, 1997), and young adults' identification with popular culture through mass media is arguably the most significant influence on young people's consumption (Fien, Neil, & Bentley, 2008). This identification has been used to illustrate the impact of globalisation on youth culture (Lukose, 2005) with the suggestion that there is little to differentiate the consumption patterns of adolescents across the developing world. Yet young people or those in emerging adulthood are free to explore their agentic abilities (Erikson, 1968) during this the period of transition. As such, it is recognised that whilst youth consumption practices have been used to illustrate homogenisation (Brake, 1985), more recent commentators have suggested that the youth market 'interpret and rework global cultural practices and meanings to fit into local contexts' (Kjeldgaard & Askegaard, 2006, p. 231). The degree to which these global practices are reworked, however, will depend on both the individual and group agency of the adolescents. Kozinets, Sherry, Storm, Nuttavuthist, and Deberry-Spence (2004) discuss two opposing views on agency: one being that individuals can be creative and subversive, the other being that agency can be overwhelmed and duped by producers. Whilst it is likely that consumer and producer interests may overlap and that co-creation can exist in certain circumstances (e.g. rituals), it is also acknowledged that individual and even group-resistant alternatives, particularly during adolescence, may be difficult to achieve. That is, although agency implies that the actors have the freedom to create, change, and influence events, factors affecting agency include pre-conditions (e.g. individual goals), processes (e.g. locus of control within peer group/s or cultural boundaries), and previous agentic actions (Titma, Tuma, & Roots, 2007). This needs further exploration in the context of the adoption or adaptation of global rituals.

Arguably one of the most significant developmental aspects for an adolescent in the UK is leaving high school or sixth form to continue with further education and/or to find employment (see, e.g., Hektner, 1995). In order to recognise this milestone in the UK, traditionally there would have been a disco in the school gym (Pyke & Bloomfield, 2004) where pupils would be expected perhaps to invest in a new pair of jeans and some hair products. This has changed in recent years, as Duffy (2007) suggests that although less than a decade ago the 'prom' was an exclusive part of American life, in the past 10 years it has become the ultimate coming of age celebration for adolescents living in the UK. The UK government has also been said to encourage the US approach to end-of-school parties believing that formal ceremonies will help motivate students across the ability range (Pyke & Bloomfield, 2004).

In a global context, a number of coming-of-age celebrations are practised. but often, contrary to the prom, these are associated with religious observances. The Bar Mitzvah, Confirmation, and 'na'ii'ees' (an apache rite of puberty) are illustrative of these. However, it may be that similar ritual elements observed as part of the high-school prom will be evident in these practices. The Quinceañera, for example, is a traditional coming-of-age celebration for Latinas and is an elegant party on the girl's 15th birthday, highlighting God, family, friends, music, food, and dance. Further exploration of these rituals in the context of glocalisation is also merited.

## The high-school prom

The principle notion of the high-school prom historically in youth culture has been to signal the transition of youths to adulthood. The school prom was inspired by the debutante ball, which was of particular significance for young women as it signalled that they were ready for marriage (Escalas, 1993). The US high-school prom in this respect is a more modern ritual, although there continues to be more formal aspects to it. Girls wear formal dresses with a corsage given to them by their partner. Boys usually dress in black tie, and traditionally girls give boys matching buttonholes to be worn on their suits. The high-school prom can have a theme (e.g. that of a popular film). Common US high-school prom activities include having photographs taken, dining, dancing, and the crowning of a prom king and queen (and having fun). The high-school prom can be a meal in hotel followed by a nightclub or can simply be an event organised by a school committee and/or by members of the school staff in the gym hall. The girls are expected to have a partner, and the partner is typically expected to pay for his partner's ticket to the event, as well as his own.

Few scholars have used the high-school prom to explore youth culture. Best (2000) notes that we have less systematic research on high-school proms and the associated rituals and practices because they are typically dismissed as 'trivial'. She suggests research in this area would generate insight into transitional behaviour, and argues that the high-school prom has wrongly been positioned as 'marginal'. Escalas (1993) has also called for an examination of rites of passage present in modern-day society (e.g. high-school proms).

## Aspects of the ritual experience

Ritual artefacts (signs and symbols), a ritual script, performance roles, and an audience have been identified by Rook (1985) as essential to a ritual experience. Escalas (1993) observes that these four components are central to the debutante ball, and they are in some respects equally relevant for the US high-school prom. The gown, the meal, the photographs, and the audience (internal and external) contribute to the overall event. Ritual artefacts, in particular, when used in a ritual context can convey specific symbolic messages. As the 'activities of getting ready [for the prom] enabled many girls to demonstrate their skills at assembling a range of signs or symbols ... in a way that transformed who they were at school' (Best, 2004, p. 199), the school prom clearly plays a role in allowing attendees to 'tell others who I am and what I want to be' (Ostergaard et al., 1999, p. 407).

A ritual script appears to be in place for the high-school prom, although it is certainly not as rigorous as that of the debutante ball. Whilst there are specific components to it (e.g. corsage, dining, having photographs taken), there are more informal elements (e.g. type of dancing, colour and style of dress). The performance roles can also be adapted. It is commonplace to have a partner for a high-school prom in the United States (although not all attendees have someone to accompany them).

The audience is also now more diverse and virtual. With the proliferation of mobile phones with cameras, digital cameras, and social-networking sites, the opportunity to illustrate this aspect of youth culture is vast. The high-school prom has not only risen in popularity but has transcended continents. How, if at all, has the high-school prom been adopted or adapted in the UK, and how does consumer agency affect the way in which this aspect of youth culture is translated and appropriated in the UK?

This study is designed to capture the practice of a recent phenomenon in the UK, namely that of the US high-school prom. By exploring the high-school prom as a ritual event, this paper will investigate if and/or how youth culture is a glocal phenomenon that depends on a dynamic cultural process of adoption and adaptation. This specific experience will be considered in an attempt to understand how this aspect of youth culture is translated and appropriated in the UK. The research reported here is an exploratory study conducted with both adolescents who currently attend a secondary school in central Scotland and young adults who have attended a high-school prom in the UK in the last three years. In order to meet the aims of the research, the following objectives were set:

- To explore the adoption and adaptation of the high-school prom in the context of the homogenisation of youth culture and to investigate if this global phenomenon impacts on local practice
- To develop a deeper understanding of the relationship between the components and the ritual experience in the context of an event that symbolises a rite of passage
- To examine the interpretation (and reworking) of the high-school prom as a cultural practice, and to appreciate the meaning of individual agency in this context.

## Method

This research employs a mixed method approach as described by Johnson and Onwuegbuzie (2004). The method used here is a mixed model design, which involves mixing qualitative and quantitative approaches within or across the stages of the research process. However, it is recognised that 'the distinction of phenomena in mixed methods research is crucial and can be clarified by labeling the phenomenon examined by each method' (Sale, Lohfeld, & Brazil, 2002, p. 50). To that end, this is a qualitative study of the appropriation of the high-school prom as a global ritual that informs a quantitative study of ritual practice. In order to appreciate further the significant findings of the questionnaire, the qualitative data is revisited to enhance our understanding of both agency and the appropriation of this cultural event. Consumer culture theorists have a commitment to multi-method investigations (Arnould & Thompson, 2005), and the approach used here supports the view of Moran-Ellis et al. (2006) who suggest mixed methods allows an in depth exploration and integration of data, and posit that when employing mixed methods data, it would appear to be important to focus on what needs to be found out as opposed to the type of method that provided the answer.

Initially, 12 interviews were organised with young adults (18–20 years of age) who had already attended a high-school prom (and the sample included those from England, Ireland, and Scotland). A semi-structured interview guide was developed for the data-collection phase. Questions ranged from an initially broad approach with questions such as 'tell me about your school prom', with later questions addressing the specific aspects of the prom as a ritual, such as 'how do you think your prom differed from that of a US prom' and 'how important was the prom for your year group' to 'why do you think some people did not attend the prom' and 'did some people feel obliged to go the prom'.

Second, a mini discussion group of three 17-year-old girls was invited to discuss how they would research this particular topic with their peers. A questionnaire was designed by the authors using the data generated by the discussion group (as well as the data from the interviews) and was underpinned by the notion of the high-school prom being a ritual experience. The questionnaire was then piloted by the members of the discussion group and changes to the wording of the questionnaire were discussed and addressed. The questionnaire was then self-administered by the female friends from the discussion group to their peers to facilitate completion of the survey and to generate interest in the research topic. Using this research approach allowed the research topic to be addressed in a more holistic way, as it not only allowed the adolescents an opportunity to add their own insights but it may also have provided a more complete knowledge of the research issue because of the creation of shared meaning with and within the respondent group.

Teenagers responding to the questionnaire were at the same high school in central Scotland and were intending to go to the high-school prom. Of a possible 178 pupils, 132 intended to go to the prom and 86 pupils completed questionnaires. Of these 86 questionnaires, 81 were usable and five were incomplete (n = 81). This provided us with responses from more than 60% of the attendees. The questionnaires included a number of open-ended questions to generate a greater level of insight than may be obtained by simply employing a closed-question approach.

The majority of adolescents completing the questionnaires were aged either 16 or 17, although a few of the youngest pupils were 15. Appropriate ethical consideration was given to this study with permission for the research to be conducted sought and given from the Head Teacher and on-going consent given by the adolescents involved in the project. The adolescents knew that they were not obliged to complete the questionnaires, although interest in doing so appeared to be widespread. The research was topical, as the questionnaires were distributed 10 days before the prom was to take place and, as such, the event was widely anticipated.

The questionnaire data were statistically analysed using SPSS and the types of tests employed included cross tabulations, correlates (bivariates), and exploratory factor analysis. Correlations were used to determine significant relationships between the variables where $p < .05$. Likert scales, ranging from 1 = 'strongly disagree' to 5 = 'strongly agree', were employed to gauge the strength of agreement or disagreement with statements about the high-school prom and the significance of the components of the ritual experience. The open-ended question responses were also considered relative to the themes of this ritual event and contributed to an understanding of the meaning of this experience and its role in youth culture.

For the analysis of the interviews, an interpretive analytic stance was adopted drawing on the transcriptions of the interviews and mini-group discussion. The analysis of the data explored themes in the responses of adolescents using the constant comparative method described by Glaser and Strauss (1967) and analytic induction (Bryman & Burgess, 1994). Once the data were collected, they were sorted before being analysed. Each interview was examined to gain a holistic understanding of the respondent, noting themes in the margin as they emerged (see Thompson & Hirschman, 1995). All the themes were reviewed through iterations of comparison and rereading. The interpretations developed were as a consequence of the relationship between emerging insights and prior assumptions (Spiggle, 1994).

# Findings

Initially, the data presented here will provide a holistic view of the practice of the high-school prom in the UK. This will include exploratory factor analysis to examine if there are different types of prom attendees with varying attitudes towards the high-school prom. There then will follow a discussion, facilitated by the qualitative data, on the appropriation of the high-school prom and the adoption or adaptation of the components of the ritual and the experience itself. The role of individual agency will also be explored. As the qualitative and quantitative stages of this research were designed to substantiate one another, the findings are structured around the key themes from the research rather than the phases of data collection.

## The practice of the high-school prom ritual elements

The ritual elements of the high-school prom include artefacts (e.g. dress, shoes, limo), a script (e.g. what happens and in what order), performance roles (e.g. expected behaviour), and an audience (e.g. peers, family, and a wider social network). The following section will explore how these manifest themselves at a UK prom, and will conclude by examining, through exploratory factor analysis, if the ritual elements are perceived differently by the attendees.

### Artefacts

Girls attending the UK prom appeared to invest in their artefacts to a greater extent than boys ($p < .05$), with 70% of the quantitative sample (and their parents) spending £80 or more on their prom outfit (including dress, shoes, jewellery, make-up). A total of 24% of respondents spent in excess of £150 – with girls appearing to research the items necessary for this ritual event to a greater degree than boys, and this was supported qualitatively:

> They [the girls] were planning it weeks before – and to be fair they looked stunning – they really made an effort. (Jamie, 19)[1]

Popular culture also played a more overt role for girls than for boys. Girls (to a greater extent than boys) were influenced by magazines when choosing an outfit, haircut, or accessories for the prom ($p < .01$). Girls were also significantly more likely than boys to travel in a limo to the event ($p < .01$) and to spend more time preparing to go to the prom ($p < .01$). As with the outdated debutante ball, there appeared to be a greater emphasis on the women and their attire, perhaps suggesting their agency in this context was more constrained as opposed to dialectical (see Kozinets et al., 2004).

### Script

Whilst the script of the US prom is evident in the data, two central components of the script appeared to have been lost in transition: that of the corsage exchange and the crowning of the prom king and queen. The latter does not feature as a component of the ritual scripts at all for this sample. This may be because the high-school prom is viewed in the UK as a celebration for everyone leaving school (and as a consequence ought not to be considered more special for people who have been chosen as king and queen), and, collectively, this particular element of the prom has been rejected (see,

[1]Respondents' names have been anonymised.

e.g., Scott, 1994). Also the choosing of the king and queen would involve organisation and may require adult contribution. The celebration appears to remain more youth-focused without additional organisation or intervention. Only two of the interviewees had a corsage exchange. As corsages are associated with weddings in the UK, it may be that corsages have not been adopted to minimise the associations between weddings and high-school proms.

*Performance roles*

Performance roles would include formal dancing and perhaps more importantly the role of a partner or boyfriend. Interestingly, there was no consensus on prom 'dates'. Results from the questionnaire demonstrate that girls strongly disagreed that the purpose of the prom was to find a boyfriend ($p < .001$), and although this was not always supported in the qualitative data, '...there was a big emphasis on who had been asked to prom and who hadn't' (Rachel, 19), generally it was accepted that a prom date was not an essential component of the evening. Indeed, the prom could be considered more as a an 'investment' to build individual social capital, as there was a significant association between those who disagreed the purpose of the senior dance is to find a girlfriend or boyfriend and those that agreed that looking good and being remembered for a great outfit is important as it gives you more confidence the following year ($p < .05$).

*Audience*

The girls' research, organisation, and planning may possibly have been influenced by the perception and expectations of 'the audience':

> it's a competition of who has the nicest dress and the most expensive dress and who has the nicest way of getting there and who has the nicest date and who has the nicest hair – that is the thing [of most importance] – nothing about the actual night – everyone is just comparing each other. (Hannah, 19)

The audience for the prom was both internal (e.g. those attending the event and their families) and external (e.g. those likely to see pictures and hear anecdotal stories about the evening).

In some respects, the internal audience could be considered as the harshest critic, with the perception that ritual practice may be borrowed from elsewhere (e.g. weddings):

> It was complete red carpet stuff. We had our pictures taken on the red carpet outside the hotel and we all watched each other having our photo taken, commenting on the dress, the date – one girl was dressed in a wedding dress – seriously – and I thought 'Are you getting married tonight?'. (Keri, 20)

Perhaps not surprisingly then, girls comparatively with boys were more worried about wearing the same outfit ($p < .01$) and looking individual ($p < .05$). As Best (2004) suggests, there is agency in this context for girls to demonstrate their skills at assembling a range of signs or symbols. However, this agency was clearly constrained by the boundaries of what was acceptable or, to a certain degree, expected in this particular social environment (Kozinets et al., 2004).

The role of the external audience could not be underestimated either, with those who agreed it was important to have a website or other type of space to show and share photos of the prom also agreeing that it was important to go to the prom because people were still talking about it the following year ($p < .01$). As 'the minute people got home [from the prom] the first thing they did was put their pictures up on Bebo' (Rachel, 18), the longevity of the event and the significance of the audience was clearly important for some, if not all, the attendees. This, in itself, illustrates the role of the high-school prom in youth culture, given the growing significance and proliferation of social-networking sites.

It appeared from both the qualitative and quantitative data that there might be differing perceptions of prom attendance. To explore this concept further, exploratory factor analysis was conducted. Byrne (2001) confirms the use of exploratory factor analysis as a tool to allow data to be explored in order to generate underlying factors that may exist within the data. This factor analysis was not designed to 'freeze meaning' (see Slater, 1997) but to illustrate the states between which adolescents would be likely to move. As discussion on identity formation in this postmodern age leads to references of multiple or fragmented identities instead of unitary or unchangeable ones (Featherstone, 2001), it is recognised that these segments are not stable.

This exploratory analysis indicated that there are four factor groupings of prom attendees, each with varying attitudes towards the high -school prom and with differing propensities for the appropriation of cross-cultural ritual practice. These groups are: those who were anxious about attending, those who thought it was an excuse for a party, those who were particularly image conscious, and those who illustrated a need to belong (see Table 1). A discussion of ritual orientation and appropriation follows.

## The appropriation of the high-school prom

Each of the groups identified in Table 1 have been classified as demonstrating a degree of appropriation or ritual orientation. That is, they have been categorised by the extent to which as groups they have adopted or adapted the high-school prom. These groups and the relationship they have with the ritual elements will now be discussed in turn.

### The 'anxious' group

This group were anxious about attending the prom, and focused on not finding a date, not looking as good as others, and were most concerned about being left out of their group. These attendees placed greater emphasis on the traditional (conveyed) meaning of the prom ritual, and as such exhibited a greater propensity for appropriation of the global ritual script without adaptation. As such, this 'anxious' group exhibited a global orientation. It would also seem that authenticity in terms of replicating (perceived) authentic US prom practice was significant in accepting the high-school prom as part of youth culture for this group, and that there were expectations of what adolescents should experience as a result of observing what happened elsewhere: 'The American Prom on TV looks amazing but my school prom was nothing like that' (Hannah, 19).

In this case, Hannah thinks her prom lacked authenticity, as it did not match her perceptions of the way in which the prom is practiced in the United States and therefore the way in which she thinks it should have been interpreted in the UK. Lesley is disappointed she cannot adopt the US practice:

> My prom wasn't as full-blown as the American prom. We tried to get a limo but couldn't. The size of the hall it was in wasn't the same size as the one on the films. Ours wasn't quite as extravagant. (Lesley, 18)

**Table 1** Types of prom attendees.

| Type of prom attendee | Ritual orientation | Corresponding statements | Cronbach's alpha | Cumulative loading |
|---|---|---|---|---|
| Anxious | Global | I am apprehensive about not finding someone to go with | .701 | 74.5% |
| | | I am anxious about not looking as good as others | | |
| | | I will be nervous about making sure I get to sit with friends | | |
| | | I am anxious about not being left out of my group | | |
| Celebratory | Local | I am very excited and full of anticipation | .656 | 78.8% |
| | | I am looking forward to really dressing up | | |
| | | I am expecting one of the best nights out so far | | |
| | | I am really looking forward to sharing the experience with all my friends | | |
| Image Conscious | 'Glocal' | I am anxious about how my partner will feel if I dance with someone else | .706 | 64.3% |
| | | I am worried about dancing with people who can't dance | | |
| | | I am concerned about how much it will all cost me | | |
| | | I'll probably get anxious about taking enough good photos | | |
| Needing to belong | 'Glocal' | I'll probably get upset if I don't get invited into a limo | * | * |
| | | I am worried someone else will be wearing the same outfit | | |

*This is a correlate as opposed to a factor score, as there are only two statements ($p < 0.01$).

Ashley also recognises that some attendees of her prom were disappointed, as the UK prom did not meet the expectations of how a prom should be practised:

> I think our prom is very different to a US high-school prom. A lot of people said before the prom that it was going to be like an American prom but after the prom lots of people said it was a big let down. (Ashley, 20)

Agency in this context was 'blindly conformist' (Hetrick & Lozada, 1994). It may be, however, that the personal anxiety associated with the prom attendance manifest itself in the expectations of this ritual event. That is, these attendees were so anxious about performing appropriately that they expected the prom to reflect their own investment. Interesting to note is Giddens's (1991) reflection that ritual often produces anxiety rather than alleviating it, as it represents a major transition in life. Perhaps the anxious group were more aware of the significance of this transitional phase.

## The 'celebratory' group

Those who thought the prom was an excuse to celebrate, however, were less concerned with the adoption of the US prom, and were excited, full of anticipation, and were just really looking forward to dressing up. In this sense, the 'celebratory' group displayed a greater preference for the local adaptation of the prom ritual, reworking it to complement their calendar of end-of-year social events, and displayed a local orientation, which was both creative and subversive in practice.

> I suppose ours was a prom but it was more like a big party – a sort of going away. It was a disco in a different location – although we were wearing gowns and kilts and we had a limo – whereas at a disco you wouldn't make that much of an effort. [It was] a glorified disco I suppose. (Ashley, 20)

There also appeared to be an acceptance that, depending on the locale of the prom, the custom would be different. Additionally, the US prom and the associated practices were recognised as being stressful or pressurised:

> I think it's important to have one [a prom] because you get to do the social thing with people from school but I also think that it's important to have fun – but not to try hard to have fun and just enjoy yourself without any pressure of the American type prom. (Joanne, 18)

There also appeared in this group to be more recognition of reworking the prom to the local culture:

> We had stretch hummers, so that definitely compares [to the US high-school prom]. They get more dressed up [but] we put a Scottish slant on it because they usually have a theme like 'Under the Sea' or things like that. We had a caleigh [sic; Scottish dancing] and then just a disco. (Lorna, 18)

## The 'image conscious' and those who 'needed to belong'

This reworking was less apparent in the groups who were 'image conscious' or those who 'needed to belong'. These groups tended to focus on specific aspects of the prom. For example, if the attendees were image conscious, they focused on getting 'good' photos taken, whereas those who needed to belong indicated that they were anxious about feeling left out of their group (e.g. not being asked to share a limo). Both these groups demonstrated a desire to adopt specific characteristics of the prom ritual whilst remaining faithful to the local cultural narratives, and could be said to have a more 'glocal' orientation. The notion of why taking pictures is so important for the 'image conscious' was elaborated on by Yasmin:

> Bebo stalking goes to the extreme [with prom pictures]. You have to have pictures galore . . . so that people who didn't go you make it look like it was more fun. When you put your pictures up you have to have millions . . . and you have to get pictures of everyone. Even if you don't know these people you just have to – and you are very glam – it's not just like going to a normal party. . . (Yasmin, 18)

Of course, not all prom attendees will fall neatly into one category, and it is likely that there may be some overlapping (e.g. Lorna in this sample appeared to be celebratory, as well as image conscious). It may be that the degree of agency varies depending on the changing social circumstances in which the ritual is being performed, for example, if a girl is unexpectedly asked to the prom by a boy, she may become more anxious, whereas previously when just attending with friends her outlook would have been more celebratory. The exploratory factor analysis, however, does confirm the presence of common groupings, which could be used for future research in this area to explore the extent to which the prom is more likely to be adopted (globalisation) or adapted (localised) depending on motivations for attending.

## The role of individual agency

Within youth culture, the notion of agency is well documented. For example, teenagers are known to engage in imaginative acts of defiance or practices of (re)appropriation (Russell & Tyler, 2005). These practices, however, may depend on the role(s) adopted by those engaged in the cultural act or process. It was evident, for example, that attendees in this sample used the prom as an opportunity to change people's opinion of them and that this could be perceived to have been a success. For example, Keri reflects on how her perception of an attendee changed as a consequence of the school prom:

> Some people looked amazing – you know those who walked along at school really quietly – they were still quite quiet at the formal [prom] but I think they had made a real effort to change people's perception of them. Some of them looked fantastic – you'd never seen them out of tracksuit bottoms and a hoodie. (Keri, 20)

There was also opportunity to build social capital for the attendees depending on their individual agency in relation to social networking sites:

> More pictures equal more [perceived] fun – and you are capturing more of it . . . the more pictures you have, it looks like it was more of a night. If you only put up five pictures, it looks like it was a bit of a pants night. The more people you have in the pictures, it looks like you have more friends. If you have massive group photos, that's good. (Yasmin, 18)

Adolescent agency was also evident in the way in which local adaptations of the high-school prom allowed this ritual event to be reworked. Practices included giving special gifts within friendship groups before going to the prom to mark the occasion and also added to the known script (and may further illustrate the symbolic meaning of gift giving, see, e.g., Belk, 1996). There also appeared to be special roles for some parents, which may reinforce the way in which this event, positioned as an aspect of youth culture, can be appropriated as part of a more dominant (familial) culture.

> My parents came home from work and we had a champagne reception for us [other parents and five girls in friendship group] before the prom. I think it was probably quite a big thing for them too. (Sarah, 20)

## Conclusion

This paper has shown not only adolescents' appropriation of a globalising cultural ritual, but also how this appropriation appears to differ by attitudes to attending, in this particular case, the high-school prom. Previous studies (see Ger & Belk, 1996) have alluded to globalisation and appropriation, but have tended only to provide examples of brand-related products. This paper contributes to our existing understanding of appropriation by illustrating not only the role of agency in appropriation, but also the extent to which homogenisation and heterogenisation are interconnected processes (Robertson, 1994; Robertson & White, 2005), and that there can be varying degrees of appropriation (e.g. global, local, or glocal) even for the same ritual practice. That is, our understanding of how and in what ways local practice has been developed and co-created in the context of the global has been illustrated here. Agency has been identified as both creative and conformist (see Kozinets et al., 2004), and as such has contributed to our notion of the ways in which the degree of glocalisation is influenced by social circumstances. Figure 1 illustrates the key concepts and interrelationships that have been explored whilst investigating the appropriation of the high-school prom in the UK.

The existing local practice in the UK, which would have involved a disco in the school hall, has not been entirely lost in the adoption or adaption of the high-school prom, and as such, appropriation of this US ritual has not completely replaced previous tradition (although it has certainly added to the notion of how to celebrate the end of school). The adaptation (or co-shaping) of the high-school prom has seen a 'Scottish slant' reported by those attending Scottish proms, and this has been reflected in artefacts (e.g. kilts) and performance roles (e.g. ceilidh dancing) illustrating that the creation of localities is indeed a standard component of globalisation (Giulianotti &

**Figure 1** Concepts and interrelationships associated with appropriation.

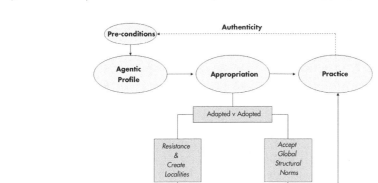

Robertson, 2007). Examination of other ritual practices, such as the coming-of-age celebrations (e.g. confirmation) mentioned earlier may also provide a more holistic understanding of the diversity of practice in relation to (re)appropriation.

Interestingly, the findings suggest that authenticity in the context of globalising rituals is twofold. That is, all the adolescents did not necessarily negotiate authenticity when appropriating the high-school prom, as suggested by Arthur (2006). Rather a number of attendees considered that when their prom did not replicate their perceptions of a US prom that their prom lacked authenticity. This contributes to our understanding of adolescent agency, as it elaborates on the way in which co-creation is influenced by both a dominant force (US producers) and conformist behaviour. Additional work on the aspects of perceived authenticity and practice authenticity and the role of appropriation in this situation would contribute further to our understanding of glocalisation. Research that considers the factors affecting agency (see Titma et al., 2007) such as individual goals, control within peer groups, self esteem, and previous experiences (taking into account the role of individual agency) would also allow a development of the typology explored in Table 1 and the framework illustrated in Figure 1.

As this paper has focused solely on the attendees of the high-school prom in the UK, a study that considers the anti- or non-consumption of this ritual event and focuses on how youth culture in this situation critically resists this practice (see Giulianotti & Robertson, 2007) could add to our understanding of both (re)appropriation and agency in relation to the high-school prom.

Finally, further research could also explore the concept of multiple identities or selves, as the prom can be a way in which teenagers can transform themselves literally overnight. The example of the girl who changed out of her tracksuit into a ball gown is evidence of this. The prom as a 'critical moment' (see Thomson et al., 2002) also needs further exploration, as critical moments in 'inventing adulthoods' appear to be socially structured and could feature the high-school prom. This will both develop and enhance our understanding of this cultural practice as a coming-of-age event. If, as Newcombe, Drummey, Fox, Lie, and Ottinger-Alberts (2000) suggest, extended memories often include prom night, the longer-term significance of the UK high-school ritual experience as a milestone may yet to be fully appreciated.

# References

Arnould, E.J., & Thompson, C.J. (2005). Consumer Culture Theory (CCT): Twenty years of research. *Journal of Consumer Research*, 31, 868–881.

Arthur, D. (2006). Authenticity and consumption in the Australian Hip Hop culture. Qualitative Market Research: *An International Journal*, 9(2), 140–156.

Belk, R.W. (1990). Halloween: An evolving American consumption ritual. *Advances in Consumer Research*, 17, 508–517.

Belk, R.W. (1996). The meaning of gifts and greetings. *Advances in Consumer Research*, 23, 13.

Belk, R.W. (2004). Men and their machines. *Advances in Consumer Research*, 31, 273–278.

Best, A.L. (2000). *Prom night: Youth, schools and popular culture*. New York: Routledge/Farmer.

Best, A.L. (2004). Girls, schooling and the discourse of self change: Negotiating meaning of the high school prom. In A. Harris (Ed.), *All about the girl: Culture power and identity* (chap. 17). New York: Routledge.

Bonsu, S. (2001). Death becomes us: Negotiating consumer identities through funerary products in Ghana. *Advances in Consumer Research*, 28, 340–346.

Brake, M. (1985). *Comparative youth culture*. London: Routledge.

Bryman, A., & Burgess, R.G. (1994). *Analyzing qualitative data*. London: Routledge.

Bynner, J. (1997). Agenda for youth research in the next century: A British Perspective. *Young*, *5*(4), 34–49.

Byrne, B.M. (2001). *Structural equation modelling with AMOS basic concepts, applications and programming*. London: Lawrence Erlbaum.

Chun, S., Gentry, J.W., & McGinnis, L.P. (2004). Cultural differences in fan ritualization: A cross-cultural perspective of the ritualization of American and Japanese baseball fans. Advances in Consumer Research, *31*, 503–508.

Chun, S., Gentry J.W., & McGinnis L.P. (2005). Ritual aspects of sports consumption: How do sports fans become ritualized? *Asia Pacific Advances in Consumer Research*, 6, 331–336.

Close, A., & Zinkhan G.M. (2006). A holiday loved and loathed: A consumer perspective of Valentine's Day. *Advances in Consumer Research*, *33*, 356–365.

Duffy, M. (2007, September 8). Fizz, frocks and limos: Get ready for the ultimate party. *The Herald*, p.15.

Eckhardt, G.M., & Mahi, H. (2004). The role of consumer agency in the globalization process in emerging markets. *Journal of Macromarketing*, *24*(2), 136–146.

Erikson, E.H. (1968). *Identity: Youth and crisis*. New York: Norton.

Escalas, J.E. (1993). The consumption of insignificant rituals: A look at debutante balls. *Advances in Consumer Research*, *20*, 709–716.

Featherstone, M. (2001). Postnational flow, identity formation and cultural space. In E.B. Rafael & Y. Sternberg (Eds.), *Identity, culture and globalization* (pp.494–526). Leiden, The Netherlands: Brill.

Fernandez, K.V., & Veer, E. (2004). The gold that binds: The ritualistic use of jewellery in a Hindu wedding. *Advances in Consumer Research*, *31*, 55.

Fien, J., Neil, C., & Bentley, M. (2008). Youth can lead the way to sustainable consumption. *Journal of Education for Sustainable Development*, *2*(1), 51–60.

Fischer, E., & Gainer, B. (1993). Baby showers: A rite of passage in transition. *Advances in Consumer Research*, *20*, 320–324.

Ger, G., & Belk, R.W. (1996). I'd like to buy the world a coke: Consumptionscapes of the less affluent world. *Journal of Consumer Policy*, *19*, 271–304.

Giddens, A. (1991). *Modernity and self identity: Self and society in the late modern age*. Cambridge, England: Polity Press.

Giulianotti, R., & Robertson, R. (2007). Forms of glocalisation: Globalization and the migration strategies of Scottish football fans in North America. *Sociology*, *1*(1), 133–152.

Glaser, B., & Strauss, A. (1967). *The discovery of grounded theory: Strategies for qualitative research*. Chicago: Aldine.

Hektner, J.M. (1995). When moving up implies moving out: Rural adolescent conflict in the transition to adulthood. *Journal of Research in Rural Education*, *11*(3), 3–14.

Hetrick, W.P., & Lozada, H.R. (1994). Constructing the critical imagination: Comments and necessary diversions. *Journal of Consumer Research*, *21*, 548–558.

Jeffries, S. (2004, October 29). Give up the ghosts. *The Guardian*. Available at http://www.guardian.co.uk/g2/story/0,,1338569,00.html.

Johnson, B.R., & Onwuegbuzie, A.J. (2004). Mixed methods research: A research paradigm whose time has come. *Educational Researcher*, *33*(7), 14–26.

Kjeldgaard, D., & Askegaard, S. (2006). The glocalization of youth culture: The global youth segment as structures of common difference. *Journal of Consumer Research*, *33*, 231–247.

Kozinets, R., Sherry, J.F., Storm, D., Nuttavuthist, K., & Deberry-Spence, B. (2004). Ludic agency and retail spectacle. *Journal of Consumer Research*, *31*, 658–672.

Lukose, R. (2005). Consuming globalization: Youth and gender in Kerala, India. *Journal of Social History*, *38*, 915–935.

McAlexander, J.H. (1991). Divorce, the disposition of the relationship and everything. *Advances in Consumer Research*, *18*, 43–48.

Moran-Ellis, J., Alexander, V.D., Cronin, A., Dickson, M., Fielding, J., Sleney J., & Thomas, H. (2006). Triangulation and integration: Processes, claims and implications. *Qualitative Research*, 6(1), 45–59.

Newcombe, N.S., Drummey, A.B., Fox, N.A., Lie, E., & Ottinger-Alberts, W. (2000). Remembering early childhood: How much, how and why (or why not). *Current Directions in Psychological Science*, 9(2), 55–58.

Ostergaard, P., Fitchett, J.A., & Jantzen, C. (1999). On appropriation and singuralisation: Two consumption processes. *Advances in Consumer Research*, 26, 405–409.

Otnes, C., & Lowrey, T.M. (1993). Til debt do us part: The selection and meaning of artifacts in the America wedding. *Advances in Consumer Research*, 20, 325–329.

Ozanne, J.L. (1992). The role of consumption and disposition during classic rites of passage: The journey of birth, initiation and death. *Advances in Consumer Research*, 19, 396–403.

Pollay, R.W. (1987). It's the thought that counts: A case study in Xmas excesses. *Advances in Consumer Research*, 14, 140–143.

Prakash, A., & Hart, J.A. (2000). *Coping with globalization*. New York: Routledge.

Pyke, N., & Bloomfield, S. (2004, July 11). The high school prom arrives in UK (via stretch limo, naturally). *The Independent*, Sunday, Education News. Available at http://www.independent.co.uk/news/education/education-news/the-high-school-prom-arrives-in-uk-via-stretch-limo-naturally-552740.html.

Ritzer, G. (1993). *The McDonaldization of society*. Newbury Park, CA: Pine Forge Press.

Robertson, R. (1994). Globalization or glocalisation? *Journal of International Communication*, 1(1), 33–52.

Robertson, R. (1995). Glocalisation: Time-space and homogeneity-heterogeniety. In M. Featherstone, S. Lash, & R. Robertson (Eds.), *Global modernities* (pp. 25–44). Sage, London.

Robertson, R., & White, K.E. (2005). Globalization: Sociology and cross-disciplinarity. In C. Calhoun, C. Rojek, & B.S. Turner (Eds.), *The Sage handbook of sociology* (pp. 345–366). London: Sage.

Rogers, R.A. (2006). From cultural exchange to transculturation: A review and reconceptualiztion of cultural appropriation. *Communication Theory*, 16, 474–503.

Rook, D.W. (1985). The ritual dimension of consumer behavior. *Journal of Consumer Research*, 12, 251–264.

Rook, D.W., & Levy, S.J. (1983). Psychosocial themes in consumer grooming rituals. *Advances in Consumer Research*, 10, 329–333.

Russell, R., & Tyler M. (2005). Branding and bricolage: Gender, consumption and translation. *Childhood*, 12(2), 221–237.

Ruth, J.A. (1995). Sad, glad and mad: The revealing role of emotions in consumer rituals. *Advances in Consumer Research*, 22, 692.

Sale, J.E.M., Lohfeld, L.H., & Brazil, K. (2002). Revisiting the quantitative–qualitative debate: Implications for mixed methods research. *Quality and Quantity*, 36, 43–53.

Scott, L. (1994). The bridge from text to mind: Adapting reader-response theory to consumer research. *Journal of Consumer Research*, 21, 461–480.

Shugart, H. (1997). Counterhegemonic acts: Appropriation as a feminist rhetorical strategy. *Quarterly Journal of Speech*, 83, 210–229.

Slater, D. (1997). *Consumer culture and modernity*. Cambridge, England: Polity Press.

Spiggle, S. (1994). Analysis and interpretation of qualitative data in consumer research. *Journal of Consumer Research*, 21, 491–503.

Thompson, C.J., & Arsel, Z. (2004). The Starbucks brandscape and consumers (anticorporate) experiences of glocalization. *Journal of Consumer Research*, 31, 631–642.

Thompson, C.J., & Hirschman, E. (1995). Understanding the socialized body: A poststructuralist analysis of consumers' self-conceptions, body images and self-care practices. *Journal of Consumer Research*, 22, 139–153.

Thomson, R., Bell, R., Holland, J., Henderson, S., McGrellis, S., & Sharpe, S. (2002). Critical moments: Choice, chance and opportunity in young people's narratives of transition. *Sociology*, 36, 335–354.

Titma, M., Tuma, N.B., & Roots, A. (2007). Adolescent agency and adult economic success in a transitional society. *International Journal of Psychology, 42*(2), 102–109.

Tomlinson, J. (1991). *Cultural imperialism*. Baltimore: John Hopkins University Press.

Watson, J. (1998). Why did you put that there?: Gender, materialism and tattoo consumption. *Advances in Consumer Research, 25*, 453–460.

# The interrelationship between desired and undesired selves and consumption: The case of Greek female consumers' experiences

Katerina Karanika, *University of Exeter Business School, UK*
Margaret K. Hogg, *Lancaster University Management School, UK*

**Abstract** Earlier work on identity, self, and consumption identified that desired and undesired selves play a significant role in the important global phenomenon of symbolic consumption, but neglected to investigate and conceptualise the interrelationship between desired and undesired selves and consumption. Phenomenological interviews with Greek women are used to elicit consumption experiences linked to positive and negative aspects of the self. The interrelationships between desired and undesired selves in consumption were characterised by two patterns (first, conflicting, and second, compatible desired and undesired selves) that could be linked to consumers' different strategies. Examining these strategies, we extend previous work on the strategies that consumers use to handle identity issues. Finally, we evaluate this theory building derived from the Greek empirical data within the context of US-generated theory about individuals' ways of dealing with self-coherence issues through symbolic consumption; we identify consumers' sense of baffled self and ambivalence in the emotions surrounding consumption.

## Background

Previous consumer research has identified that desired and undesired selves play a significant role in the important global phenomenon of symbolic consumption (e.g. Ahuvia, 2005). However, no attempt had been made to investigate and conceptualise the *interplay* between desired and undesired selves in consumption, and this paper addresses this important gap. The strategies consumers used in order to handle the interrelationships between their desired and undesired selves are examined, extending Ahuvia's theory on the strategies consumers use in handling identity issues. We note differences and similarities between Ahuvia's and our findings, and we identify the different conditions under which consumers follow different strategies. Finally, the theory building derived from this study's Greek empirical data is evaluated within the context of US-generated theory about how consumers, dealing with difficulties in creating a coherent sense of self, negotiate conflicting identities through symbolic consumption (e.g. Ahuvia, 2005; Cushman, 1990; Firat & Venkatesh, 1995). This study identifies, first, consumers' sense of baffled self, and second, more ambivalence in consumers' emotions surrounding consumption than previous studies suggest, contributing to the debates about homogeneity–heterogeneity in global consumer culture.

## Consumer culture

With the erosion of traditional forms of identity, individuals are increasingly obliged to choose and construct their own self-identity from an abundance of competing frameworks of meaning, and they do so partly through consumption (Bauman, 1991; Gergen, 1991; Giddens, 1991; Taylor, 1989). How individuals choose, construct, and communicate their identities through consumption has emerged as a central concern of consumer research (Arnould & Thompson, 2005; Belk, 1988; Dittmar, 1991; Elliott & Wattanasuwan, 1998; Holt, 2002; Richins, 1994a, 1994b; Wallendorf & Arnould, 1988).

Belk (1988) provided the foundations of this research on symbolic consumption. He used the terms 'self', 'sense of self', and 'identity' interchangeably for how a person subjectively perceives who s/he is, and Belk discussed the use of possessions for defining, extending, and strengthening the self, as well as for communicating meaning about the self to the individual and to others. Based on these assumptions, valued possessions emerged as associated with differentiation of the self from others, integration of the self with others, self-continuity, self-change, and more recently with self-coherence (e.g. Ahuvia, 2005; Belk, 1988; Csíkszentmihályi & Rochberg-Halton, 1981; Kleine, Kleine, & Allen, 1995; Myers, 1985; Schultz, Kleine, & Kernan, 1989; Wallendorf & Arnould, 1988).

## Desired and undesired selves and consumption

The notions of the desired and undesired self, which are imagined selves (Markus & Nurius, 1986) – that can be positive or negative – within identity projects, have attracted growing interest in consumer behaviour. The work on symbolic consumption in consumer behaviour confirms the role of products and services in portraying a desired self-concept (Belk, 1988; Levy, 1959; Solomon, 1983; Wright, Claiborne, & Sirgy, 1992) and the role of consumption avoidance in avoiding an undesired self-concept (Banister & Hogg, 2001, 2003; Freitas, Davis, & Kim, 1997; Wilk, 1997). The role of products and services both in approaching desired possible selves and in avoiding undesired possible selves has also been explored (Ahuvia, 2005; Patrick & MacInnis, 2002; Schouten, 1991). However, the dynamics between positive and negative selves in consumption have been neglected in studies of identity projects, even though desired and undesired selves play a significant role in symbolic consumption. We use the word dynamics to signify the way the desired and undesired self interact.

## Consumers' sense of self-coherence

Due to the contemporary difficulties in establishing self-coherence (the erosion of traditional forms of identity and the abundance of competing frameworks of meaning; e.g. Gergen, 1991; Giddens, 1991), consumers' identity projects often involve identity conflicts (e.g. Ahuvia, 2005; Arnould & Thompson, 2005; Cherrier & Murray, 2007; Fournier, 1998; Holt & Thompson, 2004; Murray, 2002; Thompson, 1996;

Thompson & Haytko, 1997; Thompson, Locander, & Pollio, 1990). Ahuvia discussed strategies that consumers in his US study used in coping with their identity conflicts related to symbolic consumption, but he neglected the conditions under which consumers follow different strategies. Moreover, since self-concept and consumption are developed within a sociocultural context, consumers in other cultures may deal differently with issues of identity and consumption.

Three discourses refer to the difficulties in establishing self-coherence: fragmented multiple selves, the empty self, and the coherent sense of self created out of synthesis of opposite identities.

Firat and Venkatesh (1995) propose that the contemporary consumer possesses fragmented multiple selves and has no need to reconcile identity contradictions; s/he is not strongly committed to identities, chooses identities (from a wide range) based on his/her momentary wants, and then discards these identities without feeling anxiety or uncertainty but rather enjoying the freedom from needing a centred, authentic self.

In contrast, Cushman (1990) argues that the contemporary consumer desires a unified and coherent identity that is difficult to construct due to the abundance of competing lifestyles and subcultures that lack shared meaning. In this view, the consumer develops feelings of self-doubt and unworthiness, and a sense of an 'empty-self', and engages in an ongoing lifestyle of consumption but never reaches fulfilment.

In the middle of these two opposing views lies the work of Gould and Lerman (1998), Thompson and Hirschman (1995), Murray (2002), Schau and Gilly (2003), and Ahuvia (2005) who explored the use of consumption to construct a coherent identity within a fragmented society. Consumers in these studies wanted a coherent identity narrative but experienced difficulties in establishing a coherent sense of self and yet did not necessarily experience an 'empty-self'. Rather, consumers were shown often to create a coherent self-narrative out of potentially disjointed material, synthesising opposite identities through consumption (Ahuvia, 2005) and flexibly incorporating dualism.

### Identity narratives

Narratives are considered a fundamental way by which the consumer structures and therefore makes sense of his/her identity, life, and consumption experiences (Ahuvia, 2005; Fournier, 1998; Giddens, 1991; Shankar, Elliott, & Goulding, 2001; Thompson, 1997; Thompson & Tambyah, 1999). Narrative theory places emphasis on the narrative structure and works on the premise that, although the narratological constructions may be marked by internal contradictions and compartmentalised beliefs, narratives nonetheless enable people to construct a sense of continuity and coherence from the flow of their life experiences (Gergen, 1991; Giddens, 1991; Thompson, 1997). This structurally oriented approach focuses on how a person frames meanings, personal concerns, and life goals in order to derive a coherent sense of personal history (Thompson, 1997). The narrative approach suggests that a coherent self-narrative represents a coherent sense of self (e.g. Ahuvia, 2005).

However, according to McAdams (2006, p. 118), 'Life is messier and more complex than the stories we tell about it'. In a similar way, Sartre maintained that the stories we tell do not need to relate easily to the lives we live; narrative coherence may signify 'bad faith'. And according to Raggatt (2006), life stories should strive to portray the rich diversity of lived experience resisting dominant cultural narratives. Therefore, calls have been made (Gubrium & Holstein, 1998; McAdams, 2006) for a focus on both the coherence and the incoherence (diversity, contrasting trends) of narratives.

McAdams (2006) maintains that a large problem in evaluating life narratives is that the coherence in a story may not reflect a respondent's own 'lived experience'.

### The phenomenological self

Because a coherent self-narrative (e.g. Ahuvia, 2005) may not necessarily represent the experience of a coherent sense of self, we draw on the phenomenological approach to the self (Reed, 2002; Thompson, Pollio, & Locander, 1989) that shares similarities with the narrative analysis (e.g. they both draw heavily on hermeneutics) but primarily focuses on the experience of self and consumption rather than the structure of these experiences (see Table 1). The self is seen as an ongoing project, a construction, recreated each moment through choices from different meanings after dialogue with different images of the self from past and future, mediated by anticipated responses of significant or generalised others (Heidegger, 1962; Sartre, 1943).

### Sociocultural context

Consumer culture theorists study consumers in consumption contexts (Arnould & Thompson, 2005). Consumers' identity projects in Mediterranean and non-American cultures such as Greece have been relatively neglected. This exploratory study into how Greeks pursue meaning and identities through consumption could therefore add to existing consumer research, which hitherto has concentrated largely on symbolic consumption in the United States, extending our understanding of the role of consumption in identity projects (Arnould & Thompson, 2005), and potentially providing a more nuanced understanding of how symbolic consumption works within global consumer culture.

### Self–object relationship

The relationship between the self and the objects often remains under-theorised (Borgerson, 2005) in consumer studies. Belk (1989, p. 130) emphasised the subject's agency (but also acknowledged a kind of agency on the part of objects) in merging identity with objects. D. Miller (1987) emphasised objects as active in subject formation. This study adopts the constructionism view on meaning (Crotty, 2003) that bridges the previous two views, emphasising the co-creation of subject and object by stating that meaning is constructed and comes out of the interplay between object and subject.

**Table 1** Narrative approach vs. Phenomenology

|  | Assumptions | Focus | Result |
| --- | --- | --- | --- |
| Narrative approach | (Coherent) self-narrative represents (coherent) sense of self | How people frame meanings to derive a coherent sense of personal history despite internal contradictions | Synthesis of potential contradictions |
| Phenomenology | Sense of self inferred through the individual's perception | Lived experience | Could potentially throw light on the dynamics of potential contradictions |

## Research design and method

This phenomenological study explored Greek female consumers' experiences with their meaningful possessions, products, and consumption activities in relation to desired and undesired selves. Because gender, as a major social category, is likely to influence self-concepts and consumption experiences, only women's consumption experiences were the focus for this study in order to reduce the complexity of examining both women's and men's consumption experiences across age groups. Convenience and snowball sampling was used to recruit 30 participants, 10 from each age span: 18–33, 34–49, and 50–65. For the purposes of this paper, we draw on the stories of 14 informants that reflect the findings of the whole data set. Their personal characteristics are summarised in Table 2 .

Phenomenological interviewing (Colaizzi, 1978; Kvale, 1983; Thompson et al., 1989, 1990) was used to elicit full descriptions of experiences. The phenomenological interview is semi-structured. The respondents largely drive the conversation. The interviewer employs short descriptive questions and specifically avoids 'why' questions. Respondents were informed that the study's purpose was to obtain insights into their experiences with their meaningful possessions, products, and consumption activities. They were also told that the interview would be audiotaped, and anonymity was assured. To stimulate discussion about themselves, their lives, and consumption, informants were invited to 'Tell the story' about their meaningful possessions, products, and/or consumption activities.

Interviews were transcribed and a phenomenological–hermeneutical analysis (Thompson et al., 1989, 1990) using a back and forth, part-to-whole interpretation

**Table 2** Informants' personal characteristics.

| Age span | Nickname | Age | Marital status | Occupation | Most important possessions/products/consumption activities |
|---|---|---|---|---|---|
| 18–33 | Victoria | 27 | Engaged | Architect assistant | Clothes, laptop, studies, cosmetics |
| | Elena | 28 | Engaged | Architect | Laptop, clothes, tennis, broach |
| | Sofia | 29 | Married | Unemployed | Clothes, furniture, tutorials, photos |
| | Nancy | 31 | Single | Clerical | Car, mobile, clothes, trips |
| | Fofika | 33 | Divorced | Middle-level manager | Mobile, car, laptop, house, studies |
| 34–49 | Nena | 36 | Single | Tour guide | Ring, heirloom, house, car |
| | Patca | 38 | Single | Pharmacist | Music CDs, (self)gifts, books, theatre |
| | Julia | 43 | Married | White-collar manager | Ring gift, organic products, house |
| | Maria | 46 | Married | Clerical | House, necklace, perfume, clothes, cafés |
| | Mina | 48 | Married | Clerical | Cosmetics, clothes, education, furniture |
| 50–65 | Andy | 53 | Married | TV/radio producer | Trips, piano, house, son's education |
| | Nana | 57 | Separated | Housewife | Music CDs, paintings, clothes, bars |
| | Joanna | 64 | Widow | Retired | Houses, lamp, furniture, books, trips |
| | Rea | 65 | Single | Retired | Diet, pet, flowers, gifts, mobile |

mode was applied to the data in order to generate theory building around the desired and undesired selves and their interrelationship in consumption.

## Findings and discussion

The findings suggest that the desired and undesired self coexist for consumers in the Greek context, colouring their consumption experiences. Table 3 presents briefly the themes around which consumers' predominant desired and undesired selves revolved. Table 4 provides a few examples of how respondents' desired and undesired selves revolved around these themes, followed by a brief discussion of these themes in regards to the context in which they emerged. Then the focus turns to identifying and conceptualising two patterns that capture the dynamic interrelationship between desired and undesired selves in consumption.

## Thematic dimensions of desired and undesired selves

Our participants' strong affiliation, security, and control needs are encouraged by the current difficult and uncertain economic climate, with factors such as high unemployment rates and the state's poor levels of support and protection for both young and elderly citizens in Greece (Eurostat, 2002). Young and elderly people in Greece and in other Mediterranean countries rely heavily on their nuclear families, in contrast to people in Scandinavian countries who are strongly supported by the state (Eurostat, 2002). Indeed, our respondents sought strong interpersonal ties with their

**Table 3** Thematic dimensions of desired and undesired selves.

| Themes | Desired selves | Undesired selves |
|---|---|---|
| Affiliation | Feelings of belonging, being accepted, and caring for others | Feelings of being excluded, rejected, alone, and not caring for others |
| Standing out | Feeling respected and proud, standing out positively | Feeling disrespected and ashamed, standing out negatively |
| Security | Feeling safe and secure | Feeling unsafe and insecure |
| Control | Being in control | Not being in control |
| Pleasure | Experiencing pleasure/enjoyment | Experiencing displeasure/pain |

**Table 4** Mapping themes across desired and undesired selves.

| Themes | Desired selves | Undesired selves |
|---|---|---|
| Affiliation | Being loved, fitting in, caring for others | Unloved, alone, negligent mother/daughter |
| Standing out | Beautiful, successful, sophisticated | Unattractive, failed, snobbish, deprived, miserly |
| Security | Financially secure, healthy, safe | Financially insecure, unhealthy, ill, unsafe |
| Control | Free, independent, powerful | Oppressed, dependent, weak |
| Pleasure | Indulgent, enjoying, relaxed | Stressed, in displeasure |

nuclear family. Moreover, our participants sought security and control in reaction to the environmental uncertainty that surrounds them; they were motivated to minimise financial uncertainty and risk in order to ensure that they achieved a degree of protection for and control over the future.

## Patterns of interrelationships between desired and undesired selves

Two dynamic patterns of interrelationship between desired and undesired selves were conceptualised from this study. This part of the paper is structured as follows. First, in section 1, we discuss pattern A, then we identify different motivations in pattern A, and subsequently we discuss two different emergent strategies linked to different motivations in pattern A. Next in section 2, we move on to pattern B, the relevant motivation, and the relevant consumers' strategies. Table 5 summarises the findings discussed further in sections 1 and 2.

### 1. Pattern A: Dynamic of conflicting desired and undesired selves

In the first pattern (A), consumers experience the dilemma of choosing between one pair of desired/undesired selves over another pair of desired/undesired selves (win–lose situations). Maria (46 years old), for example, experiences the dilemma of choosing between either 'being a caring mother but not enjoying herself' or 'enjoying herself but being a negligent mother', which are two opposite possible identities, each involving a desired and an undesired self (affiliation and pleasure themes). In this case, dilemmas and tensions are experienced, as described in earlier studies as life themes or

**Table 5** Patterns of consumers' desired and undesired selves' interrelationships, consumers' motivation, and strategies.

| Patterns | Motivation | Strategies |
|---|---|---|
| **A**: Conflicting desired and undesired selves *Existential dilemmas; **win–lose** situations; e.g. pursuing a desired self necessitates acceptance of an undesired self* | *Approach a desired self*<br>• Abandoning another desired self and/or<br>Accepting one undesired self<br>*Avoid an undesired self*<br>• accepting another undesired self and/or<br>• abandoning one desired self | Choice strategy |
| | Unclear framing around desired and undesired selves | Balance strategy<br>Transition strategy |
| **B**: Compatible desired and undesired selves *No dilemma; **win–win** situations; pursuing a desired self means avoiding an undesired self and vice versa* | Approach a desired self and avoid an undesired self | Straightforward strategy |

*identity conflicts* (e.g. Ahuvia, 2005; Fournier, 1998). Respondents with such conflicting desired and undesired selves experienced a sense of 'baffled' self (T. Miller, 2009) and often the need to compromise due to the dilemma of choosing between two possible and competing identities. Several dilemmas emerged from respondents' lifeworld descriptions such as 'enjoying myself or being a caring mother' (Maria, Andy), 'looking feminine or feeling comfortable' (Victoria), 'being healthy or indulging' (Rea).

Such existential dilemmas mirror the tensions between choosing an identity and the constraints in doing so (Shankar, Elliott, & Fitchett, 2009). Moreover, such existential dilemmas were reflected in consumers' experiences with their important possessions, products, and consumption activities. The important object or activity in this case enables and activates both a desired and an undesired self. The consumer associates the special item or activity with both her desired self and undesired self, has both positive and negative memories about it, has mixed feelings about it, and has a 'love–hate' relationship with it.

Often respondents experiencing such dilemmas of choosing between one pair of conflicting desired/undesired selves over another were more motivated either to pursue one desired self or to avoid one undesired self. However, sometimes there was a less clear framing of consumers' decisions around their desired/undesired selves.

## Pursuing a desired self

Often respondents pursued one desired self in preference to another; that is, they pursued one desired self and abandoned or neglected an alternative desired self. For example, Mina (48 years old) pursues her desired self of being 'a caring mother' rather than her other desired self of 'looking beautiful and young'. Therefore, she pays for her daughter's private education, which means that she can only afford to buy cosmetics that she considers cheap and about which she has mixed feelings. She feels that these cosmetics are not very effective in helping her to achieve her desired self of 'looking beautiful and young'. She says:

> Cosmetics are important to look beautiful and young ... if I had financial comfort I would buy more expensive and therefore more effective cosmetics, but I consider my daughter's education as a priority now.

Respondents also discussed how pursuing a desired self often required the acceptance of an undesired self. Mina, for example, discussed how she provides private education for her daughter and thus pursues her desired self as 'a caring mother' and has at the same time to accept her 'financially pressured' undesired self.

## Avoiding an undesired self

In other cases, respondents chose to avoid one undesired self but chose (accepted or reluctantly embraced, or compromised with) another undesired self, and/or abandoned/neglected one desired self.

Victoria (27 years old), for example, avoids her undesired self 'feeling uncomfortable and insecure', but at the cost of reluctantly embracing her other undesired self 'being shy and dressed conservatively' and abandoning the opportunity of achieving her desired self 'standing out as feminine' through her dressing choices. She enacts the 'shy' aspect of her self – which she considers unwanted but also impossible to avoid. Her description reveals the tension between her ability to create her identity through her choices and the constraints on her ability to do so (Shankar et al., 2009). She says:

My clothes are conservative. I only like a cheap, feminine skirt, I bought not to wear, but because it is nice. I never wore it. I like feminine clothes that reveal parts of the body but as I am shy I always wear conservative clothes; feminine clothes attract others' attention and make me feel uncomfortable and insecure ... I admire women who dare to wear feminine clothes and stand out but I cannot.

### Choice strategy – Compromising and choosing one identity over another

Respondents from pattern A (motivated either to approach a desired self or to avoid an undesired self) dealt with their dilemma of choosing between two possible identities, each of which involves simultaneously desirable and undesirable aspects of the self by making a compromising choice. They gave up what they saw as some of the attractive features of one identity and chose the other identity. Feelings of compromise and pressure were pre-eminent and reflected in consumers' love–hate relationship with the object or activity that mediated the choice.

The choice between two competing identities was often guided by a sense of the inability to pursue, cope with, or abandon one of the identities. For example, Victoria's choice of 'feeling comfortable and secure but not standing out as feminine' with her dress choices is based on her sense of inability to pursue and cope with 'standing out as feminine but feeling uncomfortable and insecure' (see also Table 6).

Nena (36 years old) chose to avoid her undesired 'oppressed' self (control theme) at the cost of abandoning her desired 'married woman' self (affiliation theme). She has mixed feelings about her ring from her broken engagement that symbolises her choice. She said: (see also Table 6)

The ring from my broken engagement is important to me. I haven't enjoyed it ... We broke up soon after the engagement. I kept this ring but I don't wear it ... The relationship became unfair for me. I was only giving. He did not want to give things back ... I was getting oppressed ... I want another engagement ring.

When faced with two conflicting desired/undesired selves, respondents often chose one identity over another because they considered the chosen identity to be more important than the abandoned identity. Maria, for example, when she became a mother for the first time, considered her desired 'caring mother' self as more important than her desired 'enjoying' self, and stopped engaging in self-grooming and entertainment activities and devoted all her free time to her child.

Moreover, a sense of obligation (or ought self) often guided the choice between two identities. Andy, for example, chose to pursue the desired self of being 'a caring mother' and therefore abandoned the opportunity to achieve her other desired self of 'enjoying' herself because she could not engage in her favourite activity of travelling. She feels she ought to make this choice and says:

I miss trips and entertainment ... I cannot do what I want because I have to stand by my son who is going to school. He needs to know that we are close to him and here for him. All our goals are on our son to study and succeed. We pay a lot for his education. We don't exist; he exists. When he is over 18 years old and starts working in parallel to his studies, we may start to exist again. (See also Table 6.)

These respondents, who followed this compromise strategy, were often trying to adapt to or prepare for a new private transition. Nena, for example, faced the

**Table 6** Mapping respondents onto the patterns & strategies.

| Name | Age | Narrative mainly about | Main themes | Pattern A: Conflicting desired and undesired selves | Pattern B: Compatible desired and undesired selves |
|---|---|---|---|---|---|
| Victoria | 27 | Feeling comfortable but not looking feminine | Security, standing out | Choice strategy | |
| Elena | 28 | Stand as successful, not ineffective, not very classical, not very modern | Standing out | | Straightforward strategy |
| Sofia | 29 | Be financially secure, not very classical, not very modern | Security Standing out | | Straightforward strategy |
| Nancy | 31 | Belong, look not too similar, not too different, be safe, independent and enjoy | Affiliation, stand out, security, control, pleasure | | Straightforward strategy |
| Fofika | 33 | Balance belonging and calm self | Affiliation, pleasure | Balance strategy | |
| Nena | 36 | Not oppressed but alone | Control, affiliation | Choice strategy | |
| Patca | 38 | Be independent, calm, not very self-focused, not very other-focused | Control | | Straightforward strategy |
| Julia | 43 | Belonging, not being alone | Affiliation | (+ aspires to transition strategy as afraid of conflicting desired – undesired selves in the future) | Straightforward strategy |
| Maria | 46 | Balance being a caring mother and enjoying | Affiliation, pleasure | Balance strategy (+ aspires to transition strategy) | |
| Mina | 48 | Caring mother but financially pressured | Affiliation, pleasure | Choice strategy (+ aspires to transition strategy) | |
| Andy | 53 | Caring mother but suppressed, not enjoying | Affiliation, control, pleasure | Choice strategy (+ aspires to transition strategy) | |
| Nana | 57 | Be internally independent | Control | | Straightforward strategy |
| Joanna | 64 | Stand as not deprived, not showing off | Standing out | | Straightforward strategy |
| Rea | 65 | Balance healthy and indulging self | Security, pleasure | Balance strategy | |

transition of getting married; Maria had faced the transition of motherhood; Andy was anticipating the transition to the state of being an empty nester.

## Less clear framing around desired/undesired selves

In some cases, respondents experiencing identity dilemmas (pattern A) expressed less clear framing in regards to their desired and undesired selves and consumption. Fofika (33 years old), for example, has mixed feelings for her mobile phone, as it enables both her desired self 'being close to loved ones' (affiliation theme) and her undesired self 'pressured and tensed' (pleasure theme). Therefore, she regulates its use. She says:

> My mobile is important as it gets me closer to my friends and family ... but it often makes me sad ... I cannot stand it. It pressures me because I receive family tension through it ... therefore I often keep it switched off.

Rea (65 years old) discussed the tension between two possible identities, that is, 'being healthy but not indulging' and 'indulging but not being healthy' (security and pleasure themes). Each of these identities involves both a desired and an undesired self. Rea tries to reconcile the tension between these two competing possible identities by watching her diet.

## Balance strategy: Compromising and pursuing the golden mean of two identities

Respondents from the first pattern (such as Fofika, Maria, and Rea) with no clear framing around desired and undesired selves dealt with the dilemma of choosing between two identities (where each identity had both desirable and undesirable aspects) in a different way. They gave up what they saw as some of the attractive features of each identity in order to achieve a middle ground between the two identities. For example, Fofika pursues the compromise or golden mean between 'being close to loved ones but experiencing family tension' and being 'calm but lonely' by making limited use of her mobile about which she has mixed feelings. Maria, after giving birth to her second child, started pursuing the golden compromise or mean between being a caring mother and enjoying herself. At times, she enjoys self-grooming activities and going out with friends, feeling, however, she neglects her children; and at other times, she takes care of her children, doing household tasks, but she feels she is not enjoying herself. Therefore, she experiences feelings of compromise and has a love–hate relationship with her house. This is in line with Thompson's (1996) findings on working mothers' efforts to balance their inner conflicts between self-indulgence and caring for others.

It can be inferred that respondents are trying to achieve a compromise between two identities because both identities are equally important and/or desirable. Moreover, the choice of this balancing strategy might be attributed to a sense of obligation: an ought self. For example, Maria tries to achieve a balance between being a caring mother and enjoying herself because she feels she ought to be youthful for her son, and she feels she achieves that by enjoying herself. She says:

> I used to stay in doing household tasks, not going out with friends to entertain in order to take care of my daughter. I was 37 years old when my son was born ... I had to stop being like before and renew myself as if I wouldn't, people would later think I'm my son's grandmother not his mother. [...] Everybody says I've changed. I have a young son and I have to be young too and enjoy. The opposite shouldn't take place.

Respondents who follow this balancing strategy tend to have relative stability in their lives, rather than being faced with transitions.

Overall, respondents in pattern A (whether following a choice or a balance strategy) experienced constraints in their identity choices associated with feelings of compromise and pressure. This tension between identity choices and identity constraints (Shankar et al., 2009) was mirrored in their consumption experiences.

## 2. Pattern B: Dynamic of compatible desired and undesired selves

The second dynamic pattern (B) of the interrelationship between the desired and undesired selves involves the enabling of the desired self and the deactivating of the undesired self via consumption (win–win situations). In this case, consumers' pursuit of their desired self meant they succeeded in avoiding an undesired self and vice versa. No dilemmas, existential tensions, or compromising feelings were experienced. Rather, possessions, products, and consumption activities were valued because they enabled a consumer's desired selves and deactivated a consumer's undesired selves. The consumer has only positive memories from and positive feelings about such objects and activities. Patca and Nana, for example (38 and 57 years old respectively), valued art-related items (music CDs and books) for enabling desired selves such as being 'calm' and 'internally independent' and for preventing or offering relief from the undesired self of feeling 'upset' and 'dependent'.

Joanna (64 years old) illustrates that the opposite of an undesired self is not necessarily the desired/ideal self. Joanna appears not to want to be associated with two equally undesirable, yet completely opposite, self-concepts. One undesired self-concept consists of being perceived as poor, while the other undesired self consists of looking too wealthy:

> On the one side is a person who has everything, shows off, and this is obvious to others. On the other side is a person who has nothing, is miserly, and this is obvious to others too. I don't want to be on either side ... I don't show off by over consuming but I am not miserly either in under consuming ... I don't want to belong or to be considered on either side.

Several respondents from pattern B revealed that they were sometimes avoiding two completely opposite undesired selves whilst simultaneously pursuing a desired self in the middle of the two opposite extremes represented by two different undesired selves. For example:

- Avoid being either very modern or very classical, but pursue a desired self in the middle (e.g. with furniture, clothing choices; Elena, Sofia)
- Avoid being too similar to others and also very different from others (e.g. with clothing choices; Nancy)
- Avoid being very self-focused, and also avoid being very other-focused at the same time (e.g. balancing self-gifts and gifts to others; Patca).

This view of the undesired self at the two extreme ends of a spectrum of the self, with the desired self in the middle (and equipoise point) of an axis, potentially provides an interesting complement to Sullivan's (1953) theorisation that the desired self is more vague and abstract than the undesired self. It also links with Ogilvie's (1987) statement that the undesired self is a more concrete and unshakeable standard against which one judges one's present level of well-being than the desired self. This view is also in line with the concept of the ideal of personhood as a centralised equilibrium-preserving structure (Erikson, 1959; Geertz, 1973, 1979; Greenwald, 1980, in Sampson, 1985).

Respondents from pattern B did not experience as problematic or difficult the pursuit of a desired self that sits at the equipoise or balancing point between two completely opposite undesired selves. In contrast, respondents from pattern A in pursuit of equilibrium between two competing identities (balance strategy) did experience the balancing act as difficult and problematic, and they expressed feelings of compromise and pressure.

### Straightforward strategy

Respondents with compatible desired and undesired selves (pattern B, e.g. Elena, Sofia, Nancy, Patca, Julia, Nana, and Joanna) approach desired selves and avoid undesired selves via consumption in a straightforward way. They do not experience tensions or compromising feelings and have only positive feelings and memories about the possessions and activities that enabled their desired selves and deactivated their undesired selves (see also Table 6).

### Transition aspiring strategy: Solving the dilemma – Transition from pattern A to B

In some cases, respondents aspired to solve the dilemma of choosing between different identities, each of which involved both a desired and an undesired self. The solution would enable the desired aspects and deactivate the undesired aspects of both identities, solving the dilemma. Thus desired and undesired selves would cease to be in conflict (pattern A) and become compatible (pattern B). Compromising feelings would be overcome (see also Table 6).

Maria, for example, aspires to solve her dilemma of choosing between caring for her loved ones and enjoying herself by taking early retirement. By doing so, she hopes to achieve both of her desired selves 'enjoying' and 'taking good care of her family', and to avoid her undesired selves 'negligent mother' and 'not enjoying herself'.

Nena (aged 36) is hoping to establish a fair and harmonious personal relationship that will solve her dilemma of having to choose between affiliation and control.

Mina who chooses the 'caring mother but financially pressured' pair of conflicting desired and undesired selves (she is paying for her daughter's private education) is hoping that her husband will find a better-paid job.

Andy is looking forward to her son becoming financially independent, hoping that this transition will solve the dilemma of choosing between caring for her son and enjoying herself.

Julia (pattern B at the time of the interview) feels that, in the future, retirement will stimulate not only her desired self, that is, 'more relaxed' but also her undesired 'lonely' self (pattern A and pleasure and affiliation themes). She intends to have a country house built on an island where her best friends are living. This way she hopes she will enable both her desired selves, 'relaxed' and 'belonging', and will prevent realisation of her undesired selves, 'lonely' and 'not relaxed' (avoid pattern A).

This strategy emerged as an aspirational strategy in our study. Respondents aspired to solve dilemmas in the future due to opportunities that they anticipated would be created by a transition to the next life stage (e.g. retirement, empty nest) or by a desired life change (e.g. find a partner) or consumption (e.g. country house).

Overall, respondents followed different strategies based on:

* The importance they placed on their different desired and undesired selves
* Their sense of obligation or ought self
* Their feelings towards their sense of identity constraints
* Their transitional or stable life state.

Table 6 maps respondents onto the two patterns and four strategies discussed above.

## Conceptualisation

Figure 1 shows the framework of how the interplay between desired and undesired selves is mediated via consumption emerged from the analysis and depicts the two dynamic interrelationship patterns (A and B) between respondents' desired and undesired selves, and the variety of strategies (I–IV) that respondents used in order to deal with these patterned interrelationships. In line with the phenomenological perspective, this framework follows the viewpoint of the respective respondents.

## Comparison with a US study (Ahuvia, 2005)

How do our findings align with earlier US work and theory building (Ahuvia, 2005)? The four strategies that our respondents in Greece used in order to handle the dynamics between their desired and undesired selves (patterns A and B) were in some ways in line with three strategies that US respondents had followed in order to deal with their identity conflicts and to create a coherent self-narrative (Ahuvia, 2005). (Note that the pattern A in our study, which identified the role of identity conflicts, i.e. conflicting desired and undesired selves, aligns with Ahuvia's study.) Table 7 summarises the differences and similarities in the strategies consumers followed, comparing Ahuvia's with our findings.

Of particular interest here is the third strategy identified in Ahuvia (2005). This is the 'synthesising' strategy where the consumer creates a synthesis of opposing identities (getting the best of both worlds). In the synthesising strategy, US consumers created a sense of self-coherence and overcame compromising feelings via consumption without really solving their identity conflicts. Their identity dilemmas continued to exist. We did not find this strategy among our Greek respondents. Rather, our Greek participants aspired to solve their identity dilemmas and conflicts via life transitions, life changes, and consumption in order to overcome compromising feelings and to create a coherent sense of self using the 'transition strategy' (to which they aspired).

This is an important emergent difference between Ahuvia's US respondents and our Greek respondents. While our Greek respondents aspired to solve their identity conflicts, the US respondents accepted their identity conflicts. While our Greek respondents needed to solve their identity conflicts in order to overcome their feelings of compromise and pressure, and also in order to experience a sense of self-coherence, the US respondents were able to overcome compromising feelings and to experience a sense of self-coherence without solving their identity conflicts. This possibly suggests that our respondents in Greece felt more uncomfortable than

**Figure 1** Interplay of desired and undesired selves mediated via consumption.

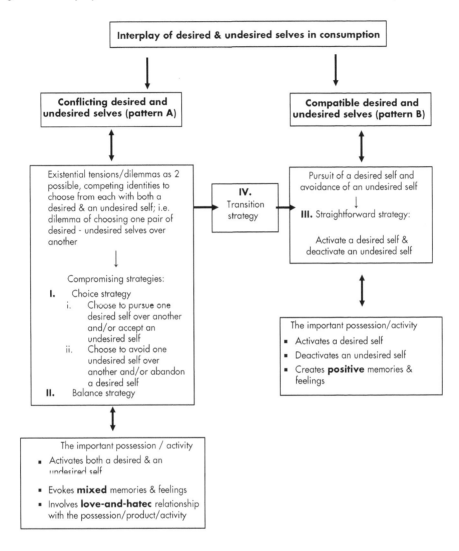

respondents in the United States with identity conflicts. Greek consumers seemed to have a sense of 'baffled' self (T. Miller, 2009) when their identity conflicts had not been solved.

## Cross-cultural issues

So, are consumers becoming increasingly homogenised in a global consumer culture? Our study reports similarities as well as differences in symbolic consumption between Greece and the United States.

The view that important items are connected to the self by both expressing and transforming the self into some new desired form was supported by Ahuvia's (2005) US-based study and is also supported by our findings for Greek consumers. Moreover, just like US respondents (Ahuvia, 2005), our respondents in Greece also have a great

**Table 7** Consumers' strategies.

| Strategies in Ahuvia (2005) – US respondents | Strategies in our study – Greek respondents | Comments |
|---|---|---|
| *Demarcating strategy*: | *1. Choice strategy*: | Ahuvia's interpretation of demarcating points to two potentially different strategies (as found in our data) and so he would seem to be offering two potentially inconsistent views of the demarcating strategy |
| The consumer chooses one identity and rejects another | In line with the first view of Ahuvia's 'demarcating strategy' | |
| *Potentially inconsistent views*: | | |
| 1. strategy used by consumers | *2. Straightforward strategy*: | |
| 2. strategy used by consumers who 'strongly prefer one identity over another' (and who thus experience no identity conflict) (p. 181) | In line with Ahuvia's second description of the 'demarcating strategy' | |
| *Compromising strategy*: Suggested, but not empirically supported, in Ahuvia's study | 3. *Balance strategy* | Our Greek study provides empirical support for this strategy |
| *Synthesising strategy* | – | For the US respondents, identity conflicts are not solved but compromising feelings are overcome to create a self-coherence sense. There was no empirical evidence for this strategy from this study of Greek consumers. |
| – | 4. *Transition strategy* | Aspiring to solve identity conflicts in order to overcome compromising feelings and create a self-coherence sense |

deal of choice about who they want to be, and experience identity conflicts (illustrated by pattern A of conflicting desired and undesired selves) that colour their consumption experiences. Our findings suggest that contemporary conditions in Greece resemble those in the United States in that they make the establishment of a coherent sense of self difficult. Just like the US respondents (Ahuvia, 2005), our Greek respondents can construct their identity from an abundance of identities and did not experience the difficulties in constructing a coherent sense of self as the liberation from an oppressive ideal of a unified self (Firat & Venkatesh, 1995) or with a sense of an 'empty' self (Cushman, 1990).

However, our Greek respondents seemed to feel more uncomfortable than the US respondents with the difficulties they faced in constructing a coherent sense of self and with their identity conflicts. Therefore, our Greek respondents seem to deal with their identity conflicts in a different way from US participants (Ahuvia, 2005), often following different strategies. Our study identifies less coherence in the concept of self and more ambivalence in the emotions surrounding consumption than Ahuvia's study. Ahuvia's US respondents managed to create a sense of self-coherence without solving their identity conflicts by combining (synthesising) conflicting standards through consumption of loved objects. Our informants aspired to solve their identity conflicts via life transitions, life changes, and consumption in order to create a sense of self-coherence. For our Greek respondents, conflicting standards are not combined (synthesised) through consumption (as for US respondents in Ahuvia, 2005; Holt & Thompson, 2004), but rather create ambivalent/mixed emotions in consumption and the sense of a 'baffled' self (T. Miller, 2009). Consumers in our study tried to achieve a compromising balance between opposing identity positions (as consumers in Thompson, 1996) or to compromise with one identity position while often aspiring to overcome the identity conflict in the future.

## Conclusion

This study sought to conceptualise the interrelationship between desired and undesired selves and to highlight how the interplay between different selves was significant in the consumption experiences of Greek women. The present interpretation focuses on the experiences of women situated in a particular context, and are supported by the transcriptions. However, we do not claim to have developed an exhaustive account. Different insights could emerge across different settings. The interplay between the desired and undesired selves of male consumers, for instance, would represent another important avenue to be explored by future research.

As discussed in the previous section, our study adds to existing consumer research, which has largely concentrated on the United States, providing a more nuanced understanding of how symbolic consumption works within global consumer culture. Consumers in this study did not experience fragmented multiple selves (Firat & Venkatesh, 1995), an 'empty-self' (Cushman, 1990), or a coherent self created out of synthesis of opposite identities (Ahuvia, 2005). Rather, they experienced the desire for a coherent self that often left them with a sense of baffled self (T. Miller, 2009) when coherence was not attained. Informants in this study aspired to solve their identity conflicts via life transitions, life changes, and consumption in order to create a sense of self-coherence. And this study identified more ambivalence in the emotions surrounding consumption than previous work (Ahuvia, 2005; Cushman, 1990; Firat & Venkatesh, 1995).

We extend theory on the desired/undesired self by mapping the desired and undesired self in terms of thematic dimensions, conceptualising two interrelationship patterns (A and B) between desired and undesired selves, and examining the impact of these interrelationships on four consumer strategies. The first pattern (A) of 'conflicting desired and undesired selves' identified in this study integrates two major developments in consumer research on identity: (1) desired and undesired self-concept (Banister & Hogg, 2001, 2003; Freitas et al., 1997; Patrick & MacInnis, 2002; Wilk, 1997); and (2) identity conflicts/tensions (e.g. Ahuvia, 2005; Fournier, 1998). We also identify consumers' mixed feelings for and often their love–hate relationship with their important possessions, products, and consumption activities. Finally, we extend Ahuvia's theory on the strategies consumers use to handle identity issues, and we identify different conditions under which consumers follow different strategies.

The findings can offer additional insights of value to marketing managers in terms of marketing segmentation, targeting, and positioning techniques. Marketing strategists need to recognise the desired and undesired selves' associations with product and service choices and anti-choices, understand the desired and undesired selves' themes and interrelationships in consumption, and exploit this understanding in the development of communication and channel strategies for the positioning and branding of their goods and services. Finally, as desired and undesired selves often relate to social roles (e.g. mother), the findings can also offer insights to role theory and more specifically to role conflict, as well as to role-related consumption. From the perspective of symbolic interactionism, the findings can throw light on how consumers as social actors pursue personal coherence across different settings (Goffman, 1959), and choose and use products as social stimuli to perform roles and to define the self (Solomon, 1983).

# References

Ahuvia, A.C. (2005). Beyond the extended self: Loved objects and consumers' identity narratives. *Journal of Consumer Research*, 32, 171–184.

Arnould, E.J., & Thompson, C.J. (2005). Consumer Culture Theory (CCT): Twenty years of research. *Journal of Consumer Research*, 31(4), 868.

Banister, E.N., & Hogg, M.K. (2001). Mapping the negative self: From 'so not me' . . . to 'just not me. *Advances in Consumer Research*, 28, 242–248.

Banister, E.N., & Hogg, M.K. (2003). Possible selves: Identifying dimensions for exploring the dialectic between positive and negative selves in consumer behaviour. *Advances in Consumer Research*, 30, 149.

Bauman, Z. (1991). *Modernity and ambivalence*. Cambridge, England: Polity Press.

Belk, R.W. (1988). Possessions and the extended self. *Journal of Consumer Research*, 15(2), 139–168.

Belk, R.W. (1989). Extended self and extending paradigmatic perspective. *Journal of Consumer Research*, 16, 129–132.

Borgerson, J. (2005). Materiality, agency, and the constitution of consuming subjects: Insights for consumer research. *Advances in Consumer Research*, 32, 439–443.

Cherrier, H., & Murray, J.F. (2007). Reflexive dispossession and the self: Constructing a processual theory of identity. *Consumption, Markets and Culture*, 10(1), 1–29.

Colaizzi, P.F. (1978). Psychological research as the phenomenologist views it. In R.W. Valle & J. King (Eds.), *Existential-phenomenological alternatives for psychology*. New York: Oxford University Press.

Crotty, M. (2003). *The foundations of social research, meaning and perspective in the research process*. London: Sage.

Csíkszentmihályi, M., & Rochberg-Halton, E. (1981). *The meaning of things: Domestic symbols and the self*. Cambridge, England: Cambridge University Press.

Cushman, P. (1990). Why the self is empty: Toward a historically situated psychology. *American Psychologist*, 45(5), 599–611.

Dittmar, H. (1991). Meanings of material possessions as reflections of identity: Gender and social material position in society. To have possessions: A handbook of ownership and property [Special issue]. *Journal of Social Behaviour and Personality*, 6, 165–186.

Elliott, R., & Wattanasuwan, K. (1998). Consumption and the symbolic project of the self. In B. Englis & A. Olofsson (Eds.), *European Advances in Consumer Research* (pp. 17–20). Provo, UT: Association for Consumer Research.

Erikson, E.H. (1959). Identity and the life cycle. New York: International Universities Press.

Eurostat (2002). *The life of women and men in Europe*. Luxembourg: European Communities.

Firat, F.A., & Venkatesh, A. (1995). Liberatory postmodernism and the reenchantment of consumption. *Journal of Consumer Research*, 22(3), 239–267.

Fournier, S. (1998). Consumers and their brands: Developing relationship theory in consumer research. *Journal of Consumer Research*, 24(4), 343.

Freitas, A., Davis, C.H., & Kim, J.W. (1997). Appearance management as border construction: Least favorite clothing, group distancing and identity ... Not! *Sociological Inquiry*, 67(3), 323–335.

Gergen, K.J. (1991). *The saturated self: Dilemmas of identity in contemporary life*. New York: Basic Books.

Geertz, C. (1979). From the native's point of view: On the nature of anthropological understanding. In P. Rabinow & W.M. Sullivan (Eds.), Interpretive social science (pp. 225–241). Berkeley: University of California Press.

Geertz, C. (1973). The interpretation of cultures. New York: Basic Books.

Greenwald, A.G. (1980). The totalitarian ego: Fabrication and revision of personal history. American Psychologist, 35, 603–618.

Giddens, A. (1991). *Modernity and self-identity*. Cambridge, England: Polity Press.

Goffman, E. (1959). *The presentation of self in everyday life*. New York: Anchor.

Gould, S.J., & Lerman, D.B. (1998). 'Postmodern' versus 'long-standing' cultural narratives in consumer behavior: An empirical study of NetGirl online. *European Journal of Marketing*, 32(7/8), 644–654.

Gubrium, J.F., & Holstein, J.A. (1998). Narrative practice and the coherence of personal stories. *Sociological Quarterly*, 39(1), 163–187.

Heidegger, M. (1962). *Being and time*. New York: Harper & Row.

Holt, D.B. (2002). Why do brands cause trouble? A dialectical theory of consumer culture and branding. *Journal of Consumer Research*, 29(1), 70.

Holt, D.B., & Thompson, C.J. (2004). Man-of-action heroes: The pursuit of heroic masculinity in everyday consumption. *Journal of Consumer Research*, 31, 425–440.

Kleine, S.S., Kleine, R.E., & Allen, C.T. (1995). How is a possession 'me' or 'not me'? Characterizing types and an antecedent of material possession attachment. *Journal of Consumer Research*, 22(3), 327–343.

Kvale, S. (1983). The qualitative research interview: A phenomenological & hermeneutical mode of understanding. *Journal of Phenomenological Psychology*, 14, 17.

Levy, S.J. (1959). Symbols for sale. *Harvard Business Review*, 37(4), 117.

Markus, H., & Nurius, P. (1986). Possible selves. *American Psychologist*, 41(9), 954.

McAdams, D.P. (2006). The problem of narrative coherence. *Journal of Constructivist Psychology*, 19(2), 109–125.

Miller, D. (1987). *Material culture and mass consumption*. Oxford, England: Berg.

Miller, T. (2009, May). *Engaging with the maternal: Tentative mothering acts and the props of performance*. Paper presented in the Motherhood, Consumption and Transition, 2nd seminar, Lancaster University.

Murray, J.B. (2002). The politics of consumption: A re-inquiry on Thompson and Haytko's (1997) 'Speaking of Fashion'. *Journal of Consumer Research*, 29, 427.

Myers, E. (1985). Phenomenological analysis of the importance of special possessions. *Advances in Consumer Research*, 12, 560–565.

Ogilvie, D.M. (1987). The undesired self: A neglected variable in personality research. *Journal of Personality and Social Psychology*, 52(2), 379–385.

Patrick, V.M., & MacInnis, D.J. (2002). Approaching what we hope for and avoiding what we fear: The role of possible selves in consumer behaviour. *Advances in Consumer Research*, 29, 270–276.

Raggatt, P. (2006). Multiplicity and conflict in the dialogical self: A life narrative approach. In D.P. McAdams, R. Josselson, & A. Lieblich (Eds.), *Identity and story: Creating self in narrative*. Washington, DC: American Psychological Association Books.

Reed, A. (2002). Social identity as a useful perspective for self-concept based consumer research. *Psychology and Marketing*, 19(3), 235.

Richins, M.L. (1994a). Valuing things: The public and private meanings of possession. *Journal of Consumer Research, 21*, 504–521.

Richins, M.L. (1994b). Special possessions and the expression of material values. *Journal of Consumer Research, 21*, 522–533.

Sampson, E.E. (1985). The decentralization of identity – Toward a revised concept of personal and social order. *American Psychologist, 40*(11), 1203–1211.

Sartre, J.P. (1943). Being and Nothingness: An Essay on Phenomenological Ontology, Trans. H. Barnes, London: Routledge.

Schau, H.J., & Gilly M.C. (2003). We are what we post? Self-presentation in personal web space. *Journal of Consumer Research, 30*, 385–404.

Schouten, J. (1991). Selves in transition: Symbolic consumption in personal rites of passage and identity reconstruction. *Journal of Consumer Research, 17*, 412.

Schultz, S.E., Kleine, R.E., III, & Kernan, J.B. (1989). 'These are a few of my favorite things': Toward an explication of attachment as a consumer behavior construct. In T. Srull (Ed.), *Advances in Consumer Research* (Vol. 16, pp. 359–366). Provo, UT: Association for Consumer Research.

Shankar, A., Elliott, R., & Fitchett, J.A. (2009). Identity, consumption and narratives of socialization. *Marketing Theory, 9*(1), 75–94.

Shankar, A., Elliott, R., & Goulding, C. (2001). Understanding consumption: Contributions from a narrative perspective. *Journal of Marketing Management, 17*(3–4), pp. 420–453.

Solomon, M.R. (1983). The role of products as social stimuli: A symbolic interactionism perspective. *Journal of Consumer Research, 10*, 319–329.

Sullivan, H.S. (1953). *The interpersonal theory of psychiatry.* New York: Norton.

Taylor, C. (1989). *Sources of the self: The making of modern identity.* Cambridge, England: Cambridge University Press.

Thompson, C.J. (1996). Caring consumers: Gendered consumption meanings and the juggling lifestyle. *Journal of Consumer Research, 22*(4), 388–407.

Thompson, C.J. (1997). Interpreting consumers: A hermeneutical framework for deriving marketing insights from the texts of consumers' consumption stories. *Journal of Marketing Research, 34*, 438–455.

Thompson, C.J., & Haytko, D.L. (1997). Speaking of fashion: Consumers' uses of fashion discourses and the appropriation of countervailing cultural meanings. *Journal of Consumer Research, 24*, 15.

Thompson, C.J., & Hirschman, E.C. (1995). Understanding the socialized body: A poststructuralist analysis of consumers' self-conceptions, body images, and self-care practices. *Journal of Consumer Research, 22*(2), 139–153.

Thompson, C.J., Locander, W., & Pollio, H. (1990). The lived meaning of free choice: An existential-phenomenological description of everyday consumer experiences of contemporary married women. *Journal of Consumer Research, 17*, 346.

Thompson, C.J., Pollio, H.R., & Locander, W.B. (1989). Putting consumer experience back into consumer research: The philosophy and method of existential-phenomenology. *Journal of Consumer Research, 16*, 133–146.

Thompson, C.J., & Tambyah, S.K. (1999). Trying to be cosmopolitan. *Journal of Consumer Research, 26*, 214–241.

Wallendorf, M., & Arnould, E. (1988). My favorite things: A cross-cultural inquiry into object attachment, possessiveness and social linkage. *Journal of Consumer Research, 14*, 531–547.

Wilk, R.R (1997). A critique of desire: Distaste and dislike in consumer behavior. *Consumption, Markets and Culture, 1*(2), 175–196.

Wright, N.D., Claiborne, C.B., & Sirgy, M.J. (1992). The effects of product symbolism on consumer self-concept. *Advances in Consumer Research, 19*, 311.

# Self-gift giving in China and the UK: Collectivist versus individualist orientations

Caroline Tynan, *Nottingham University Business School, UK*
M. Teresa Pereira Heath, *Universidade do Minho, Portugal*
Christine Ennew, *Nottingham University Business School, UK*
Fangfang Wang, *Nottingham University Business School, UK*
Luping Sun, *Shandong University, PR China*

**Abstract** While research on self-gift consumer behaviour (SGCB) has shown evidence of the importance of this behaviour in Western cultures, particularly that of the United States, there is no understanding of self-gift giving in collectivist cultures. Given the self-oriented nature of this behaviour, research is required to address its possible differences in a collectivist society. In this paper, we use personal interviews with consumers to establish the existence of SGCB in China, and further to compare motivations for and the emotions associated with SGCB in positive-related contexts in the UK and mainland China, with a particular focus on the Chinese side. We also address the nature of this behaviour for Chinese participants. Findings indicate that SGCB is less self-oriented for the Chinese than for the British, and suggest that academics should reflect on the meaning of this behaviour in non-Western countries. Implications from these findings for practitioners are also presented.

## Introduction

Research on self-gift consumer behaviour (SGCB), while still limited, has shown clear evidence of the importance of self-gifts for consumers in dealing with positive events in their lives. However, this evidence has been almost exclusively collected in individualistic cultures, particularly that of North America.

While a few authors have addressed the need to redefine the understanding of gift-giving behaviour in China and other non-Western contexts (e.g. Chan, Denton & Tsang, 2003; Joy, 2001; Qian, Razzaque, & Keng, 2007; Wang, Piron, & Xuan, 2001; Yan, 1996), surprisingly no study has focused on exploring self-gift giving in such contexts. This paper responds to calls for a better understanding of consumer behaviour in collectivist cultures (e.g. Wang et al., 2001; Wong & Ahuvia, 1998). It also responds directly to Mick and DeMoss's (1990b) call for 'cross-cultural self-gift research' (p. 330) and to Olshavsky and Lee's (1993) suggestion to consider the influence of the 'cultural milieu' (p. 551) on this behaviour, by gaining insights into SGCB in China in comparison to that of the UK.

In this paper, we use interviews with consumers to establish the existence of self-gifting behaviour in China, and further to compare motivations for and the emotions associated with SGCB in positive-related contexts in the UK and mainland China, with a particular focus on the Chinese side. We also aim to gain insights into the nature of this behaviour for Chinese participants. We begin with a brief review of relevant literature on SGCB and gift giving in a Confucian culture, and subsequently report the main findings obtained from the interviews. In the last section, we discuss the findings in light of existing literature and their implications.

## Literature

While gift giving has been extensively addressed in the literature, the topic of self-gifts, that is, 'products, services, or experiences . . . partly differentiated from other personal acquisitions by their situational and motivational contexts' (Mick & DeMoss, 1990a, p. 681), has been far less frequently considered (Mick & DeMoss, 1990b; Schwartz, 1967). Much of the work on gift giving in general, and on self-gifts in particular, has been 'conducted in and limited to the American culture' (Park, 1998, p. 578). The nature and role of gift giving varies with the financial, emotional, and symbolic significance accorded it by different cultures (Joy, 2001) and is thus culturally specific. Hence, the understandings, which are almost exclusively limited to the North American context of an individualist rather than a collectivist culture (Hofstede, 1980), indicate that the academy's knowledge of this phenomenon is partial. Noting that 'the very existence of self-gifts as well as their places in consumers' lives may depend on an individually centred versus group-centred view of self as in non-Western societies' (Belk, 1984; Tuan, 1982), Mick and DeMoss (1990b, p. 130) call for self-gift research that is cross-cultural. This paper represents an attempt to reconsider and redevelop existing consumer behaviour understandings that have emerged from North America.

Recently, authors have begun to study gift giving in Asian contexts, including China (A.K. Chan, Denton, & Tsang, 2003; Qian et al., 2007; Wang et al., 2001; Yan, 1996; Zhou & Guang, 2007), Korea (Park. 1998), Hong Kong (Joy, 2001; Yau, Chan, & Lau, 1999), and Japan (Lotz, Shim, & Gehrt, 2003). Other relevant work being stimulated by interest in the impact of *guanxi*, that is, the system of personal relationship networks with attendant obligations and expectations, particularly studied in business-to-business contexts (e.g. Leung, Heung, & Wong, 2008; Millington, Ebrhardt, & Wilkinson, 2005). Qian et al. (2007) argue that is essential to understand the Chinese cultural context in order to understand the consumption patterns of the Chinese people. The context of research in China offers an opportunity to explore aspects of self-gift giving in a Confucian culture. Confucianism is the foundation of the Chinese value system, which supports stability and harmony as the foundation of the society where the community comes before the individual. According to Confucian beliefs, loyalty, respect for older or senior individuals, and service to the family are essential to live properly. The notion of self is one of the most fundamental assumptions shared within a culture (Kitayama, Markus, Matsumoto, & Norasakkunkit, 1997) and underpinning SGCB behaviour (Mick & DeMoss, 1990a, 1992; Olshavsky & Lee, 1993). Belk (1984) first noted the significant difference in the concept of self in the individualistic societies of the West as compared to the more group-based understanding of identity where cultures' sense of self is governed more by their perspective of 'being part of cohesive whole, whether it be (that of) a family, clan, tribe, or nation' (Belk, 1984, p. 754). In Western society, including the United States and the UK, the self is seen as independent, without obligations to fulfil the needs and expectations of others, where individuals are encouraged to be proud and reward themselves for their own achievements (Mesquita & Karasawa, 2004). Chinese society by comparison is interdependent, where self is a relational entity and the individual's social obligations to family and other networks is prime. Park (1998) suggests that this primacy of group over individual goals, evident in collectivist cultures, will lead to greater conformity and to the prevalence of face-saving behaviour and its corollary, a feeling of *ch'i* or shame. While the five cultural values identified in a work-related environment by Hofstede have been widely used in cross-cultural studies (Bond & Hofstede, 1989; Hofstede, 1980), Yau et al. (1999) consider that the authors misunderstand Chinese philosophy and highlight the limitations of the work as being too succinct and omitting key variables including fate and reciprocity. Therefore, this study adopts Chinese cultural values that relate more directly to gift giving.

The human universals (Lee & Green, 1991), face saving and shame, are important aspects of Confucian cultures and thought to be crucial in explaining much behaviour. Maintaining personal status in society depends on others and not on the self (Yau et al., 1999), and upon keeping their good regard by fulfilling expectations of personal conduct or performance of particular roles. Therefore, to maintain face, it is important that an individual be judged to behave well, with integrity, and meet social expectations. Group influence promotes conformity, and so any deviation from these expectations is seen as a failure to achieve an acceptable standard of behaviour for the moral individual and the resulting loss of face induces shame, an outcome that disturbingly has been compared to physical mutilation of one's eyes, nose, or mouth (Qian et al., 2007). Shame is regarded as an important and healthy contribution to achieving social control and child rearing in China according to Fung (1999). It is not only an emotion, but also a mechanism for behavioural regulation and adjustment. Shame signals an individual's acknowledgement of the social rules (W.T. Chan, 1963), and provides an ongoing incentive and motivation to act morally and is thus a driver for appropriate gift giving.

Salient aspects of Chinese cultural values that influence gift-giving behaviours include family orientation (Qian et al., 2007), *guanxi*, *renqing*, face, harmony, and reciprocity (Zhou & Guang, 2007). Family orientation extends beyond the biological definition of family (Qian et al., 2007) and includes relatives, classmates, work colleagues, old friends, and those from the same town (Yau et al., 1999) as part of the social network. The degree of closeness between these individuals can be viewed as a set of concentric circles (Qian et al., 2007) with gift-giving behaviour decreasing in frequency and value for more distant 'family' members. *Renqing*, related to *guanxi*, is another central concept of Chinese culture, which can be interpreted as meaning appropriate emotion, but also denotes 'the *tao* or "way" of interpersonal interactions' (A.K. Chan et al., 2003, p. 48), which harmonise relationships and maintain balance within the social network. Traditionally, Chinese culture is characterised by a very restrained display of emotion.

Yau et al. (1999) note that the Chinese are inveterate gift givers, using gifts variously to express friendship, maintain a long-term relationship, recognise the successful conclusion of a project, acknowledge generosity, or communicate thanks for a favour. It is also a 'face act' offering the opportunity for enhancing relationships (Yau et al., 1999, p. 99). Gifts must both reflect the income and status of the giver and symbolise the prestigious status of the recipient to give him face, with any mistakes forcing the wrongdoing to break the relationship (Yau, 1988; Yau et al., 1999). In Chinese society, the occasions upon which gifts should be offered traditionally include birthdays, weddings and betrothals, funerals, visiting, festivals including the Chinese New Year, house construction, to acknowledge achievements like graduation, and, more recently, female sterilisation and abortion (Qian et al., 2007; Yan, 1996; Yau et al., 1999; Zhou & Guang, 2007). Gift giving is also governed by the cultural understanding that there is an obligation to reciprocate gifts (A.K. Chan et al., 2003; Yau et al., 1999; Zhou & Guang, 2007). Reciprocity, or *bao*, binds the giver and recipient in an ongoing cycle of indebtedness (Yau et al., 1999), where gifts and favours are given and returned, and repayment can be claimed. Correct timing is important (A.K. Chan et al., 2003), as gifting at the appropriate juncture can enhance the value of a gift for both giver and receiver (Yau et al., 1999).

Additionally, as the third largest economy after the United States and Japan (Fung, 1999), with a growth rate of 9.0% in 2008 (Euromonitor, 2009), and 7.9% in mid 2009, which is 'the envy of the world' in the current recession (The Economist, 2009, p. 57), China represents an immensely important target for many companies. According to the Chairman of the UK Parliament's All Party China Group, it has a population of 1.3bn, enjoyed real GDP growth of 10.1% between 2002–2006, has a labour market that increases by 20 million people each year, has more people studying English as a second language than the entire population of the UK, and enjoys a consumer market consisting of over 500 million middle-class Chinese (Chapman, 2007). Therefore, it is important for practitioners, as well as academics, to understand the complexity of SGCB in China.

Earlier studies have analysed contexts in which SGCB is likely to occur (e.g. Mick & DeMoss, 1990b). The most frequently identified positive situation refers to *reward* self-gifts where an achievement has prompted the behaviour as 'a reward for having accomplished a personal goal' (Mick & DeMoss, 1990a, 1990b, p. 323). This positive emphasis is important in self-gifts (Luomala & Laaksonen, 1997, 1999) in that the individuals feel that the self-gift is deserved because it has been earned through sacrifice or personal effort (Williams & Burns, 1994). This behaviour can be justified at a sociocultural level by Western cultural and religious beliefs encouraging the delay of gratification (Mick & DeMoss, 1990b). However, this focus on the individual achievements and delayed gratification as both a stimulus for, and a justification of, self-gifting behaviour is unlikely to pertain in a collectivist society.

Existing research conducted in the West has identified SGCB as being used to maintain a good mood and also as a way of alleviating or repairing a bad mood (Luomala, 1998; Luomala & Laaksonen, 1999) so it can be both triggered by emotions and used to regulate them (Pereira, 2006). Additionally, a wide variety of emotions have been reported as stimulating, accompanying, and resulting from SGCB (e.g. Pereira, Ennew, & Tynan, 2005; Williams & Burns, 1994). Mood maintenance behaviour is essentially socially or outwardly directed, whereas mood-repair activities are more inwardly directed (Luomala & Laaksonen, 1999). Acceptable behaviour in a collectivist society that values group achievements over individual ones, esteems self-effacement, and eschews self-aggrandisement, and which sets great store by shame is likely to experience different forms of SGCB than an individualistic society. Therefore, an exploration of the emotions following SGCB will greatly add to our understanding of the behaviour in the Chinese context.

## Purpose of research and methodology

This exploratory research aims to uncover differences between SGCB in the UK and mainland China, particularly in the motivations for this behaviour in positive contexts, in the nature of the behaviour, and in the emotions associated with it. We focus on positive contexts, since, in both countries, these were found to be the predominant circumstances for self-gift giving.

Critical incident technique (CIT) was selected as appropriate for this study because it is a 'procedure which facilitates the investigation of significant occurrences (events, incidents, processes, or issues) identified by the respondent, the way they are managed, and the outcomes in terms of perceived effects' (Gremler, 2004, p. 66) and so apt for our study of the contexts judged as significant by our participants in leading to acts of SGCB. Additionally, the work meets the criteria of being a topic that has been sparingly documented, where an exploratory method is being employed about a little-known phenomenon (e.g. Walker & Truly, 1992), and also one where a thorough understanding is needed, and so on all three counts, a context where CIT is seen as useful according to Gremler (2004). The open-ended nature of critical incident questions facilitates the gathering of rich and complete data of respondents' own experiences (e.g. Harris & Reynolds, 2004), while their accounts are not forced into any pre-established framework (Stauss & Weinlich, 1997). Moreover, Stauss and Mang (1999) commend CIT as well suited for use in assessing the perception of consumers from different cultures and de Ruyter, Perkins, and Wetzel (1995) endorse it as a culturally neutral method and therefore suitable for a cross-cultural consumer study. Finally, it is the method adopted by Mick and DeMoss (1990a) in the seminal SGCB paper, although they used questionnaires and not interviews to collect data.

Following guidance from Flanagan (1954) and Bitner, Booms, and Tetreault (1990) that it is crucial to develop a clear definition of critical incidents for the study, in this study a critical incident is defined as 'those life experiences (positive or negative) which the participants believe to have made a contribution to their engagement in SGCB (self-gift consumer behaviour) activities'. In this paper, we focus on the positive incidents only. Not all life experiences were included, and those that were met four criteria employed in the study:

1.  Only those incidents that were memorable enough for the consumers to recall in detail (Bitner et al., 1990)

2.  Those that consumers saw as positive or negative, with the neutral ones being excluded

3.  Those that led to self-gift consumer behaviour (Mick & DeMoss, 1990a)

4.  Those that had sufficient detail to be fully contextualised and understood by the analysts (after Bitner et al., 1990).

We conducted 102 personal interviews in the UK using CIT, after having conducted 14 in-depth, exploratory interviews. The exploratory interviews allowed us to investigate participants' awareness of self-gift giving and to enhance our understanding of this behaviour. Insights derived from these interviews were valuable in preparing the CIT interview guide and in learning the importance of focusing on specific experiences as a means of facilitating the emergence of important data (e.g. Chell & Pittaway, 1998). The focus provided by the CIT allowed us to obtain detailed descriptions of participants 'lived' experiences, rather than letting the dialogue to become abstract or 'experience-distant' (Thompson & Haytko, 1997). As described above, the incidents observed focused on the 'life circumstances' in which participants have given themselves a gift. An informal and brief description of what a 'gift to oneself' (or self-gift) meant was provided and, when needed, examples were given. Drawing on an interpretivist approach and believing that 'social beings construct reality and give it meaning based on context' (Hudson & Ozanne, 1988, p. 510), a contextual understanding of the incidents is essential to understand the phenomenon under study (see Gremler, 2004; Hopkinson & Hogarth-Scott, 2001; Walker & Truly, 1992). Accordingly, participants' description of the circumstances that led to self-gift giving comprised rich details about their context (e.g. the people involved, participants' perception of responsibility for the situation and of its importance, the emotions and motivations experienced). Besides the contexts for self-gift giving, the CIT interview guide further focused on the nature of the self-gift experiences in such contexts and on the emotions experienced throughout them. Probing was used to encourage detailed accounts (e.g. Chell, 2004; Edvardsson & Roos, 2001) and to enrich the picture of both participants' life incidents and self-gift experiences.

These interviews were conducted until theoretical saturation was reached (e.g. Strauss & Corbin, 1998), which provided a solid understanding of the context and nature of SGCB in the UK. We then conducted 12 in-depth, exploratory interviews followed by 54 personal interviews in China using CIT. The number of these interviews was limited by constraints on the time available for data collection. The interview guides (in both stages of interviews) used in China covered similar topics to those in the UK. However, in general, UK participants gave more details than their Chinese counterparts about their self-gift experiences, and often talked about more than one experience. The average length of CIT interviews was 16 minutes for the UK and 12 minutes for China. In both countries, we used convenience samples, which included participants of both genders with a variety of occupations and ages.

The data were all transcribed and subjected to interpretative analysis. Chinese interviews were translated by native Mandarin speakers who were completing the final stage of their cognate master's degree in the UK and possessed a good knowledge of the English language. Further assistance from a native English speaker was given. In agreement with an interpretivist stance, we were committed to interpret the events 'through the eyes' of the people involved in them (Bryman, 2004), trying to illuminate the meanings they attached to the phenomenon under study (Holbrook & O'Shaughnessy, 1988; Kvale, 1990; Spiggle, 1994). Drawing on authors such as Rubin and Rubin (1995), Thompson, Locander, and Pollio (1990), and Banister and Piacentini (2006), data analysis involved reading and rereading each interview transcription carefully, organising the information into themes based on the perceived patterns or commonalities, and critically discussing and reflecting upon the interpretations reached. This analysis was approached as a dynamic and iterative process, where we continually refined our interpretations (Taylor & Bogdan, 1998). In order to convey the authenticity of the study (see Golden-Biddle & Locke, 1993; Hogg & Maclaran, 2008) and in keeping with an *emic* approach (Spiggle, 1994; Thompson, Locander, & Pollio, 1989), we support our findings with examples of participants' accounts.

## Findings

In the following section, we compare the main motivations for engaging in SGCB in positive contexts for Chinese and UK participants, and discuss the nature of the self-gift experiences and the emotions that follow this behaviour.

### Motivations for SGCB in positive contexts

Although SGCB was found to exist in China, as well as in the UK, our findings suggest important differences in the motivations that underlie this behaviour in the two countries' samples. In both countries, the most common positive context is *work-related* (e.g. being promoted at work, finishing an important task or exam, finding a new job). These achievements often demanded a great deal of sacrifice and hard work, which motivates the reward. However, several of the Chinese *work-related* achievements are collective, whilst the UK achievements are typically self-attributed. The following transcriptions (from Chinese and UK participants respectively) illustrate this observation. Note Shen's use of the first-person plural in the former case and John's use of the first-person singular in the latter:

> ... *our team* successfully dealt with a criminal case ... All my *team members* were worried about this case ... after two months of hard work *we* finally arrested the criminal. (China, Shen, male, 29; emphasis added)
> Most recently, there was a positive situation when *I* bought *myself* a *digital camera*. *I* had just completed a *successful consulting contract* and *got a new job* as a business consultant. So *I rewarded myself* ... (UK, John, male, 40; emphasis added)

The next passage further illustrates that, even when the achievements are of a more individual nature, Chinese participants acknowledge the contribution of others. Although Fang seems to attribute the prize to her own effort (she 'worked hard'), she soon mentions ('but at the same time') how others (e.g. students) had a part on it (e.g. by having good marks):

> Last June I was awarded the model teacher prize ... I'm grateful to my *school* and my *students* ... I worked hard, *but at the same time* my *students* got *good marks* ... *Above all*, I was grateful to my *school* and *other teachers* for their *encouragement* to me ... as well as my *family* ... sometimes, if I am busy at the school, I cannot set aside *enough time to care* for my children, I'm grateful to my *husband*, his *encouragement* ... (China, Fang, female, 46; emphasis added)

Additionally, some of the Chinese participants suggested that 'luck' helped on the achievements, which is possibly linked to the value placed on modesty and self-effacement (Yau, 1988). The benefit of the achievements for others (e.g. for the company where they work) was also mentioned by some participants from this country.

Another common, work-related, positive event that triggers self-gift giving both in China and in the UK is the achievement of *receiving money* from work salary or bonus. On some of these occasions, Chinese interviewees bought a gift for a family member, together with the self-gift. This is illustrated, in the following account, of Jing's behaviour upon receiving her first month's salary. Jing mentions the gift for her mother before acknowledging her own self-gift and focusing the description on how she felt she owed this to her mother:

> ... I bought an *anti-aging moisturizer* for my *mum* and a *purse* for *myself* after I got the first month's salary ... wherever I go, I *will think of my mum*. I just want to *make her happy*. Maybe it is the *time to pay her back. She sacrificed* too much for me. (China, Jing, female, 25; emphasis added)

Receiving one's salary is also an important self-gift context for British participants, but this is described with a more self-oriented and indulgent focus, as if participants feel they owe it to themselves:

> ... at the end of the month, when I get paid, I think *'let's get myself* something *rather than just paying the bills'*. I did it at the end of last month, as soon as I got paid ... *probably as a reward* ... just to make *yourself feel better* after working all those days. (UK, Alice, female, 21; emphasis added)

Additionally, for both Chinese and British participants, buying self-gifts while on *holiday or away from home* enhances the travelling experience and offers the opportunity to bring home something different, which will be a symbolic reminder of that experience. Some descriptions of this context further reflect Chinese, collectivist culture. For example, one Chinese participant adds that bringing self-gifts from a holiday is a way of showing others the things she had seen, while another mentions the souvenirs he happily purchased for his wife and daughter, together with his self-gift, from a business trip to Holland.

Furthermore, several positive contexts for self-gift giving in Chinese interviews refer to circumstances of *reunions*, such as gatherings of family and friends. In these, self-gifts are purchased during the reunion or prior to it, almost as a way of honouring the special occasion and the person who is being met. This is the case, for instance, for a participant who purchased new clothes to meet his girlfriend after spending a week apart, since he wanted the give her a 'delightful' surprise, or for a participant who purchased new clothes because she 'wanted to look good' when picking up her daughter at the airport. In contrast, in the UK interviews, the *reunion* motivation for self-gift giving did not emerge, despite the greater number of interviews conducted.

### Nature of SGCB

In both sets of interviews, self-gifts include a wide range of products (e.g. clothes, mobiles, compact discs, sweets) and services (e.g. eating or drinking out, travelling). Also, in both cases, the self-gifts tend to involve hedonic experiences, often viewed as special. Even when they are relatively cheap items, self-gifts are usually associated with a certain degree of specialness, for instance, buying a better brand of a product than usual. Chen's transcript (below) illustrates how consuming a product as ordinary as coffee can be a pleasurable self-gift experience when this is enjoyed in a place different from normal and in the context of an important achievement (see also Mick & DeMoss, 1990b). Chen's description also suggests that this was a special and private experience of pleasure and tranquillity:

> ... I like drinking coffee, but it is more expensive to drink in coffee bars. Thus I usually buy some instant coffee from supermarkets, it is cheaper ... After work, I went directly to Starbucks to have a cup of coffee ... I remember I sat on a chair near the back wall of the coffee bar, it was quite quiet ... I was so delighted; because of the approval of the project plan ... I felt peace of mind, relaxed, just having a rest ... (China, Chen, male, 37)

Self-gifts often have an important symbolic value, which further highlights their hedonic nature. For several UK and Chinese participants, self-gifts were said to be a 'reminder' of a person, place, or event. Additionally, they were associated with a means of asserting one's identity. However, in UK interviews, this typically happened with self-gifts purchased in negative contexts, where the items purchased were often a means of asserting a different self to cope with separations. In contrast, Chinese participants reported diverse self-gift experiences in which they bought top brands of certain products, associated with high status and specifically said to be 'more expensive', as a way of affirming and communicating an ideal self in positive contexts:

> . . . the mobile phone is important to me . . . such as, if I have dinner with *my friends* or *business partners*, I always answer the phone. The phone *can stand* for *my identity*, if the phone is the *old style*, it is *not good*. I prefer to choose a recent stylish phone . . . (China, Huan, male, 41; emphasis added)

The fact that not many people possessed such top-branded goods was said to make these self-gifts particularly special.

Additionally, gifts reported by Chinese participants were, in many cases, *other* (as well as *self*) oriented, often as a means of celebrating the achievement or positive event with others, whilst thanking them for their support. Indeed, when asked to describe their self-gift experiences, it was typical of these participants to describe gifts that were, in fact, not 'myself-' but rather 'ourselves-directed', as if they attached a different meaning to the concept of 'self-gift'. That was for example the case of Fang who was awarded the model teacher prize and compensated her family (and herself) for the lack of shared time they had endured because of her job by carefully choosing and cooking 'a special meal for myself as well as my family' (China, Fang, female, 46).

Although UK participants were in general more self-directed in their choices, there are also those who described celebrating work and other personal achievements with others (e.g. friends, relatives) as an appreciation of the support received. Those celebrations usually included meals or drinks out.

Travelling, alone, with relatives, or friends was an important self-gift for both UK and Chinese participants. Additionally, for a few Chinese participants, the travelling was, in fact, a means of meeting relatives (usually parents) from whom they were geographically separated. In those cases, the meeting of family was the actual self-gift. For example, one of these interviewees was planning to go on holiday to stay with her parents to celebrate her admission to her first-choice university.

### Emotions following SGCB in positive contexts

For the UK participants, the positive contexts described (especially when these involve earned achievements) justify self-gift giving. Expressions such as 'it was justified' (UK, Anne, female, 19), 'so it was fair enough' (UK, Peter, male, 20), 'I felt I deserved and it was OK to reward myself' (UK, Bob, male, 20) abound as spontaneous justifications for self-gift giving. The emotions experienced after SGCB were usually positive and intense, including happiness, excitement, and feelings of deservedness. Most Chinese participants described the same kind of positive emotions, although they never mentioned feelings of deservedness, and some referred to experiencing some guilt and/or regret for their purchases.

An important difference in Chinese post self-gift emotions is the fact that, for many of these participants, the satisfaction with self-gifts seemed to be dependent on the approval of others (colleagues, friends, and family). Specifically, that approval made participants proud and happy, whilst the disapproval of others caused the opposite effect.

Several Chinese interviewees further explained that the top-branded self-gifts made them feel different, more confident, and more likely to be successful. Positive emotions were reinforced by other people's recognition. Note the associations Lee makes between the brand (Boss) and his feelings of self-confidence, as well as between the compliments he received from his children and his positive emotions:

> ... Before meeting the client, I decided to go shopping to relax my mind. I bought myself a new Boss three-piece suit and a tie ... Boss was a popular brand designed for a *mature* and *successful* person, I thought. When I was in Boss, I got *a sense of achievement* ... – I was *happy*, it was really nice. I *felt more confident* ... [I thought] I must try my best to negotiate with the client. I ... They [clothes] were really good, making me *confident of success* ... my children said, 'Wow, dad, you look full of vigour, looking handsome' I was very *happy* and *proud* ... (China, Lee, male, 46; emphasis added)

The importance of others for the enjoyment of the gifts is also related to the aforementioned collective orientation of some purchases. Below, Wen describes his satisfaction in watching his wife's contentment with a gift he had bought for them both:

> ... Sometimes, I open the [music] box, with the old Chinese couple dancing... My wife and I can stay happily looking at them. At these moments, I am *delighted* ... It *was worth buying it ... looking at my wife's smiling face, I feel so happy.* (China, Wen, male, 58; emphasis added)

In contrast, in the UK interviews, others' comments on participants' self-gifts did not emerge as a factor affecting participants' satisfaction.

## Discussion and implications

Chinese SGCB seems to be particularly affected by the importance of the family, by the Chinese, group-based notion of the self, and by the significance of the 'face' concept (see Joy, 2001; Qian et al., 2007; Wong & Ahuvia, 1998). This is apparent in the preferred self-gift occasions (e.g. group reunions, group-related achievements), in the gifts chosen, which in several cases were not purely self-oriented, and also in the emotions experienced after self-gift giving, which were dependent upon the approval of others. The evidence adds support to the findings of Wang et al. (2001) that gifts are used as a tangible evidence of love and affection, given that open demonstrations of affection are not customary in China.

Contexts related to work, holiday, or receiving money are amongst the main positive circumstances for self-gift giving shared by both sets of participants. There are, however, important differences underlying the self-gift behaviour. For UK participants, these self-gifts are noticeably perceived as deserved by the self-attribution of the achievements. As referred to by Faure and Mick (1993), drawing on research on social psychology, the perceived responsibility for an outcome (see Weiner, 1995), together with the positively valued behaviour attributed to the action (in this case, usually hard work), are found to influence judgments of deservingness of the outcome (Feather, 1992). UK participants' internal *locus* (e.g. Weiner, 1980) of achievements contrasts with a Chinese emphasis on external *locus* (Qian et al., 2007).

Our results suggest that aspects such as 'luck' and, especially, other people's contributions are often held as co-responsible for the Chinese positive outcomes. In such circumstances, the motivation for self-gift giving seems to be more about the celebration of the events with the others to whom the giver is inherently connected than the individuals' feelings of deservedness, which are seen as inappropriate in a society that values modesty and self-effacement (Yau, 1988). Accordingly, and agreeing with the Chinese, interdependent notion of the self, the gifts chosen are often not purely self-oriented. Several descriptions of those gifts support Belk's (1984, p. 757) assertion that when the 'concept of self is group-based rather than individual-based, gift giving within the clan or family takes on a unique meaning. Under these circumstances, giving to others may be seen as giving to self'. In particular, participants' parents, husbands, or wives are often included in self-gift descriptions, also in tune with Chinese, Confucian values of loyalty and family orientation (e.g. Joy, 2001; Qian et al., 2007).

The types of self-gifts chosen by the two sets of participants include the same kind of varied items and services. In both cases, self-gift giving involves special, hedonic experiences, adding support to Mick and DeMoss's (1990b) US findings. However, Chinese participants seem particularly to value luxury brands, and these play an important conspicuous role in their personal and professional relations by visibly demonstrating expensiveness and prestige, thus honouring the receiver (Yau et al., 1999). It is also consistent with the brand loyalty and brand orientation identified in Yau (1988) and Qian et al.'s (2007) studies respectively. Wong and Ahuvia (1998) believe that Eastern Asian cultural notion of interdependent self and the importance attached to preserving 'face' help to explain the significance given to possessions that are public and visible, such as designer-labelled goods and other expensive brands. Several of our participants' spontaneous expressions illustrate the reflection of these cultural values on self-gift giving, such is the case of one participant who felt 'ashamed' for not having a brand of clothes as luxurious as the one that his friend was wearing, or of the several participants who felt proud because of others' positive comments.

Regarding the emotions that follow SGCB, for both sets of participants these tend to be positive. For UK participants, self-gifts are mostly seen as a 'fair reward' for the personal effort and therefore any post-purchase guilt tends to be diverted. This may be related to Western cultural beliefs of delayed gratification (e.g. Mick & DeMoss, 1990b) and of that 'people get what they deserve (or earn) and deserve what they get' (Mick, 1991, p. 151). Amongst Chinese participants, post-purchase negative emotions are relatively more frequent than for their British counterparts, and these are associated with the fear of having been too self-indulgent and the shame that could induce or with disapproval of the gift by others. In particular, other people's reactions to self-gifts seem to have an important role in participants' satisfaction (and dissatisfaction) with them, which is an additional indication of the others-oriented nature of some of these gifts. Chinese cultural values may also help the understanding of this finding. Indeed, the importance of individuals' public image and 'the concern for not losing one's face' (Qian et al., 2007, p. 216) means that individuals are more concerned with other people's perceptions of themselves and with maintaining their status (Lee & Green, 1991). As well as agreeing with Qian et al. (2007) in that the concept of 'face' is likely to influence consumers' buying decisions, these findings further suggest that it is also likely to affect consumers' post-purchase satisfaction.

As in the UK, self-gift behaviour seems to be relevant for Chinese consumers in a variety of positive contexts, especially related to work-related achievement. A closer look reveals, however, important differences in this behaviour between these two countries' participants. Overall, self-gift giving seems to be less self-oriented for Chinese than for British consumers. Wong and Ahuvia (1998) remind us that 'existing consumer theory is steeped in Western cultural values' (p. 425) and alert us to the need to consider the influence of collectivism on consumption. In particular, self-gift giving is a type of consumer behaviour where cultural aspects, such as the interdependent notion of the self and the importance attributed to 'face', are critical. On this subject, Mick and DeMoss (1990b) have suggested that the very existence of self-gifts may depend on an individually centred versus group-centred view of self. In a similar vein, Olshavsky and Lee (1993) had suggested that, in certain Asian countries that are influenced by Confucian, collectivistic culture, 'it may be socially inappropriate to act on this individualistic desire (i.e. to buy gifts for oneself)' (p. 551). While our findings confirm the existence of self-gift behaviour in China, they also indicate that a redefinition of the concept is needed to reflect the Confucian, collectivist culture as called for by Hofstede (1980). Marketing scholars should pay attention to the implications of these cultural differences on the concept of self-gift giving, which has been constructed against a Western (and more individualistic) cultural background. We further draw attention to the fact that, even though the interview guides used in the two countries were the same, participants' interpretations of the expression of 'self-gift' are expected to have reflected these countries' cultural differences and the possible different meanings attached to the concept. This may help explaining the 'others orientation' dimension of the behaviour in Chinese interviews, which expresses the Chinese group-based concept of self.

These findings, although exploratory, also have important implications for practitioners. We agree with Qian et al. (2007) in that Western international managers must become familiar with Chinese culture values when extending their activities to that country. Specifically, we believe that marketers targeting China may benefit from using communication strategies that combine meaningful self-gift themes (e.g. work-related) with collectivist appeals, to which Chinese consumers may relate better. In particular, colleagues', friends', or relatives' commendation of one's self-gift choices could be successfully used in some communications. At the same time, those appeals may reduce post-purchase cognitive dissonance associated with a consumer behaviour that, by its self-indulgent nature, may be uncomfortable in that culture.

This research has also some limitations. Although this study was exploratory, insights on SGCB in China would have been enhanced by a larger sample. Additionally, a focus on both positive and negative contexts for self-gift giving might produce a more complete picture of this behaviour. Nevertheless, to the best of our knowledge, this paper was pioneering in addressing this distinct form of consumer behaviour on a collectivist culture like China. Future studies, using larger samples and combined qualitative and quantitative methodologies, should further explore the implications of the concept of self on SGCB in China, as well as on other collectivist-oriented countries. Further research should also address the need for a new definition of self-gift consumer behaviour in China that better expresses this country's cultural context.

## Acknowledgements

The authors would like thank the editors, particularly Maria Piacentini, for their helpful comments on the manuscript and also to acknowledge the useful and considered suggestions of the two anonymous reviewers.

# References

Banister, E., & Piacentini, M. (2006). Binge drinking – Do they mean us? Living life to the full in students' own words. In C. Pechmann & L. Price (Eds.), *Advances in consumer research* (Vol. 33, pp. 390–398). Duluth, MN: Association for Consumer Research.

Belk, R.E. (1984). Cultural and historical differences in concepts of self and their effects on attitudes toward 'having and giving'. In T.C. Kinnear (Ed.), *Advances in consumer research*, (Vol. 11, pp. 753–760). Provo, UT: Association for Consumer Research.

Bitner, M.J., Booms, B.H., & Tetreault, M.S. (1990). The service encounter: Diagnosing favourable and unfavourable incidents. *Journal of Marketing*, 54(1), 71–84.

Bond, M.H., & Hofstede, G. (1989). The cast value of Confucian values. *Human Systems Management*, 8(3), 195–199.

Bryman, A. (2004). *Social research methods* (2nd ed.). Oxford, England: Oxford University Press.

Chan, A.K., Denton, L.T., & Tsang, A.S.L. (2003). The art of gift giving in China. *Business Horizons*, 46(4), July–August, 47–52.

Chan, W.T. (1963). *A source book of Chinese philosophy*. Princeton, NJ: Princeton University Press.

Chapman, B. (2007, October). China challenges and opportunities: Wake up and smell the green tea. *The Bridge, Industry and Parliamentary Trust*, pp. 4–5.

Chell, E., & Pittaway, L. (1998). A study of entrepreneurship in the restaurant and café industry: Exploratory work using the critical incident technique as a methodology. *Hospitality Management*, 17, 23–32.

de Ruyter, K., Perkins, D.S., & Wetzel, M. (1995). Consumer-defined service expectations and post purchase dissatisfaction in moderately priced restaurants: A cross-national study. *Journal of Consumer Satisfaction, Dissatisfaction and Complaining Behaviour*, 8, 177–187.

Edvardsson, B., & Roos, I. (2001). Critical incident techniques: Towards a framework for analysing the criticality of critical incidents. *International Journal of Service Industry Management*, 12(3/4), 251–268.

Euromonitor International (2009). G20: In focus. Euromonitor International Countries and Consumers. Retrieved April 2, 2009, from http://www.euromonitor.com/factfile.aspx?country=CN

Feather, N.T. (1992). An attributional and value analysis of deservingness in success and failure situations. *British Journal of Social Psychology*, 31(2), 125–145.

Fung, H. (1999). Becoming a moral child: The socialization of shame among young Chinese children. *Ethos*, 27(2), 180–209.

Faure, C., & Mick, D.G. (1993). Self-gifts through the lens of attribution theory. *Advances in Consumer Research*, 20(1), 553–556.

Flanagan, J.C. (1954). The critical incident technique. *Psychological Bulletin*, 51(4), 327–357.

Gremler, D. (2004). The critical incident technique in service research. *Journal of Service Research*, 7(1), 65–89.

Golden-Biddle, K., & Locke, K. (1993). Appealing work: An investigation in how ethnographic texts convince. *Organization Science*, 4(4), 595–616.

Harris, L., & Reynolds, K. (2004). Jaycustomer behavior: An exploration of types and motives in the hospitality industry. *Journal of Services Marketing*, 18(5), 339–357.

Hofstede, G. (1980). *Culture's consequences: International differences in work related values*. Beverley Hills, CA: Sage.

Hogg, M., & Maclaran, P. (2008). Rhetorical issues in writing interpretivist consumer research. *Qualitative Market Research*, 11(2), 130–146.

Holbrook, M., & O'Shaughnessy, J. (1988). On the scientific status of consumer research and the need for an interpretive approach to studying consumption behavior. *Journal of Consumer Research*, 15(3), 398–402.

Hopkinson, G., & Hogarth-Scott, S. (2001). 'What happened was...': Broadening the agenda for storied research. *Journal of Marketing Management*, 17(1), 27–47.

Hudson, L., & Ozanne, J. (1988). Alternative ways of seeking knowledge in consumer research. *Journal of Consumer Research*, 14(4), 508–521.

Joy, A. (2001). Gift giving in Hong Kong and the continuum of social ties. *Journal of Consumer Research*, 28(2), 239–256.

Kitayama, S., Markus, H.R., Matsumoto, H., & Norasakkunkit, V. (1997). Individual and collective processes in the construction of the self: Self-enhancement in the United States and self-criticism in Japan. *Journal of Personality and Social Psychology*, 72(6), 1245–1267.

Kvale, S. (1990). The qualitative research interview: A phenomenological and a hermeneutical mode of understanding. *Journal of Phenomenological Psychology*, 14(2), 171–196.

Lee, C., & Green, R.T. (1991). Cross-cultural examination of the Fishbein behavioral intentions model. *Journal of International Business Studies*, 22(2), 289–305.

Leung, T.K.P., Heung, V.C.S., & Wong, Y.H. (2008). One possible consequence of guanxi for an insider: How to obtain and maintain it? *European Journal of Marketing*, 42(1/2), 23–34.

Lotz, S.L., Shim, S., & Gehrt, K. (2003). A study of Japanese consumers' cognitive hierarchies in formal and informal gift giving situations. *Psychology and Marketing*, 20(1), 59–71.

Luomala, H. (1998). A mood-alleviative perspective on self-gift behaviours: Stimulating consumer behaviour theory development. *Journal of Marketing Management*, 14(1/3), 109–132.

Luomala, H., & Laaksonen, M. (1997). Mood-regulatory self-gifts: Development of a conceptual framework. *Journal of Economic Psychology*, 18(4), 407–434.

Luomala, H., & Laaksonen, M. (1999). A qualitative exploration of mood-regulatory self-gift behaviours. *Journal of Economic Psychology*, 20(2), 147–182.

Mesquita, B., & Karasawa, M. (2004). Self-conscious emotions as dynamic cultural processes. *Psychological Inquiry*, 15(2), 161–166.

Mick, D. (1991). Giving gifts to ourselves: A Greimassian analysis leading to testable propositions. In H.H. Larsen, D.G. Mick, & C. Alsted (Eds.), *Proceedings of marketing and semiotics: The Copenhagen symposium* (pp. 142–159). Copenhagen: Handel-Shojskolens Forlag,.

Mick, D., & DeMoss, M. (1990a). To me from me: A descriptive phenomenology of self-gifts. In M.E. Goldberg, G. Gorn, & R.W. Pollay (Eds.), *Advances in consumer eesearch* (Vol. 17, pp. 677–682). Provo, UT: Association for Consumer Research.

Mick, D., & DeMoss, M. (1990b). Self-gifts: Phenomenological insights from four contexts. *Journal of Consumer Research*, 17(3), 322–332.

Mick, D., & DeMoss, M. (1992). Further findings on self-gifts: Products, qualities and socioeconomic correlates. In J.F. Sherry & B. Sternthal (Eds.), *Advances in consumer research* (Vol. 19, pp. 140–146). Provo, UT: Association for Consumer Research.

Millington, A., Eberhardt, M., & Wilkinson, B. (2005). Gift giving, guanxi and illicit payments in buyer–supplier relations in China: Analysing the experience of UK companies. *Journal of Business Ethics*, 57(3), 255–268.

Olshavsky, R.W., & Lee, D.H. (1993). Self-gifts: A metacognition perspective. In L. McAlister & M.L. Rothschild (Eds.), *Advances in consumer research* (Vol. 20, pp. 547–552). Provo, UT: Association for Consumer Research.

Park, S.Y. (1998). A comparison of Korean and American gift-giving behaviours. *Psychology and Marketing*, 15(6), 577–593.

Pereira, M.T. (2006). *Understanding self-gift consumer behavior*. Unpublished PhD thesis, University of Nottingham.

Pereira, M.T., Ennew, C., & Tynan, C. (2005, July). *Self-gift consumer behaviour: Does it make you feel better?* In Proceedings of the Academy of Marketing Conference, Dublin Institute of Technology, Dublin.

Qian, W., Razzaque, M., & Keng, K. (2007). Chinese cultural values and gift-giving behaviour. *Journal of Consumer Marketing*, 24(4), 214–228.

Rubin, H., & Rubin, I. (1995). *Qualitative interviewing: The art of hearing data*. London: Sage.

Schwartz, B. (1967). The social psychology of the gift. *American Journal of Sociology*, 73(1), 1–11.

Spiggle, S. (1994). Analysis and interpretation of qualitative data in consumer research. *Journal of Consumer Research*, 21(3), 491–503.

Stauss, B., & Mang, P. (1999). Culture shocks in inter-cultural service encounters? *Journal of Services Marketing*, 13(4/5), 329–346.

Stauss, B., & Weinlich, B. (1997). Process-oriented measurement of services quality: Applying the sequential incident technique. *European Journal of Marketing*, 31(1), 33–55.

Strauss, A., & Corbin, J. (1998). *Basics of qualitative research – Techniques and procedures for developing grounded theory.* Thousand Oaks, CA: Sage.

Taylor, S., & Bodgan, R. (1998). *Introduction to qualitative research methods: A guidebook and resource* (3rd ed.). New York: John Wiley.

The Economist (2009, July 18–24). China's recovery: A fine balancing act. *Economist*, pp. 57–58.

Thompson, C., & Haytko, D. (1997). Speaking of fashion: Consumers' uses of fashion discourses and the appropriation of countervailing cultural meanings. *Journal of Consumer Research*, 24(1), 15–42.

Thompson, C., Locander, W., & Pollio, H. (1989). Putting consumer experience back into consumer research: The philosophy and method of existential-phenomenology. *Journal of Consumer Research*, 16(2), 133–146.

Thompson, C., Locander, W., & Pollio, H. (1990). The lived meaning of free choice: An existential-phenomenological description of everyday consumer experiences of contemporary married women. *Journal of Consumer Research*, 17(3), 346–361.

Tuan, Y.-F. (1982). *Segmented worlds and self: Group life and individual consciousness.* Minneapolis: University of Minnesota Press.

Walker, S., & Truly, E. (1992). *The critical incidents technique: Philosophical foundations and methodological implications.* In C. Allen & T. Madden (Eds.), American Marketing Association Winter Educators' Conference, Chicago, pp. 270–275.

Wang, J., Piron, F., & Xuan, M.V. (2001). Faring one thousand miles to give goose feathers: Gift giving in the Peoples Republic of China. In M.C. Gilly & J. Meyers-Levy (Eds.), *Advances in consumer research* (Vol. 28, pp. 58–63). Valdosta, GA: Association for Consumer Research.

Weiner, B. (1980). A cognitive (attribution)–emotion–action model of motivated behavior: An analysis of judgments of help-giving. *Journal of Personality and Social Psychology*, 39(2), 186–200.

Weiner, B. (1995). *Judgments of responsibility – A foundation for a theory of social conduct.* New York: Guilford Press.

Williams, L.A., & Burns, A.C. (1994). The halcyon days of youth: A phenomenological account of experiences and feelings accompanying spring break on the beach. In C.T. Allen& D.R. John (Eds.), *Advances in consumer research* (Vol. 21, pp. 98–103). Provo, UT: Association for Consumer Research.

Wong, N.Y., & Ahuvia, A.C. (1998). Personal taste and family face: Luxury consumption in Confucian and Western societies. *Psychology and Marketing*, 15(5), 423–441.

Yan, Y. (1996). *The flow of gifts: Reciprocity and social networks in a Chinese village.* Stanford, CA: Stanford University Press.

Yau, O.H.M. (1988). Chinese cultural values. *European Journal of Marketing*, 22(5), 44–55.

Yau, O.H.M., Chan, T.S., & Lau, K.F. (1999). Influence of Chinese cultural values on consumer behavior: A proposed model of gift-purchasing. *Journal of International Consumer Marketing*, 11(1), 97–116.

Zhou, C., & Guang, H. (2007). Gift giving culture in China and its cultural values. *Intercultural Communication Studies*, 16(2), 81–93.

# Death and disposal: The universal, environmental dilemma

Louise Canning, *University of Birmingham, UK*
Isabelle Szmigin, *University of Birmingham, UK*

**Abstract** Individuals around the world engage in one common yet fundamental activity that is of personal, emotional, social, and environmental significance –disposal of the dead. As the global landscape becomes increasingly populated, so disposal choice becomes a critical environmental issue. Disposal of the dead is an essential aspect of our existence; it is an inevitable activity, which cannot be avoided. This paper contributes to an emerging body of work written from a consumer culture theory and marketing perspective on disposal of the dead. The paper examines the convergence of the consumer decision with environmental factors from a multicultural viewpoint. We add to existing literature in this area through a perspective that highlights key environmental issues that cross cultural and spatial boundaries, namely land use, land space, and pollution implications. These in turn are seen within the context of cultural norms, individual memorialisation practice, and specific regulations pertaining to body disposal.

## Introduction

The environmental consequences of man's actions ignore geographic boundaries and have the potential to present us with long-term problems that are essentially irreversible and are therefore of paramount importance (Lash & Wellington, 2007). Increasing awareness of the effect of climate change may result in conscious changes in consumption behaviour by some, yet there are certain activities over which individual self-management is constrained. One such activity is the disposal of the dead. While cultural mores may dictate differences in disposal rites, all individuals around the world engage in this one common yet fundamental activity that is of personal, emotional, social, and environmental significance. In 2005, the world population stood at 6515 million, and by 2050 it is expected to reach 9191 million (United Nations, 2007). As the global landscape is increasingly populated, so the removal of human remains becomes a critical environmental issue for all cultures and nations. Disposal of the dead is a fundamental aspect of our existence; it is an inevitable activity, which cannot be avoided. But in practice, the funeral and disposal ritual is essentially mutable, with different meanings across cultures and religions, the nature and meaning of burial or memorial space changing over time (Rugg, 2000) and reflecting structural and regulatory requirements.

Whilst there is a body of literature on death and dying largely emanating from the disciplines of sociology and anthropology, relatively little has been written from the business and more specifically marketing perspective (Turley, 1997). This has started to change with, for example, the examination of death-related consumption (Bonsu & Belk, 2003; Gabel, Mansfield, & Westbrook, 1996; Gentry, Kennedy, Paul, & Hill, 1994), marketing's treatment of death in advertising (O'Donohoe & Turley, 2000), and encounters between the bereaved and service providers (O'Donohoe & Turley, 2006). Historically, the most significant cross-cultural debate was that instigated by Mitford (1963, 1997), revealing the Anglo-American cultural divide in dealing with the process of death and disposal.

This paper contributes to the emerging body of work written from a consumer theory and marketing perspective on disposal of the dead, examining the convergence of the consumer decision with environmental factors from a multicultural and sociohistorical viewpoint. We consider some of the current issues that are both specific to particular cultural contexts and cross-cultural boundaries with regard to the removal of the dead. In doing so, we review a range of literature from consumer behaviour, sociology, and anthropology, with our discussion being informed in particular by the Consumer Culture Theory (CCT) perspective (Arnould & Thompson, 2005). Our focus is primarily on the act of disposal, recognising that cultural differences in funeral rites impact on the removal decision. We begin with an examination of issues relating to individual choice with regards the disposal decision. From this, we explore some of the supply side constraints impacting on this decision and the environmental outcomes associated with removal practices. In particular, we suggest that debate should indeed revolve around key environmental issues, which cross cultural and spatial boundaries, namely land use, land space, and pollution implications. This debate, however, has to be seen within the context of cultural norms, individual memorialisation practice, and specific regulations pertaining to body disposal. The paper concludes with suggestions for future research.

## Consumer decision processes and disposal of the dead

Although consumer research has paid relatively scant attention to removal of the dead (Bonsu & Belk, 2003; Gabel et al., 1996; Gentry et al., 1994), there is both practical and theoretical significance in this area of decision making for consumer research. Decisions regarding what to do with the dead are part of the consumption cycle, which includes disposal and is also a subject that falls into CCT's call for focus to 'investigate the neglected experiential, social and cultural dimensions of consumption in context' (Arnould & Thompson, 2005, p. 869). Some see consumer behaviour in such a context as recourse to accepted or market-driven rituals, which avoid the need to make choices or result in reduced decision-making skills (Gentry et al., 1994). This is primarily the case when the consumer is the person dealing with the deceased, although many deceased have effectively avoided the decision process by not making clear their requirements before death. For those who do plan ahead, it seems likely that the decision process is highly involved and specific in terms of disposal preferences. Unlike most major purchases, social and cultural norms require decision making that might seem inappropriate in other situations (Bonsu & Belk, 2003), and normal market activities such as price comparisons may be perceived as socially and culturally taboo (Gentry et al., 1994; Mitford, 1997). Not only is the decision likely to be made from a new consumption role as widowed, single parent, and so on (Gabel et al., 1996), but it is at a time of intense emotional pressure when grieving may prevent the consumer from taking an active role in the decision or affect their decision-making abilities. Whether symbolically demonstrating one's relationship to the deceased or for the purpose of displaying social or cultural capital, avoiding a complex decision-making process by spending money may act as a satisfactory default, which also implies vulnerability in the marketplace that may be exploited (Mitford, 1997). Death and the activities following death, as a focus of consumption, whether of a ritual or disposal nature are particular, culturally imbued, regulated, and relatively rare for those involved in the process. When consumers lack experience to guide their decisions, and are less aware of the choices available and their own motivations in the decision-making process, the standard cultural modes of disposal are likely to dominate with significant guidance from market providers.

While removal of the dead can be placed within the broader context of disposal, be it mobile phones, cars, or other consumer goods, it is also a unique process in that alternative choices of the repair or replace kind do not exist. Consumer behaviour around removal choice must be set within the context of particular social and cultural constraints. As such, the subject of the disposal of the dead is central to the CCT sociohistorical theme of meanings being 'embodied and negotiated in particular social situations, roles and relationships' (Arnould & Thompson, 2005, p. 869). As Walter (2005) identifies, while religion might appear as the most obvious variable, other factors such as the dominant municipalisation of disposal in European countries as compared to the more prevalent private enterprise model of the United States (although local communities and religious groups also own cemeteries in the United States) have shaped differences in behaviour. Walter (2005) describes the municipal model found in, for example, France, Germany, Italy, and Spain as having mixed success and in some cases leading to conflict with priests. But above all, this municipal model downplays the role of the corpse as compared to the American counterpart where the public display of the body enhanced by embalming techniques is central to the funeral process. Where a municipal context is the norm, constraints on individual actions frame and restrict but may also lead to improvisation within those constraints (Bourdieu, 1990). German regulations forbidding the burial of remains outside of an approved cemetery where plots are expensive has resulted in many Germans scattering ashes in Switzerland where rules are more relaxed. This, however, has led to consternation from inhabitants near Lake Constance, a drinking water reservoir, who fear the lake will become contaminated from the continual scattering of ashes (Pancevski, 2008). A significant factor in individual behaviour determining choice, say, of cremation or burial is the freedom it gives the mourner, but municipalisation or market practice means that this is by no means universal. While it has become commonplace in Britain for ashes to be scattered, in Belgium, Denmark, Sweden, and Germany, the placement of ashes, as discussed above, is far more restricted, and in Italy it is illegal to scatter ashes anywhere other than in a designated space, which is usually a cemetery (Kellaher, Prendergast, & Hockey, 2005).

Culturally, there is a range of social and historical differentiations affecting choice. Mitford (1963, 1997), for example, distinguished between the largely celebratory and costly American model and the more utilitarian approach of the British. Jupp's (1993, p. 186) comparison of the funeral choices of a city and village identified social class differences between 'a lingering burial choice' associated with working class and local identity and an adoption of cremation amongst the more mobile middle classes. In contrast, cremation in the United States was presented as a cheap alternative and 'by portraying cremation as tawdry, un-Christian and un-American, and by simply not suggesting it to customers as an option, funeral directors were highly successful in resisting it' (Walter, 2005, p. 179). Thus the British model of choice as depicted by Jupp is one of modern innovative behaviour by middle-class consumers, whereas the US funeral as presented by Walter is one where the consumer is effectively managed (or manipulated) by the dominant supplier. This fear of market manipulation has been noted by other American scholars, and contrasts with narratives of empowered, symbolic practices, such as Bonsu and Belk's (2003) description of conspicuous ritual consumption in Ghana. This raises interesting issues regarding consumer identity projects in terms of the marketplace positions that consumers may choose, or find themselves inhabiting, and questions the ubiquity of a consumer-driven global economy (Arnould & Thompson, 2005).

Part of the identity project is the need of the bereaved to maintain the individuality of the deceased through some kind of personal space or memory. A cemetery enshrines the identity of individuals through grave markers giving their name and dates of birth and death (Rugg, 2000). So while this is readily available in a burial plot, many may be 'unable to accept the anonymity of ashes strewn in a collective area' (Kellaher et al., 2005, p. 238). Kellaher et al. reveal a wide variety of opinions regarding the benefits of cremation or burial, but most of their participants reflected a desire to retain an embodiment of the dead, whether this is having somewhere to go to talk to their loved ones, or a fear of either burning or decaying. Given that the consumer is often depicted as having a fragmented sense of self (Belk, 1988), acknowledging the impact that the nature of disposal has on the maintenance of identity beyond death is critical to understanding the cultural and social imperatives felt by many in a constrained place of decision making. This in turn leads to a variety of behaviours that go far beyond the point of disposal. Kellaher et al. (2005) describe how one family had ashes buried in the garden with a memorial but felt they could remove them if they ever moved house, despite such action not being countenanced by existing regulations around exhumation. Others wanted to share the ashes between family members allowing individuals to memorialise the loved one in their own fashion. But such freedom of choice is likely to be reflected by the cultural and regulatory constraints impacting on such behaviour.

## Disposal choice and environmental impact

Disposal of the dead, while having received relatively little attention in the marketing literature, is replete with diverse cultural and consumption issues and subject to varied regulations, differences in availability of alternative provision, and changing consumer behaviour. Nevertheless, death is often a taboo subject controlled by social and cultural norms leading to relatively rare marketplace presence in public space (Bonsu & Belk, 2003). Whatever the religious or cultural settings, removal of the dead can essentially take two forms: burial and cremation. The following discussion examines burial and cremation from a multicultural perspective, paying particular attention to the environmental constraints of these disposal methods.

### Traditional burial

Burial as a means of removing the dead has been practiced since the Stone Age (Davies, 2004), and is common around the world and across religions, although rituals associated with it vary. This latter point is of particular interest to us because of the environmental consequences of these rituals. Where burials are influenced by Islamic and Jewish faiths, preparation involves the washing of the corpse and dressing in a shroud and, where used, containment in a simple wooden coffin (Jewish ritual also includes the removal of any lining inside the coffin). Other cultures and religions may require more elaborate handling of the corpse, where emphasis is placed on preserving the body, this having been a dominant theme in burials influenced by Confucian beliefs in Asia. So, for example, the traditional preference in China was for methods of disposal that would delay decay, including the use of thick wooden coffins into which clothing and shrouds were packed. These coffins were then contained in tombs made of wood, stone, or brick (Ebrery, 1990). Christian practices in Europe and North America generally involve the corpse being dressed in normal clothing, although traditionally Catholics were dressed in a shroud, contained within a coffin (made of chipboard, wood, or metal), and, in some cases, preservation of the corpse via embalming, though not primarily to preserve the body after burial, but rather to slow its rate of decay before internment. Embalming in its current form consists of the injection of formaldehyde solution into the corpse and is not a Christian tradition. However, it became a dominant practice in US funeral rites following the American Civil War of the nineteenth century when Abraham Lincoln introduced the requirement in order to preserve the bodies to allow transportation of the Union dead to their homes in the North. From this initial trigger, embalming was promoted in the United States by the funeral industry as a means of extending the period of display of the dead in open caskets when family and friends could visit the funeral home to pay their respects and celebrate the life of the deceased (Mitford 1963, 1997). This extended period of display is not so common in the UK, and so the need for preservation is less, although of all corpses buried in Britain, around half are embalmed (Environment Agency UK, 2004).

From an environmental perspective, the simpler the method of preparing the corpse for burial, the fewer natural resources are used and the fewer substances can subsequently contaminate the area surrounding the burial sites, which would typically be designated cemeteries in the vicinity of residential areas. Possible contaminants from coffins include preservatives, varnishes, and sealers on wood coffins, and lead, zinc, copper, and steel in metal coffins (Spongberg & Becks, 2000). Historically, the marketing of hardwood or metal caskets promoted their capacity to protect the body from the elements of nature (Walter, 2005), and, as Mitford (1963, 1997) reported, this preservation of the corpse over time was in some cases used by American funeral directors as a positive attribute. Where preservatives are not used, a wooden coffin might not be a major contaminant source, but an untreated coffin will decompose and leach its contents more quickly (Spongberg & Becks, 2000), an important issue in any country where water and land resources can be contaminated by the leachate.

Not only do the processes of burial affect the land in which the bodies are placed, but using land for burial purposes also has important environmental consequences because:

- cemeteries require maintenance, such that they provide an acceptable setting in which to honour and maintain relationships with the dead
- that land is then restricted in being able to support other activities
- cemeteries have capacity constraints.

Land is a valuable resource (for many life forms) with man's use of burial and location of sites conflicting at times with farming, industrial, residential, and leisure activities. Cemeteries have to be located such that they do not impinge on these other activities yet have sufficient capacity for and are readily accessible to the communities they are meant to serve. The nature of land usage and cemetery capacity provides two particular tensions with regards burial in different countries. For example, the importance of land for food production in the Micronesian island nation the Marshall Islands meant that traditionally only chiefs were given land burials, with commoners rafted out to sea. However, once Christianity was established on the islands, burial customs changed so that rafting of commoners stopped and churches set up cemeteries in shore areas. More recently, rapid population growth has meant that capacity for burial is constrained, and weather events such as El Nino risk burial sites being exposed or completely destroyed (Spennemann, 1999). The apparent tension in using land to sustain various human activities is also apparent in China where haphazard placing of tombs took up large areas of cultivable land. This contributed to the promotion of cremation from the 1950s onwards, and the levelling of more than 100 million tombs located on arable land and along railroads allowed 6.7 million hectares of cultivable land to be reclaimed (People's Daily Online, 2001).

The social and cultural issues impinging on the supply side of disposal practices cannot be underestimated. Walter (2005) recounts how, from the late eighteenth century, with a rising population and as yet no improvement in mortality, the number of deaths in Europe and the United States increased such that there was a real social problem in terms of how to deal with the dead. Public health requirements often led the state to take over from the church to ensure a more rationalised approach to disposal and the building of new cemeteries on 'principles of hygiene, rationality and aesthetics' (Walter, 2005, p. 177). Cemeteries were located away from towns, as the corpse was seen as a danger to public health (Rugg, 2000). Countries such as France, Spain, and Portugal all replaced the traditional churchyard with new municipally run cemeteries.

Space for cemeteries is a particular issue for countries large and small. Some cemeteries are huge, covering, in the case of York in the UK, more than 25 acres, and in the United States and Australia more than double this (Rugg, 2000), although such coverage does not necessarily resolve capacity issues in the long term. In the UK, there are between 12,000 and 20,000 graveyards, cemeteries, and burial grounds (CABE, 2007), but in spite of this number, the country is facing major constraints, with some cemeteries reaching capacity and others having run out of space completely. This means that families either have to pay increased fees for the remaining burial plots (price being one way in which public bodies regulate demand) or have to locate plots at sites that are some distance away, breaking the relationship between the dead and the living (CABE, 2007). Thus while across cultures the spatially oriented problems of burial are similar but with different degrees of criticality depending on land availability, how consumer demand is managed is likely to be different according to cultural and social requirements, as well as economic and market contexts.

## Cremation

Britain saw a dramatic increase in cremation following the Second World War, rising from 6% of all deaths in 1945 to 72% by 2002 (Davies & Mates, 2005). This was not directly associated with religious or cultural factors; rather it was a means by which local authorities could address capacity constraints and provide the public with an economical means of disposal. Between 1951 and 1961, there was an almost threefold increase in the number of crematoria built in Britain (Jupp, 1993). Other countries, for example, China and Hong Kong, have also introduced cremation in part as a means of resolving physical land constraints associated with land burial.

The use of cremation is also culturally embedded. For example, cremation is the traditional method of disposing of the dead in countries influenced by Hindu and Sikh religions, and is the common form of removing corpses in regions informed by the Buddhist faith. In Bali, the cremation ritual, based on a combination of Hindu and Balinese culture, is a purification rite that frees the spirit. The ceremony is elaborate and joyous and one in which the whole village participates. The body is bathed and left to rest in a special house. Meals are prepared and offered to the deceased as normal. Following cremation, the final separation of the soul and the body is symbolised through the placing of the ashes in the sea (Australian Museum, 2009).

The separation of the body and soul has also influenced disposal choices in the Christian religion. For Catholics, the body and soul have traditionally been viewed as symbolically connected after death, and therefore destruction of the body could break this link; it was only in 1963 that the Pope agreed to cremation as an acceptable form of disposal (Walter, 2005). Having been legalised in 1884, cremation is now the most common form of disposal in Britain (Kellaher et al., 2005), and while it is not an accepted practice amongst the Jewish and Muslim religions (Jonker, 1996), in many countries it is becoming or has become the predominant or at least an accepted disposal method, as Table 1 indicates. Walter (2005) suggests that, in the West, cremation has become the norm where there has been state encouragement and no significant resistance of a religious or commercial nature. While in countries such as Bali cremation can be elaborate and expensive, it does provide an affordable means of disposal in many countries.

Whatever influences the use of cremation as a means of disposal, there are environmental consequences in terms of both energy consumption and emissions. The transformation of the corpse into bone fragments and the destruction of materials used to contain the body (where a coffin is used) takes up to two hours in modern industrial cremators with temperatures reaching in excess of 800°C (DEFRA, 2006). This clearly represents a significant level of fuel consumption, and incineration results in the emission of a range of chemical compounds and particulate matter (DEFRA, 2004). High incineration temperatures can reduce the release of some pollutants, with emissions being further controlled via filtering systems. Of particular concern in many developed countries is the release of mercury from dental fillings resulting from cremation. This has led, for example, to regulation in the EU, minimum incineration temperatures, and the fitting of mercury abatement equipment in crematoria in the UK (DEFRA, 2005, 2006). As noted above, disposal by cremation poses a range of cultural and religious issues concerning the relationship of the body and soul, and it is here that major confrontations between culture and environmental concerns are evident. For example, the demand from some Hindus in Britain for cremation using open-air pyres in order for their souls to be liberated from the body has created a legal dilemma of human rights on the one hand, and potentially unpleasant and harmful emissions to be suffered for those living close by on the other (Anglo-Asian Society, 2009).

Following cremation, the final disposal of a body might be by scattering remains at a site symbolic to the dead or their mourners, or discarding the ashes into water (such as in the Sikh and Hindu tradition), but can also involve the containment of ashes in urns

**Table 1** Cremation rates around the world.

| Country | Year | Cremation as a % of deaths |
|---|---|---|
| Argentina | 2002 | 13.73 |
| Austria | 2002 | 22.63 |
| Belgium | 2002 | 37.26 |
| Bulgaria | 2002 | 4.67 |
| China | 2002 | 50.6 |
| Czech Republic | 2002 | 77.05 |
| Denmark | 2002 | 72.36 |
| Finland | 2002 | 29.05 |
| France | 2002 | 29.05 |
| Hong Kong | 2002 | 82.87 |
| Hungary | 2002 | 35.57 |
| Ireland | 2002 | 6.41 |
| Netherlands | 2002 | 49.61 |
| New Zealand | 2002 | 60.38 |
| Norway | 2002 | 31.81 |
| Portugal | 2002 | 23.18 |
| Singapore | 2002 | 76.6 |
| Slovenia | 2002 | 48.14 |
| South Korea | 2002 | 42 |
| Spain | 2002 | 16.9 |
| Sweden | 2002 | 70.0 |
| Switzerland | 2002 | 75.15 |
| United Kingdom | 2002 · | 71.89 |
| USA | 2002 | 27.78 |
| | 2025 | 57.27 (predicted)* |

Source: Davies and Mates (2005); *CANA (2006).

and burial in columbaria. Cremation might reduce the amount of land actually required to dispose of corpses, but burial of remains in ceremonial containers and the construction of memorial sites that can be visited by the bereaved presents problems akin to cemeteries, that is, land requirements, the landscaping and maintenance of sites, and the costs (natural and financial) incurred in doing this (CABE, 2007; Sui, 2005). While scattering of ashes might seem a logical response to this, as noted above, the management of the final remains is carefully controlled in some countries, and mourners' requirements for ways to memorialise the deceased may lead them to seek a permanent repository for ashes. This is particularly significant for consumers in countries such as Japan where land is at a premium and the placement of ashes in columbaria represents a substantial cost.

### Natural burial: The alternative choice?

There are clearly environmental constraints in disposing of the dead via traditional forms of land burial and cremation. In recent years, alternative ways in which bodies might be removed and the deceased remembered have emerged in which a closer connection with the natural environment is sought and efforts are made to reduce the impact of disposal practices on that environment. Additionally, an increased understanding that choosing a funeral and method of removal is a consumption choice has led to a greater provision of information, including that which shows ways in which disposal can be more eco-friendly. So, for example, in the UK, the Institute of Cemetery and Crematoria Management (ICCM, 2008) and its members provide information to the public on environmental issues as they relate specifically to burial and cremation. The Natural Death Centre in the UK provides advice and information on how death and the rituals associated with it can be dignified and in tune with nature (Natural Death Centre, 2008). This has seen the coining of the term *natural burial* and the establishment in the UK of the Association of Natural Burial Grounds, with the ideas that underpin the Natural Death Centre having spread beyond the UK such that similar initiatives now exist in Italy, the United States, Canada, and New Zealand (Wienrich & Speyer, 2003).

The degree to which various aspects of funeral rites change as a result of these efforts does differ. So, for example, in the Tongzhou District of Beijing, villagers are encouraged to plant trees at a forest cemetery next to urns containing ashes of the deceased, rather than burying those ashes (People's Daily Online, 2001). New methods have been developed in Hong Kong for dealing with ashes, which allow the burial of those ashes underground (rather than above ground in a columbaria) using biodegradable urns (Sui, 2005). Some cemeteries in Beijing now not only offer burials under trees but also sea burials (People's Daily Online, 2001). Compared to disposing of ashes at sea, dealing with an uncremated corpse at sea does bring with it some complications. These include locations where it can be practiced (minimum depth to the seabed and distance from land), preparation of the corpse (biodegradable shroud or body bag, no embalming), drilling of holes in and weighting of the coffin (where one is used), and certification that the corpse is free from fever and infection (Facing Bereavement UK, 2008). Sea burial would obviously address land constraints and avoid the environmental consequences of cremation. It is, however, a relatively unusual choice amongst consumers, with few organisations able to provide the service and which itself can be cost prohibitive for the consumer (Facing Bereavement UK, 2008; Sea Services, 2008).

Consumers in the UK might opt for current cremation practices or burial at a site on land owned and managed by a local authority or a church, but in doing so are unlikely to choose for the body of the deceased to be embalmed, and may avoid coffins made of wood, chipboard, or metal in preference for alternative materials such as cardboard, wicker, or even banana leaves. Importantly, the introduction of such alternatives widens the consumer's 'horizons of conceivable action' (Arnould & Thompson, 2005, p. 869) away from what has been perceived by some as an hegemonic relationship between funeral director and bereaved (Mitford, 1997). Since the early 1990s, the British funeral consumer has come to play an increasingly active role in funeral rites with a significant growth in 'alternative funerals' and a stronger element of celebration (Walter, 1993, 1996). With regards disposal as part of this ritual, for those wishing to make even small steps towards helping their environment, the ability to choose from materials that are sustainable or which will not require a huge amount of energy when burnt is significant and may well increase their feeling of control.

Natural burial also involves disposal without the use of chemical preservatives and the containment of the corpse using biodegradable material (a coffin or simply a shroud). In addition to these practices, a fundamental and defining aspect of this form of burial is the site at which a body is interred such that

- where grave markers are used, they do not impose on the natural landscape in the way that tombs and headstones do; rather they typically consist of plants, shrubs, or trees (although trees tend to be the predominant marker, Clayden & Dixon, 2007)
- irrigation, pesticides, and herbicides are not used to maintain the site
- natural burial grounds may be located in existing cemeteries, woodlands, or a newly established woodland (Clayden & Dixon, 2007)
- cemetery and conservation legislation protects the site from future development or change in usage (Centre for Natural Burial, 2008).

The first natural burial ground was established in the UK in 1993 as part of an existing Victorian cemetery (Clayden & Dixon, 2007), and by 2004, there were more than 190, the majority of these being owned and managed by local authorities. Whilst their expansion is notable, there are no overarching principles that guide the practice of natural burial, meaning that location, ownership, landscaping, and management of natural burial grounds vary, and the experience of users of these sites can differ significantly (Clayden & Dixon, 2007).

Where religious practices do not dominate choice, the growth of natural burial can be seen as a direct response to ecological concerns and an opportunity for individuals to sidestep what may be perceived as the structuring influence of the marketplace where limited consumer positions were previously available for them to inhabit (Arnould & Thompson, 2005). While there may be sound ecological motives for natural burial, this choice may also be informed by personal reasons to do with the identity of the deceased and how their family and friends can memorialise them (Clayden & Dixon, 2007). Perhaps understandably, natural burial has been heralded as the future disposal choice of many baby boomers (Jones, 2008). Importantly, however, it does not address long-term land-capacity constraints (unless plots can be reused), and future scarcity could make this less economically viable.

## Conclusion

The disposal of the dead occupies a difficult and usually unwelcome place in most people's lives. Recognition of the need for disposal puts us in touch with our own mortality. We can refuse to plan our own funerals and allow others to take the responsibility. However, the process of planning a funeral and considering disposal options also affords us with choices of both a personal and environmental nature with which consumers may increasingly wish to engage. As Jones (2008) suggests, the baby-boomer generation were the first generation who took environmental concerns seriously, and they are now moving into a time where their parents and also their partners will be dying. It is quite likely that they will wish to be more engaged and take more control in the disposal process. Consumers are beginning to explore different variants of the funeral (Walter, 1996), but we should not exaggerate the consumer's active role where the zones of manoeuvre may be limited by religious and legal requirements. There has also been increased media interest in issues related to the disposal of the dead both in fictions such as *Six Feet Under* and in programmes that invite living celebrities to discuss their preferred funeral. Bringing the issues, whether environmental, cultural, or emotional, out into the open can only benefit those who use and provide funeral services. Awareness of people's fears, as well as their preferences, is the route to better understanding and better information and provision.

The bigger environmental issue that faces all cultures, however, remains. Whatever the efforts to reduce its impact, disposal of the dead continues to be by either cremation or burial, both of which have significant environmental consequences. Natural burial can relieve pressure in urban cemeteries and graveyards, and provide the deceased with a route to ecological immortality (Davies, 2004). It may also provide the bereaved with a pleasant and sympathetic environment in which to maintain relationships with and memorialise the deceased. Such forms of disposal, however, will not necessarily address the long-term physical constraints and economic consequences of continued land burial. The future may offer more choices that reduce the impact on land usage and pollution, but this is one cultural and environmental issue that will continue to be a dilemma for humankind. To address the problems posed by disposal, the first step is for us all to have a better understanding of alternative disposal choices and their environmental consequences. While not wanting to trivialise the religious and emotional significance of disposal practices, such an accumulation of knowledge and understanding of the effect of our decisions on the natural environment has been seen to impact on consumer behaviour in other areas. It is only once consumers have the knowledge to make informed choices that innovative solutions that challenge traditional practices associated with disposal may be considered. These could include, for example, the harvesting of trees at natural burial sites, the elimination of permanent memorials or the introduction of biodegradable memorials at traditional burial sites, and the reuse of all burial grounds. More radical practices could include the harnessing of heat generated via cremation for alternative energy uses[1] and the exploration of the feasibility of reducing corpses to disposable ashes via freeze-drying.

## Research implications

Consumers' responses to the disposal decision will continue to be framed by very different cultural and social contexts that are played out in the marketplace, whether through religious and spiritual requirements, ostentatious displays of wealth, environmentally driven choice making, or emotional vulnerability. All, though, are choices informed by the constitution and framing of the consumer society of that culture. Increasingly, environmental issues are likely to impinge on that framing and restrict or inhibit some, while others will have greater opportunities for overcoming the social taboos of disposal and fulfil an identity project for themselves or their loved ones. The issue of disposal is a classic example of how the structuring influence of the marketplace frames consumer positions (Arnould & Thompson, 2005), but also how consumers are culture producers developing their own (and their loved ones) identity projects within existing marketplace structures. Future research could identify more closely such individual disposal practices and how they reflect the interplay between the individual and the market.

Marketing and consumer behaviour researchers need to develop an understanding of disposal decisions and the different social and cultural contexts in which these are played out. While disposal practices do change and developments have been noted in recent years due, in part, to environmental constraints, there is still a need to determine ways in which more environmentally benign (and viable) forms of

[1]This is reported already to be in use in some parts of Sweden (Dijkshoorn, 2008).

removal might be married with requirements in different social and cultural contexts. Similarly, we need to understand how and whether social and cultural conditions might shift to accommodate the environmental imperative. Finally, as we see the so-called baby-boomer generation move into middle and old age, researchers could engage with these consumers to identify how a generation who have framed and been framed by choice and environmental issues are thinking about their own disposal.

# References

Anglo-Asian Society (2009). Natural cremation: Faith, freedom and choice [online]. Retrieved February 18, 2009, from http://www.anglo-asian.moonfruit.com/#/funeralpyrecampaign/4529275628

Arnould, E.J., & Thompson, C.J. (2005). Consumer Culture Theory (CCT): Twenty years of research. *Journal of Consumer Research, 31*(4), 868–882.

Australian Museum (2009). Death the last taboo [online]. Retrieved March 10, 2009, from http://www.deathonline.net/disposal/cremation/balinese.cfm

Belk, R. (1988). Possessions and the extended self. *Journal of Consumer Research, 15*(2), 139–168.

Bonsu, S.K., & Belk, R.W. (2003). Don't go cheaply into that good night: Death-ritual consumption in Asante, Ghana. *Journal of Consumer Behaviour, 30*(1), 41–55.

Bourdieu, P. (1990). *In other words: Essays toward a reflexive sociology.* Stanford, CA: Stanford University Press.

CABE (2007). *Briefing: Cemeteries, churchyards and burial grounds* [online]. Commission for Architecture and the Built Environment. Retrieved March 20, 2008, from http://www.cabe.org.uk/AssetLibrary/10701.pdf

CANA (2006). Final 2005 statistics and projections to the year 2025 [online]. Cremation Association of North America. Retrieved July 22, 2008, from http://www.cremationassociation.org/docs/CANA-Final06Prelim.pdf

Centre for Natural Burial (2008). [online]. Retrieved July 22, 2008, from http://www.naturalburial.coop

Clayden, A., & Dixon, K. (2007). Woodland burial: Memorial arboretum versus native woodland? *Mortality, 12*(3), 240–260.

Davies, D.J. (2004). *A brief history of death.* Oxford, England: Blackwell.

Davies, D.J., & Mates, L.H. (2005). *Encyclopaedia of cremation.* London: Ashgate.

DEFRA (2004). Secretary of State's guidance on crematoria. Process Guidance Note 5/2, issue 1, September [online]. Department for Environment, Food and Rural Affairs. Retrieved July 22, 2008, from http://www.defra.gov.uk/environment/ppc/localauth/pubs/guidance/notes/pgnotes/pdf/pg5-02.pdf

DEFRA (2005). Control of mercury emissions from crematoria, AQ1 (05) [online]. Department for Environment, Food and Rural Affairs. Retrieved July 22, 2008, from http://www.defra.gov.uk/environment/ppc/localauth/pubs/guidance/notes/aqnotes/aq01(05).htm

DEFRA (2006). Cremation temperature. AQ19 (06) Amendment of PG5/2 (04), [online]. Department for Environment, Food and Rural Affairs. Retrieved July 22, 2008, from http://www.defra.gov.uk/environment/ppc/localauth/pubs/guidance/notes/aqnotes/pdf/aq19-06.pdf

Dijkshoorn, J. (2008). Personal email communication to the authors.

Ebrery, P. (1990). Cremation in Sung China. *The American Historical Review, 95*(2), 406–428.

Environment Agency UK (2004). Assessing the groundwater pollution potential of cemetery developments [online]. Environment Agency UK. Retrieved July 22, 2008, from http://publications.environment-agency.gov.uk/pdf/SCHO0404BGLA-e-e.pdf

Facing Bereavement UK (2008). Burial at sea, [online]. Retrieved August 13, 2008, from http://www.facingbereavement.co.uk/BurialAtSea

Gabel, T., Mansfield, P., & Westbrook, K. (1996). The disposal of consumers: An exploratory analysis of death-related consumption. *Advances in Consumer Research*, 23(1), 361–367.

Gentry, J.W., Kennedy, P.F., Paul, K., & Hill, R.P. (1994). The vulnerability of those grieving the death of a loved one: Implications for public policy. *Journal of Public Policy and Marketing*, 13(2), 128–142.

ICCM (2008). Environmental issues affecting burial and cremation. *Charter for the bereaved* [online]. Institute of Cemetery and Crematoria Management. Retrieved July 22, 2008, from http://www.iccm-uk.com/downloads/Reference%20Charter.doc

Jones, S. (2008, April 29). Green baby-boomers, from cradle to grave. *The Guardian*, p. 9.

Jonker, G. (1996). The knife's edge: Muslim burial in the diaspora. *Mortality*, 1(1), 27–43.

Jupp, P.C. (1993). Cremation or burial? Contemporary choice in city and village. In D. Clark (Ed.), *The sociology of death: Theory, culture, practice* (pp.169–197). Oxford, England: Blackwell.

Kellaher, L., Prendergast, D., & Hockey, J. (2005). In the shadow of the traditional grave. *Mortality*, 10(4), 237–250.

Lash, J., & Wellington, F. (2007). Competitive advantage on a warming planet. *Harvard Business Review*, 85(3), 94–102.

Mitford, J. (1963). *The American way of death*. New York: Simon and Schuster.

Mitford, J. (1997). *The American way of death revisited*. New York: Virago.

Natural Death Centre (2008). [online]. Retrieved July 22, 2008, from http://www.naturaldeath.org.uk

O'Donohoe, S., & Turley, D. (2000). Dealing with death: Art, mortality and the marketplace. In S. Brown & A. Patterson (Eds.), *Imagining marketing: Art, aesthetics and the avant-garde* (pp. 86–106), London: Routledge.

O'Donohoe, S., & Turley, D. (2006). Compassion at the counter: Service providers and bereaved consumers. *Human Relations*, 59(10), 1429–1448.

Pancevski, B. (2008). Ashes from German cremations turn Lake Constance into 'lake of the dead'. Daily Telegraph Online. Retrieved April 18, 2009, from http://www.telegraph.co.uk/news/worldnews/europe/germany/2435926/Ashes-from-German-cremations-turn-Lake-Constance-into-lake-of-the-dead.html

People's Daily Online (2001, April 26). Chinese turn to new ways of burial. Retrieved June 10, 2008, from http://english.people.com.cn/200104/06/eng20010406_66968.html

Rugg, J. (2000). Defining the place of burial: What makes a cemetery a cemetery? *Mortality*, 5(3), 259–276.

Sea Services (2008). Direct burial [online]. Retrieved August 13, 2008, from http://www.seaservices.com/directburial.htm

Spennemann, D.H.R. (1999). No room for the dead. *Anthropos*, 94(1–3), 35–56.

Spongberg, A.L., & Becks, P.M. (2000). Inorganic soil contamination from cemetery leachate. *Water, Air and Soil Pollution*, 117(1–4), 313–327.

Sui, K.W.M. (2005). Culture and design: A new burial concept in a densely populated metropolitan area. *Design Issues*, 21(2), 79–89.

Turley, D. (1997). A postcard from the very edge: Mortality and marketing. In S. Brown & D. Turley (Eds.), *Consumer research: Postcards from the edge* (pp. 350–377). London: Routledge.

United Nations (2007). World population prospects: The 2006 revision population database [online]. 20th September. Retrieved June 18, 2008, from http://esa.un.org/unpp/p2k0data.asp

Walter, T. (1993). Dust not ashes. The American preference for burial. *Landscape*, 32(1), 42–48.

Walter, T. (1996). Keep on listening: The neo-modern management of death. In G. Howarth & P.C. Jupp (Eds.), *Contemporary issues in the sociology of death, dying and disposal* (pp. 149–163). New York: St. Martins Press.

Walter, T. (2005). Three ways to arrange a funeral: Mortuary variation in the modern West. *Mortality*, 10(3), 173–192.

Wienrich, S., & Speyer, J. (2003). *The natural death handbook* (4th ed.). London: Random House.

# Researching consumers in multicultural societies: Emerging methodological issues*

Stephanie Slater, *Cardiff University, UK*
Mirella Yani-de-Soriano, *Cardiff University, UK*

**Abstract** The paper presents a critical review of the main studies in cross-cultural consumer behaviour and marketing research, and identifies the methodological issues that frequently undermine the quality of research in this area. The paper offers suggestions for addressing these issues, which are becoming even more complex due to growing Internet-based marketing research and increasingly multicultural societies. The authors discuss the relevance of cross-cultural marketing research and the challenges associated with it in the context of a changing global environment, and explain how, by understanding and addressing these concerns, marketers will be able to achieve superior marketing research findings through improved validity of results.

## Introduction

In order to understand the methodological problems associated with cross-cultural marketing research, the relationship between research design and culture needs to be investigated. All too often scholars and practitioners highlight the importance of understanding culture when making marketing decisions, but fail to take account of cultural differences when they design their marketing research project.

We know that the theories and models relating to marketing and consumer behaviour have been mainly developed in an Anglo-Saxon context, notably the United States and the UK. However, these theories have rarely been tested in cultures having different languages and traditions and confronted with diverse environmental conditions, such as Asia, Africa, and Latin America. The reason for the lack of this type of research lies fundamentally in the difficulties arising when any method or theory in the behavioural sciences is applied outside its area of origin (Brislin, Lonner, & Thorndike, 1973). Boddewyn (1981) provides clear evidence for this argument in his study of the first 25 years of comparative marketing. He found that in consumer behaviour studies, researchers used the research designs tested in the United States without taking into consideration the circumstances particular to other cultures.

During the 1980s, a healthy trend towards asserting the generalisability of the existing consumer behaviour theories and findings emerged in the United States. During this period, most theory-based empirical consumer behaviour studies involved testing of the external validity of findings (Aulakh & Kotabe, 1992). This trend continued into the 1990s. Cross-cultural marketing research gained great importance due to the globalisation of marketing activities and the cross-cultural use of advertisements (Malhotra, Agarwal, & Peterson, 1996; Manrai & Manrai, 1996). Nevertheless, at the end of this decade, the number of studies in cross-cultural marketing research remained limited (Sin, Cheung, & Lee, 1999).

In the twenty-first century, the role of cross-cultural marketing research has become increasingly critical in guiding business decision making. The increased pace of globalisation and the dramatic advancements in technology are creating new challenges for firms and researchers. From a managerial point of view, firms need to understand the cultural variation between countries and cultures to be able to devise sound marketing strategies based on these variations if they are to succeed in the global marketplace (Craig & Douglas, 2001; Malhotra, 2001). From a theoretical perspective, researchers need to conduct cross-cultural marketing research to establish the validity and generalisability of marketing and consumer behaviour theories and models. The argument that it is crucial to establish whether a theory or model can be used outside its area of origin has been raised for many years and in a number of studies. More than 40 years ago, Whiting (1968) argued that since most sociopsychological studies were undertaken within the framework of Western European cultures, it was not possible to be certain whether the discovered relationships were universally valid.

In the last 20 years, significant progress has been made regarding conceptual/theoretical issues and empirical findings. Methodologically, however, recurrent and emerging issues are a key concern. To enable comparability of data and measurement equivalence, scholars need to establish a framework for evaluating the validity and rigour of data. This is paramount so that we can better understand and address the problems of conducting business and marketing research in global markets, which are often characterised by increasingly multicultural societies.

The objective of this paper is to draw closer attention to the main methodological issues confronting cross-cultural marketing research and the need to address them competently, since failure to do so could lead to confounding alternative explanations, limiting the usefulness of the marketing research project (Malhotra et al., 1996). The paper starts with a discussion of the two major general concerns in cross-cultural research and moves on to discuss more specific issues, both recurrent, which are unsolved or simply ignored, and emergent. The paper provides guidelines for addressing these problems. A summary of the main methodological concerns is presented in Table 1.

## The cultural context

This section discusses the two major general concerns in cross-cultural research: the emic–etic issue and the independence of sample issue. These are important problems that are closely connected and need to be considered if methodological developments in cross-cultural research are to demonstrate cross-cultural generalisability.

**Table 1** Literature review summary of cross-cultural methodological concerns.

| Methodological concern | Rationale | Key studies |
| --- | --- | --- |
| Cultural dimension | Highlights differences in social values and culture and provide us with an explanation as to why companies who wish to exploit market potential need to consider cross-cultural influence. | Chang (2003); Chong and Park (2003); Geletkanycz (1997); Hofstede (1980, 1991); Malhotra (2001); McCort and Malhotra (1993); Saka (2004); Trompenaars and Hampden Turner (1997); |
| Generalisability | To achieve generalisability of existing psychological knowledge, theory, laws and propositions. | Berry (1980); Berry, Poortinga, Segall, and Dasen (1992); Evans et al. (2004); Haeckel (2001); Mitchell (2001); Sekran (1983); Triandis (1980); Triandis, Malpass, and Davidson (1972); Woodside (2005) |
| Comparability | To ensure valid comparisons of datasets across countries/cultures. | Aulakh and Kotabe (1992); Bhalla and Lin (1987); Boddewyn (1981); Douglas and Craig (1983, 2007); Malhotra (2001) |
| Metric equivalence | The psychometric properties of two or more data sets from two or more cultural groups exhibit essentially the same coherence of structure. | Berry (1980); Davis, Douglas, and Silk (1981); Heeler and Ray (1972); Sekaran (1983) |
| Functional equivalence | Similar activities should have similar functions in different societies if parameters are comparable. | Berry et al. (1992); Soriano and Foxall (2002) |
| Conceptual equivalence | Subjects need to have an equal understanding or interpretation of the meaning of behaviour, product, or stimuli. | Barnard (1982); Berry (1980); Brislin, Lonner, and Thorndike (1973); Streiner and Norman (1995); Malhotra et al. (1996); Small et al. (1999) |
| Translation equivalence | The scales and other verbal stimuli should be translated so that they can be understood in different cultures and have equivalent meaning. | |
| Response bias | The instrument should produce answers that are free of response set bias. | Baumgartner and Steenkamp (2001); Caruanna et al. (1998); Heide and Gronhaug (1992) |
| Return rate | Internet survey return rate could be lower than traditional methods as respondents become more apathetic to these studies. | Backmann et al. (2000) |

*(Continued)*

**Table I.** (Continued)

| Methodological concern | Rationale | Key studies |
| --- | --- | --- |
| Ethical issues in preventing subject fraud | Subject fraud can be avoided by installing cookies. in respondents' browsers or by using passwords, but these practices would compromise confidentiality and anonymity (unethical). | Siah (2005) |
| Sample representation | Respondents not representative of target population. | Spyridakis et al. (2005) |
| Multicultural issues | Research in multicultural contexts should be sensitive to groups' ethnic or racial differences to understand better the meaning of their consumption behaviour. | Cleveland and Laroche (2007); Fletcher (2006); Jamal (2003); Nevid and Sta. Maria (1999); Villegas and Shah (2005); |
| Emerging issues in international research | Emerging issues in cross-cultural marketing research, particularly in developing environments. | Craig and Douglas (2001); Malhotra and Peterson (2001); Stening and Zhang (2007) |

### The emic–etic issue

Cross-cultural research has two objectives. One is to describe a culture by studying specific behaviours or concepts from within such culture; this is the emic approach. The other objective aims at theory building, that is, to make generalisations across cultures that take into account all human behaviour; this is the etic approach (Berry, 1990; Douglas & Craig, 1983; Triandis, Malpass, & Davidson, 1971). The importance of comparative marketing studies is that they have the potential for enriching the understanding of what marketing is all about by helping to refine and check the generality of our existing marketing concepts, hypotheses, and theories (Berry, 1980; Boddewyn, 1981). Triandis (1980, p. 3) stated that 'it is imperative to establish cross-cultural generalities in order to understand whatever cultural differences are observed'. When researchers apply an etic approach, they are imposing constructs developed in one culture to all cultures (Berry, 1990; Douglas & Craig, 1983; Triandis et al., 1971). When constructs are imposed in this way, they are referred to as the 'imposed etic' (Berry, 1969, 1990) or 'pseudo etic' (Triandis et al., 1971). This is the case when theories and models developed in the United States are applied outside their area of origin. The problem is that the concepts that are been tested may have different meanings in non-Western cultures. A derived etic approach is essential to enable understanding of cultural variations, and it is achieved when researchers adapt their constructs to fit the relevant culture under study (emic approach) (Rogoff, 2003).

Personal construct theory (Kelly, 1955) offers support to the claim that individuals perceive their environment differently and that this has implications for construct elicitation. Translation from one language to another may not mean that words are perceived by the recipient as having the same meaning. Etic characteristics have also been found to influence behavioural intent. For example, Triandis et al. (1971, p. 30) describe the way 'superordination–subordination' mimic behaviours that show status whereas 'intimacy–formality' are symbolic of interpersonal familiarity. In cultures such as Japan, status has historically been influenced by Confucian philosophy (Chen, 1995) and will therefore impact on the way Japanese society perceive and respond to certain questionnaire constructs. Cultural variables impact on scale reliability. The meaning associated with the data set in question becomes invalid because of differences in the way the two cultures associate meaning.

The emic–etic dilemma asks whether behaviour has to be understood in the context of the culture in which it occurs (emic approach) or whether cultural differences can be conceived of as variations of a common or universal theme (etic approach) (Berry, 1990; Douglas & Craig, 1983; Triandis et al., 1971). The emic–etic dilemma continues to challenge the field of psychology by posing the central question on how generalisable psychological findings are (Lonner, 1999). It also raises important questions about the design of a measurement tool that has universal application across the cultures under investigation. A number of papers address this problem, offering potential solutions.

Osgood suggests one way of dealing with semantic differentials is to use a universal construct and then use emic constructs to measure it (Osgood, 1965; Triandis et al., 1971, p. 7). Tucker (1966) also offers a potential solution to the emic–etic dilemma. He proposed that one way to alleviate bias is to adopt a three-mode factor analysis to study the intercorrelation patterns of sample respondents. The emic–etic approach requires 'respondent factors' to be analysed as part of the research process, as this provides the researcher with information that functions to identify the behavioural orientation of respondents (Triandis et al., 1971).

Another solution to the emic–etic apparent contradiction suggests that the emic approach could become a rich potential source for understanding the etic underpinnings in cross-cultural research, that is, formulating universalistic theories and hypotheses that can be tested. This presupposes that each culture is not so unique that comparison among cultures is futile or totally meaningless (Sekaran, 1983, p. 65). Finally, Berry (1990) suggests combining the two approaches rather than applying emic dimensions of one culture to other cultures, which requires researchers to get familiar with the relevant differences in each culture, putting aside their own cultural biases (Berry, 1990).

Whilst there is no 'one size fits all' approach to address the emic–etic issue, if cross-national etic factors and culture-specific emic factors are not given appropriate attention in the design process, data interpretation is likely to yield results that lack meaning. When rigour and relevance are lost, the value of the issues under examination becomes questionable. The next section discusses another major concern in cross-cultural research – the independence of sample issue.

## The independence of sample issue

The cultural studies conducted by scholars such as Hofstede (1980, 1991) and Trompenaars and Hampden-Turner (1997) highlight differences in social values and culture, and provide us with an explanation of why companies who wish to exploit market potential at a global level need to consider cross-cultural influence. However, independence of samples in relevant cultures represents another major challenge for cross-cultural researchers. The problem happens when values and behaviours become transfused among cultures to the degree that it is difficult to differentiate the emic from the etic (Sekaran, 1983). This problem is particularly relevant in the present age of globalisation and rapid technological advances, as people around the globe have been adopting similar values and behaviours (Nasif, Al-Daeaj, Ebrahimi, & Thibodeaux, 1991). The borders among cultures are becoming blurred due to cultural diffusion (or cultural convergence), and therefore the samples taken from different cultures might not be independent, leading to biased results (Yeganeh, Su, & Chrysostome, 2004).

Sir Francis Galton was one of the first scholars to question the validity of statistical inference from cross-cultural surveys (Naroll, 1961; Strauss et al., 1995; Tylor, 1889). His case was based on the non-independence of observations in the sample, leading to spurious correlation because of autocorrelation. Galton argued that if sample independence could not be achieved or methods of correction were not applied, then the research findings were of no value. The non-independence of observations in this and other non-experimental questionnaire-based research became known as Galton's problem.

In the context of cross-cultural research relating to heredity, Galton argued that the cultural similarity observed in a sample could be related to cultural diffusion. For instance, asking two people from the same family the same question does not provide the researcher with responses that are statistically independent. Similarly, cross-cultural sample clusters may not control for factors such as borrowing and common descent. Galton's problem is that the issue of sample group independence is essential for valid cross-cultural research, but is never achievable in practice. Galton's problem, therefore, is often cited as a criticism of empirical comparative studies of culture: the results are inherently uninterpretable. It undermines all cross-cultural research, forcing researchers to make important methodological decisions.

Whilst a number of scholars agree with the need to achieve sample group independence, there are conflicting views as to whether or not Galton's problem is solvable. A number of studies have put forward solutions, arguing that by using appropriate method design techniques, it is possible to control for diffusion (Denton, 2007; Naroll, 1961; Naroll & D'Andrade, 1963; Schaffer & Riordan, 2003; Strauss et al., 1975; Vandenberg & Lance, 2000). The Bimodal Sift method (Naroll, 1961) and the Interval Sift method (Naroll & D'Andrade, 1963) propose two solutions to the problem. These methods allow the researcher to treat the sample as independent 'once the validity of the sift' has been confirmed. The cluster method (Naroll & D'Andrade, 1961, p. 1054) and the matched pair method (Naroll & D'Andrade, 1961, p. 1054), whilst 'statistically less flexible' than the sifting methods, offer an alternative. They constitute a fairly 'rigorous way' (Naroll & D'Andrade, 1961, p. 1054) of measuring diffusion because they enable the researcher to distinguish between both the functional and historical associations of the culture and yield information about the importance of each association.

Galton's original studies were important because they introduced the importance of sample independence in cross-cultural surveys. However, future cross-cultural research needs to extend the issues raised by Galton in the context of a global marketing environment. A key challenge for the future is how diffusion might be measured in multicultural societies. The issues that emerge from acculturation and the globalisation of consumer behaviour mean that culture may no longer be an appropriate unit of analysis for 'cross-cultural' surveys. The next section discusses the main methodological issues confronting cross-cultural marketing research and offers suggestions for addressing them.

## The issue of comparability of data and measurement equivalence

While the paper by Malhotra et al. (1996) offers an excellent account of the methodological issues associated with cross-cultural marketing, the approach is somewhat biased towards survey techniques that use numbers and can therefore demonstrate statistical relevance. A key observation of the Malhotra et al. paper is the North American emphasis that is associated with the manuscript's research orientation. In fairness to the authors, the emphasis on North America was probably more a reflection of when the paper was written than of the author's intention to restrict sample randomness to a certain geographical region. Nevertheless, the point is worthy of attention now that current marketing theory and business decisions have become more global in their market orientation.

The issue of comparability is critical to cross-cultural research. Comparability has been defined by Douglas and Craig (1983, pp. 131–132) as 'data that have, as far as possible, the same meaning, interpretation, and the same level of accuracy, precision of measurement and reliability in all countries and cultures'. They add that 'comparability of data is important irrespective of whether research is conducted in a single country, for it is important to bear in mind that research relating to a similar problem may subsequently be conducted in another country'. Bhalla and Lin (1987) concurred with these authors in that the need for comparability is a key issue confronting marketing researchers, regardless of whether the research is conducted in one country or a number of countries simultaneously.

The major methodological challenges of cross-cultural research have been underscored by Sekaran (1983) to ensure functional equivalence, problems of instrumentation, data-collection methods, sampling design issues, and data analysis. Likewise, Parameswaran and Yaprak (1987) acknowledged the need to establish construct, functional, conceptual, instrument, translation, and sampling equivalence of research measures in cross-cultural research before inferring statistical and practical conclusions. Although 'comparability' and 'equivalence' are often used interchangeably, comparability is the more generic term; equivalence refers more precisely to measurement. Lack of data equivalence could lead to wrong conclusions. Observed differences in measures might be attributed to true differences in the latent variables, although they are solely caused by differential response behaviour; or true differences might be masked by differential response behaviour and thus remain undetected, causing an uncontrollable increase in type one and type two errors (Salzberger & Sinkovics, 2006, p. 392).

### Functional equivalence

Functional equivalence refers to the fact that similar activities should have similar functions in different societies if their parameters are to be compared. According to Sekaran (1983, p. 62), 'valid cross-cultural behaviour comparisons can be made only when the behaviour in question has developed in the different cultures in response to similar problems shared by the different social or cultural groups'. For instance, bicycles are used in the Netherlands as a means of transportation, whereas in Venezuela they are used primarily for recreation or sport. In this case, functional equivalence cannot be achieved because the goals of behaviour towards the same product are different across these two cultures.

## Conceptual equivalence

Conceptual equivalence refers to the fact that subjects have an equal understanding or interpretation of the meaning of behaviour, product, or marketing stimuli. As an example, price markdowns are regular events in the United States. However, they might be seen with suspicion by consumers in developing countries. Similarly, Soriano and Foxall (2002) found that saving-up behaviour in Venezuela and England was conceptually non-equivalent. While saving up is seen as a positive behaviour in England, in Venezuela, due to high levels of inflation, it is seen negatively or as a not-desired behaviour.

Due to these types of problems, Berry, Poortinga, Segall, & Dasen (1992, p. 237) have suggested that 'a close scrutiny of each stimulus is necessary to identify positive peculiarities in meaning or other reasons that a stimulus might be inappropriate in a particular culture and should not be used'. Furthermore, problems of conceptual equivalence are not limited to countries with different languages, but they also affect countries who share the same language. Therefore, this paper argues against the practice of directly transferring an instrument developed in the UK to the United States or from Spain to Latin America, for example. Instead, it is vital to make necessary adjustments and pretests, despite the common language base. Clinton and Calantone (1996) found conceptual problems between English-speaking countries. Equally, it is important to note that cross-cultural research issues are not limited to research in different countries but can arise in research within the same country. Advertising studies on African American and white Americans highlighted major differences in the way these two groups perceived and reacted to advertising campaigns (Bush, Smith, & Martin, 1999). A study by Soley and Reid (1983) showed similar findings. African Americans were more satisfied with the advertising content that was presented in TV commercials and magazines than white Americans. Given that the two groups were not separated by languages or significant distances, we can conclude that the differences observed were more distinctly cultural, rather than linguistic or geographical. Given that countries around the world are becoming increasingly multicultural, this problem receives special attention in the emerging methodological issues section of this paper.

## Translation equivalence

A way to operationalise conceptual equivalence is to test for translation equivalence. This can be achieved using translation and back translation of instruments (Brislin et al., 1973). Berry (1980, p. 10) explained translation equivalence as 'a technique which involves an initial translation to a target language by one bilingual person, and a back translation to the original language by another; discrepancies will often indicate the presence of conceptual non-equivalence'. Sekaran (1983) has added that the equivalence of source and target version of the instrument can be ensured with good back translations conducted by people who should be not only proficient with the different languages involved but are also familiar with the cultures in question and with the usage of the concepts and their meanings in such cultures. The problem of translation equivalence (linguistic) is a difficult one as some linguistic concepts do not translate directly into other tongues and important nuances of meanings can be put at risk (Barnard, 1982). Erkut, Alarcon, Garcia-Coll, Tropp, and Vazquez-Garcia (1999) suggest a concept-driven rather than translation-driven approach to creating bilingual measures, which requires a bilingual/bicultural research team with indigenous researchers from the cultures being studied, in order to reduce researchers' cultural bias and achieve both conceptual and linguistic equivalence.

## Metric equivalence

Metric equivalence exists when psychometric properties of two or more sets of data from two or more cultural groups exhibit essentially the same coherence of structure. There are two requirements for this type of equivalence: first, that statistical relationships remain fairly constant among independent and dependent variables; second, that statistical relationships among dependent variables should be patterned similarly in two or more cultural groups before comparisons are allowed. Similarity in correlation matrices or common factor structures can serve to demonstrate this type of equivalence (Berry, 1980, p. 10). Metric equivalence, however, is no guarantee of invariance. Byrne and Campbell (1999) have warned against the presumption of equivalent measurement and theoretical structure in cross-cultural comparisons because although the factorial structure of an instrument may replicate across cultures, this is no guarantee that the item measurements and theoretical structure are invariant across groups. They showed that, in fact, item score data can vary across cultures, despite measurements from an instrument for which the factorial structure has been equivalently specified in each group. Therefore, researchers and practitioners should also question the philosophical and conceptual appropriateness of an instrument that has been developed in a culture that differs from the one in which it is to be used.

Fontaine, Poortinga, Delbeke, and Schwartz (2008, p. 363) emphasise that researchers need to interpret equivalent measurements appropriately, arguing that 'such an assessment is more than a technical, psychometric exercise'. Based on their findings from evaluating the structural equivalence of the values domain across 38 countries, they demonstrated that patterns of non-equivalence are not sampling fluctuations, but can be attributed to meaningful variations, which generate insights into the relationship between the structure of the values domain and other aspects of society and culture. One of their findings revealed that the size of the structural deviations related more strongly to societal development in the teacher than in the student samples, which means that it is critical to include non-student samples in cross-cultural research studies.

# Complementary approaches to improve comparability

## Pretests

In addition to the methods already discussed, other approaches should be applied to improve comparability of data, including pretests, sample equivalence, sampling methods, and data-collection procedures. Brislin et al. (1973) state that multiple techniques should be used in all cross-cultural research, since the back translation as a single method is no panacea; all materials should be pretested with respondents similar to those of the proposed main sample, since there will always be items that simply do not work well in actual use (Brislin, 1986, p. 161). Douglas and Craig (2007) found that, in marketing, back translation is still, by far, the main method used to check translation accuracy. Because the translation process is complex, a single back translation does not ensure a valid and reliable instrument in the target language, since the objective is not that the words translate literally but that they have the same meaning across cultures. Therefore, a team approach is required to minimise bias. Unfortunately, although the use of pretests is particularly useful in cross-cultural research, it is not widely being employed, with less than one-third of studies conducted between 1993 and 2005 shown to have used it (Douglas & Craig, 2007).

### Sample equivalence

It is important to achieve sample equivalence, given that homogeneity of the sample reduces alternative explanations of the results (Lonner & Berry, 1986) and therefore the sample should be chosen to maximise equivalence rather than, for example, representativity. Sample equivalence can be satisfied if respondents in each study share similar demographic and socio-economic characteristics. However, Sin et al. (1999) warns that unless the researcher knows well the cultures under study, sometimes subjects coming from the same sampling frame may not guarantee sampling equivalence, such as in the case of undergraduate students. In addition, sample equivalence facilitates neutral response styles and validates cross-national comparisons between countries. One problem with this type of study is that it ignores the potential cumulative effect of efforts when targeting behaviour and leads to ethnocentric evaluations (Triandis et al., 1971). It can be argued that in the Hong Kong American study, dependent variables of interest might well be factored out when using differential sampling systems. For these reasons whilst scholars need to eliminate non-equivalence variables, methodological design procedures need to ensure that when controlling for non-equivalence researchers do not neutralise the key variables of interest to users of the research given an important aim of market research is to probe for market differences.

### Sampling methods and data-collection procedures

Sampling methods and procedures for data collection are also essential aspects in improving comparability of data. In some developed countries, particularly in the United States where consumer research is a major function of business, the collection of data tends to be highly professional. However, this is not true in developing countries, where, in addition to the lack of a research tradition, cultural factors play an important role in the collection of information. This includes attitudes towards security and privacy (e.g. people are wary of strangers and might not feel comfortable providing information about themselves) and issues of accessibility (e.g. boundary walls).

Quota sampling in marketing research has been used widely both in developed and developing countries (Malhotra & Peterson, 2001) and can be combined with other methods. Webster (1966) studied five Western European countries, employing probability sampling in four countries from readily available lists, and quota sampling in one country where random sampling needed the purchase of a special list at a very high price. She argued quota sampling could produce acceptably correct and meaningful results comparable with those obtained by probability sampling in other countries, and that sameness of method of collection by no means assures comparable data for analysis. Webster (1966) stated that data are comparable if they have the same degree of reliability and one has used the most efficient rather than the same method of data collection in each country.

Dunn (1974) extended Webster's (1966) arguments by pointing out that if the local alternative methods are all equally good, one should use the same methods in one or more countries, but if they may lead to some bias, one might deliberately choose different methods to check whether and how potential bias operates. A crucial point has been made by Osgood, May, and Miron (1975) in that the purpose of the research determines the sampling strategy, that is, whether the investigator wants representativeness within each country or equivalence across countries. They warn that maximising representativeness within a country usually means minimising equivalence between countries and vice versa. In a cross-cultural study, it is possible to use one method such as quota sampling in a developing country, and another method such as a random walk in a developed country. An advantage is achieved when comparing results between the two studies, as 'the differences in sampling methods can also be utilised to provide a check on the reliability of results and the potential bias inherent in different methods' (Douglas & Craig, 1983, p. 219). If different methods in different countries produce similar results, it means that the measurement instrument utilised is reliable. Hence, it may be not only possible but also desirable to use different sampling techniques in different countries to achieve sample equivalence and representativeness (Malhotra & Peterson, 2001). This is particularly relevant today, as marketing researchers must develop the capability to conduct research that spans diverse research environments to benefit from growth opportunities outside developed countries (Craig & Douglas, 2001).

## Emerging trends and methodological issues

### Internet-based research

The accelerated growth of the Internet has opened many new opportunities for academic and marketing research reaching populations all around the world. Research has shown that web surveys and experiments are faster, easier, cheaper, and more flexible compared to traditional methods (McCullough, 1998; Pitkow & Recker, 1995). However, there are methodological and ethical issues that must be addressed if the medium is to provide meaningful information. The main issues include sampling and generalisability of results, participant behaviour (such as drop-out rates for panels, incomprehension, response set bias, low response rate, and subject fraud), data integrity (e.g. caused by technical problems), and ethics (keeping privacy, anonymity, confidentiality, and avoiding stress related to sensitive questions).

The Internet, as a research device, is growing, and the quality of the research depends on the perceived credibility and trust both participants and researchers have in this medium (Montgomery & Richie, 2002; Siah, 2005; Spyridakis, Wei, Barrick, Cuddihy, & Maust, 2005).

There is a lack of consensus on the pre-eminence of the Internet as a research medium in the future. Wilson and Laskey (2003) found that most of the companies in the UK had used online studies in the previous year, but only as an additional supporting methodology rather than as a substitute to traditional approaches in certain special types of research (e.g., website evaluation). They also found that research companies had concerns about the weaknesses already mentioned, in particular, the issue of representativeness, given the nature of Internet sample frames.

Recent research in social marketing studying UK adolescents argues that Internet-based research has the potential to generate data that are comparable to those generated by conventional research methods and with improved efficiency in terms of time, cost, quality, and quantity of responses (De Meyrick, 2007). Tingling, Parent, and Wade (2003) believe that the Internet survey is an under-exploited resource, arguing that it can be used to reduce potential bias by randomly assigning choices along the screen and/or by generating more complex randomised display patterns than allowed in paper surveys. The Internet offers a whole new way of engaging with consumers. It is therefore not surprising that in twenty-first century marketing, well-known brands such as British Airways, Philips, and $O_2$ are launching their own community websites to engage consumers and gauge their responses to new products, designs, and advertisements (Benady, 2008). However, website content, design, and structure needs to take into account cultural sensitivity to improve its communication effectiveness both at global and multicultural levels (Fletcher, 2006).

### Diverse marketing-research contexts

Technological advances improve the basic infrastructure of developing nations opening up new marketing opportunities for global companies. Emerging economies such as China and India offer immense market potential. Marketing researchers need a clear understanding of these potential markets in order to be able to conduct valid research studies. They should also be careful not to interpret and generalise results based on their own cultural experience in developed countries. Chinese, for example, think in a holistic way, whilst Westerners think in an analytical way (Needham, 1978; Nisbet, 2003) posing a challenge to data interpretation (Stening & Zhang, 2007). Consumer behaviour needs to be studied and interpreted by researchers from the culture being studied, who deeply understand the context of consumption.

### The global and multicultural perspectives of consumer behaviour research

The twenty-first century is seeing a growing trend towards more countries becoming increasingly ethnically diverse. For example, citizens in the United States and the UK are multicultural in their ethnicity. Although there is a great emphasis on international marketing, little research has been conducted to understand diversity within a specific country (Nevid & Sta. Maria, 1999). Cleveland and Laroche (2007) argue that it is no longer appropriate to use countries as the cultural unit of analysis or market segmentation, since most of the world's countries are already highly multicultural. Globalisation thus seems to reduce the homogeneity of consumer behaviour within countries, while increasing commonalities across the globe.

Findings from recent multicultural research have shown interesting results. Two Hispanic groups (Cuban American and Mexican American), which traditionally have been treated as one group, have shown differences affecting advertising effectiveness (Villegas & Shah, 2005). Jamal (2003) found groups of different ethnic backgrounds in the UK engage in culture swapping to taste different cultures. This could cause a traditional ethnic segmentation approach ineffective, as consumers do not conform to any one specific segment.

## Summary and conclusions

This paper presents a critical review of the main studies in cross-cultural consumer behaviour and marketing research. It identifies both recurrent and emerging methodological issues, which are often undermining the quality of research, and offers suggestions for addressing these issues. The main thesis of the paper is the heightened importance of this area of research in twenty-first century marketing, characterised by an increased pace of globalisation, the exponential growth of the

Internet, diversity of marketing-research contexts, and growing multicultural societies. The paper is an attempt to encourage researchers towards a more sensitive awareness of the methodological issues associated with cross-cultural research design both at the global context and within individual multicultural societies such as the UK and the United States. We argue that by understanding and addressing these issues, it is possible to achieve superior marketing research findings through improved validity of results.

A major criticism of cross-cultural studies in the area of consumer behaviour is that researchers transfer theories, conceptual frameworks, and models from one culture to another without previous appropriate validation. A key issue in the cross-cultural discussion is whether behaviour should be understood in the cultural context in which it takes place (emic approach) or whether cultural differences can be thought of as variations of a universal theme (etic approach). Galton's problem recognised that sample group independence is central to cross-cultural research but is never achievable. Particularly problematic is the issue of cultural diffusion (or cultural convergence) taking place today and how to minimise the bias it can introduce in research.

In the present study, we found that although in the last 20 years significant progress has been made regarding conceptual/theoretical issues and empirical findings in cross-cultural marketing research, recurrent and emerging methodological issues are a key concern. Despite the increasing recognition of the need to demonstrate cross-cultural generalisability of theories and findings, applying a conceptual framework and research design outside its original context continues to be challenging. This is because of the comparability issues that surround all consumer research, and today's global environment and multicultural societies, which present new opportunities, as well as challenges.

The paper highlights the main methodological difficulties concerning cross-cultural research in a changing global environment and discusses how they can be overcome. Data comparability is of uttermost importance if scholars are to ascertain cross-cultural research is to be useful. We argue that this can be achieved by ensuring various types of data equivalence (conceptual, functional, translation, and metric) and by employing other complementary approaches to improve comparability (sample equivalence, pretests, appropriate sampling methods, and procedures for data collection). A strong emphasis should be placed on pretesting and the researcher's judgement to detect response set bias and other threats to measurement equivalence. Consequently, it seems plausible for scholars to consider a method design that encapsulates the use of multiple methods. This approach widens the degree of interpretation that can be attached to the research findings because method design focuses on generating datasets of measurement equivalence (Horn & McArdle, 1992; Vandenberg, 2002).

Cross-cultural research has become problematic, as many approach the design without proper foundation. Greater attention to measurement constructs will enable marketers to achieve superior research through improved cross-cultural research design. Concentrating on cultural variation-sensitive methodologies for market research will enable marketers to become more aware of cultural diversity. The next profitable direction for cross-cultural research requires measurement constructs to combine etic and emic indicators given the significance of cultural variation. This approach offers an opportunity for researchers to improve scale items and re-evaluate the way marketing research theory is built and enacted in globalised and multi-cultural environments.

The growth of the e-commerce industry has increased the complexity associated with conducting cross-cultural studies. Internet research techniques are now, for some companies, the dominant medium through which they conduct their marketing research. The Internet raises distinctive cross-cultural and equivalence issues whilst it mitigates some of the problems outlined with some of the traditional techniques, such as sample equivalence.

Twenty-first century marketing research should enable companies to take advantage of emerging opportunities in a fast-changing and increasingly diverse marketplace in both the global and local contexts. Advances in technology facilitate but make more complex the collection of data at the global level. Future research directions in consumer research need to be more inclusive of people of different racial and ethnic backgrounds in order to be able to understand ethnic differences in relation to norms, attitudes, cultural expectations, and acculturation status, which can have an effect on consumer behaviour, and important implications for marketing strategy.

## Acknowledgements

The authors are grateful to the editor(s) and the reviewers for their invaluable suggestions, support, and extensive feedback during the writing of this manuscript. They would also like to thank Martin Evans and Professor Mike Wallace for the constructive criticism they offered on earlier drafts.

## References

Aulakh, P.S., & Kotabe, M. (1992). An assessment of the theoretical and methodological developments in international marketing: 1980–1990. *Journal of International Marketing, 1*(2), 5–28.

Backmann, D.P., Elfrink, J., & Vazzana, G. (2000). E-mail and snail mail face off in rematch. *Marketing Research, 11*(4), 10–15.

Barnard, P. (1982). Conducting and co-ordinating multi-country quantitative studies across Europe. *Journal of the Market Research Society, 24,* 46–64.

Baumgartner, H., & SteenKamp, J.B.E.M. (2001). Response styles in marketing research: A cross-national investigation. *Journal of Marketing Research, 38,* 143–156.

Benady, D. (2008, April 3). Online market research: In search of an honest opinion. *Marketing Week,* p. 31.

Berry, J.W. (1969). On cross-cultural comparability. *International Journal of Psychology, 4,* 119–128.

Berry, J.W. (1980). Introduction to methodology. In H.C. Triandis & J.W. Berry (Eds.), *Handbook of cross-cultural psychology* (Vol. 2, pp. 1–28). Boston: Allyn and Bacon.

Berry, J.W. (1990). Imposed etics, emics and derived emics: Their conceptual and operational status in cross-cultural psychology. In T.N. Headland & M. Harris (Eds.), *Emics and etics: The insider/outsider debate* (pp. 84–89). Newbury Park, CA: Sage.

Berry, J.W., Poortinga, Y.H., Segall, M.H., & Dasen, P.R. (1992). *Cross-cultural psychology: Research and applications.* Cambridge, England: Cambridge University Press.

Bhalla, G., & Lin, L. (1987). Cross-cultural marketing research: A discussion of equivalence issues and measurement strategies. *Psychology and Marketing, 4*(4), 275–285.

Boddewyn, J. (1981). Comparative marketing: The first twenty-five years. *Journal of International Business Studies, 12,* 61–79.

Brislin, R.W. (1986). The wording and translation of research instruments. In W.J. Lonner & J.W. Berry (Eds.), *Field methods in cross-cultural research* (Vol. 8, pp. 137–164). Cross-cultural Research and Methodology Series. Beverley Hills, CA: Sage.

Brislin, R.W., Lonner, W.J., & Thorndike, R.M. (1973). *Cross-cultural research methods.* New York: John Wiley.

Bush, A.J., Smith, R., & Martin, C. (1999). The influence of consumer socialisation variables on attitudes toward advertising: A comparison of African-Americans and Caucasians. *Journal of Advertising, 28*(3), 13–24.

Byrne, B.M., & Campbell, T.L. (1999). Cross-cultural comparisons and the presumption of equivalent measurement and theoretical structure: A look beneath the surface. *Journal of Cross-Cultural Psychology, 30*(5), 555–574.

Caruanna, A., Ramaseshan, B., Ewing, M.T., & Rouhani, F. (1998). Expectations about management consultancy services: Testing the assumption of equivalence across Australian and Singaporean Firms. *Journal of Professional Services Marketing, 18*(1), 1–10.

Chang, L.C. (2003). An examination of cross-cultural negotiation: Using Hofstede framework. *Journal of American Academy of Business, 2*(2), 567–570.

Chen, M. (1995). *Asian management systems: Chinese, Japanese and Korean styles of business.* London: Routledge.

Chong, J.K.S., & Park, J. (2003). National culture and classical principles of planning. *Cross-Cultural Management: An International Journal, 10*(1), 29–39.

Cleveland, M., & Laroche, M. (2007). Acculturation to the global consumer culture: Scale development and research paradigm. *Journal of Business Research, 60*(3), 249–259.

Clinton, S.R., & Calantone, R.J. (1996). Logistics strategy: Does it travel well? *International Marketing Review, 13*(5), 98–112.

Craig, C.S., & Douglas, S.P. (2001). Conducting international marketing research in the twenty-first century. *International Marketing Review, 18*(1), 80–90.

Davis, H.L., Douglas, S.P., & Silk, A.J. (1981). Measure unreliability: A hidden threat to cross-national marketing research? *Journal of Marketing, 45,* 98–109.

De Meyrick, J. (2007). The Internet in social marketing research. *Journal of Nonprofit and Public Sector Marketing, 17*(1/2), 103–120.

Denton, T. (2007). Yet another solution to Galton's problem. *Cross-cultural Research, 41*(1), 32–45.

Douglas, S.P., & Craig, C.S. (1983). *International marketing research.* Englewood Cliffs, NJ: Prentice-Hall.

Douglas, S.P., & Craig, C.S. (2007). Collaborative and iterative translation: An alternative approach to back translation. *Journal of International Marketing, 15*(1), 30–43.

Dunn, W.S. (1974). Problems of cross-cultural research. In R. Ferber (Ed.), *The handbook of marketing research* ( pp. 360–371). New York: McGraw-Hill.

Erkut, S., Alarcon, O., Garcia-Coll, C., Tropp, L.R., & Vazquez-Garcia, H.A. (1999). The dual-focus approach to creating bilingual measures. *Journal of Cross-Cultural Psychology, 30*(2), 206–218.

Evans, M., O'Malley, L., & Patterson, M. (2004). *Exploring direct and customer relationship marketing.* London: Thomson.

Fletcher, R. (2006). The impact of culture on web site content, design, and structure: An international and a multicultural perspective. *Journal of Communication Management, 10*(33), 259–273.

Fontaine, J.R.J., Poortinga, Y.H., Delbeke, L., & Schwartz, S.H. (2008). Structural equivalence of values domain, across cultures: Distinguishing sampling fluctuations from meaningful variation. *Journal of Cross-Cultural Psychology, 39*(4), 345–365.

Geletkanycz, M.A. (1997). The salience of 'culture's consequences'. The effects of cultural values on top executive commitment to the status quo. *Strategic Management Journal, 18*(8), 615–634.

Haeckel, S. (2001) in Mitchell, A. (2001, March 16). Playing cat and mouse games with marketing. *Precision Marketing,* p. 14.

Heeler, R.M., & Ray, M.L. (1972). Measure validation in marketing. *Journal of Marketing Research*, 9, 361–370.

Heide, M., & Grohaug, K. (1992). The impact of response styles in surveys: A simulation study. *Journal of the Market Research Society*, 34(3), 215–230.

Hofstede, G. (1980). *Cultures consequences: International differences in work-related values*. Beverly Hills, CA: Sage.

Hofstede, G. (1991). *Cultures and organisations*. London: HarperCollins.

Horn, J.L., & McArdle, J.J. (1992).A practical and theoretical guide to measurement invariance in ageing research. *Experimental Ageing Research*, 18, 117–144.

Jamal, A. (2003). Marketing in a multicultural world: The interplay of marketing, ethnicity and consumption. *European Journal of Marketing*, 37(11/12), 1599–1620.

Kelly, G. (1955). *The psychology of personal construct*. New York: N.W. Norton.

Lonner, W.J. (1999). Helfrich's 'Principle of Triarchic Resonance': A commentary on yet another perspective on the ongoing and tenacious etic–emic debate. *Culture Psychology*, 5(2), 173–181.

Lonner, W.J., & Berry, J.W. (1986). Sampling and surveying. In W.J. Lonner & J.W. Berry (Eds.), *Field methods in cross-cultural research* (Vol. 8, pp. 85–110). Cross-cultural Research and Methodology Series. Beverly Hills, CA: Sage.

Malhotra, N.K. (2001). Cross-cultural marketing research in the twenty-first century. *International Marketing Review*, 18(3), 230–234.

Malhotra, N.K., Agarwal, J., & Peterson, M. (1996). Methodological issues in cross-cultural marketing research. *International Marketing Review*, 13(5), 7–43.

Malhotra, N.K., & Peterson, M. (2001). Marketing research in the new millennium: Emerging issues and trends. *Marketing Intelligence and Planning*, 19(4), 216–235.

Manrai, L., & Manrai, A.K. (1996). Current issues in cross-cultural and cross-national research. *International Journal of Consumer Marketing*, 8(3/4), 9–22.

McCort, D.J., & Malhotra, N.K. (1993). Culture and consumer behaviour: Toward an understanding of cross-cultural consumer behaviour in international marketing. *Journal of International Consumer Marketing*, 6(2), 91–128.

McCullough, D. (1998). Web-based marketing research. *Direct Marketing*, 61(8), 36–39.

Mitchell, A. (2001, March 16). Playing cat and mouse games with marketing. *Precision Marketing*, p. 14.

Montgomery, P., & Ritchie, D. (2002). Kermit: Conducting an experiment on the web. *Journal of Technology in Human Services*, 19(2/3), 135–149.

Naroll, R. (1961). Two solutions to Galton's problem. In F. Moore (Ed.), *Readings in cross-cultural methodology*. New Haven, CT: HRAF Press.

Naroll, R., & D'Andrade, R.G. (1963). Two further solutions to Galton's problem. *American Anthropologist, New Series*, 65(5), 1053–1067.

Nasif, E.G., Al-Daeaj, H., Ebrahimi, B., & Thibodeaux, M.S. (1991). Methodological problems in cross-cultural research: An updated review. *Management International Review*, 31(1), 79–91.

Needham, J. (1978). *The shorter science and civilization in China* (abridged by C.A. Ronan). Cambridge, England: Cambridge University Press.

Nisbet, R.E. (2003). *The geography of thought: How Asians and Westerners think differently . . . and why*. London: Nicholas Brealey.

Nevid, J.S., & Sta. Maria, N.L. (1999). Multicultural issues in qualitative research. *Psychology and Marketing*, 16(4), 305–325.

Osgood, C.E. (1965). Cross-cultural comparability in attitude measurement via multilingual semantic differentials. In I.D. Steiner & M. Fishbein (Eds.), *Current studies in social psychology*. Chicago: Holt, Rinehart and Winston.

Osgood, C.E., May, W.H., & Miron, M.S. (1975). *Cross-cultural universals of affective meaning*. Urbana: University of Illinois Press.

Parameswaran, R., & Yaprak, A. (1987). A cross-national comparison of consumer research measures, *Journal of International Business Studies*, 18(1), 35–49.

Pitkow, J.E., & Recker, M.M. (1995). Using the Web as a survey tool: Results from the Second WWW user survey. *Computer Networks and ISDN Systems, 27*(6), 809–822.

Rogoff, B. (2003). *The cultural nature of human development.* Oxford, England: Oxford University Press.

Saka, A. (2004). The cross national diffusion of work systems: Translation of Japanese operations in the UK. *Organisation Studies, 25*(2), 209–228.

Salzberger, T., & Sinkovics, R.R. (2006). Reconsidering the problem of data equivalence in international marketing research: Contrasting approaches based on CFA and the Rasch model for measurement. *International Marketing Review, 23*(4), 390–417.

Schaffer, B.S., & Riordan, C.M. (2003). A review of cross-cultural methodologies for organisational research: A best-practice approach. *Organisational Research Methods, 6*(2), 169–215.

Sekaran, U. (1983). Methodological and theoretical issues and advancements in cross-cultural research. *Journal of International Business Studies, 14*, 61–73.

Siah, C.Y. (2005). All that glitters is not gold: Examining the perils and obstacles in collecting data on the Internet. *International Negotiation, 10*, 115–130.

Sin, L.Y.M., Cheung, G.W.H., & Lee, R. (1999). Methodology in cross-cultural consumer research: A review and critical assessment. *Journal of International Consumer Marketing, 11*(4), 75–96.

Small, R., Yelland, J., Lumley, J.L., Lamputtong-Rice, P., Cotronel, V., & Warren, R. (1999). Enhancing data quality. Cross-cultural research: Trying to do it better, part 2. *Australian and New Zealand Journal of Public Health, 23*(4), 385–389.

Soley, L.C., & Reid, L.N. (1983). Satisfaction with the informational value of magazine and television advertising. *Journal of Advertising, 12*(3). 27–31.

Soriano, M.Y., & Foxall, G.R. (2002). A Spanish translation of Mehrabian and Russell's emotionality scales for environmental consumer psychology. *Journal of Consumer Behaviour, 2*(1), 23–36.

Spyridakis, J.H., Wei, C., Barrick, J., Cuddihy, E., & Maust, B. (2005). Internet-based research: Providing a foundation for web-design guidelines. *IEEE Transactions on Professional communication, 48*(3), 242–260.

Stening, B.W., & Zhang, M.Y. (2007). Methodological challenges confronted when conducting management research in China. *International Journal of Cross-cultural Management, 7*(1), 121–142.

Strauss, D.J., Orans, M., Barnes, J.A., Chaney, P., de Leeuwe, J., Ember, M., et al. (1975). Mighty shifts: A critical appraisal of solutions to Galton's problem and a partial solution. *Current Anthropology, 16*(4), 573–594.

Streiner, D.L., & Norman, G.R. (1995). *With measurement scales: A practical guide to their development and use.* Oxford, England: Oxford University Press.

Tingling, P., Parent, M., & Wade, M. (2003). Extending of capabilities of Internet-based research: Lessons from the field. *Internet Research, 13*(3), 223–235.

Triandis, H.C. (1980). Introduction to handbook of cross-cultural psychology. In H.C. Triandis & W.W. Lambert (Eds.), *Handbook of cross-cultural psychology* (Vol. 1; pp. 1–14). Boston: Allyn and Bacon.

Triandis, H.C., Malpass, R.S., & Davidson, A.R. (1971). Cross-cultural psychology. In B. Siegel (Ed.), *Biennial Review of Anthropology* (pp. 1–84). Stanford, CA: Stanford University Press.

Trompenaars, F., & Hampden-Turner, C. (1997). *Riding the waves of culture: Understanding cultural diversity in business* (2nd ed.). London: Nicholas Brealey.

Tucker, L.R. (1966). Some mathematical notes on three-mode factor analysis. *Psychometrika, 31*, 279–311.

Tylor, E. (1889). On a method of investigating the development of institutions applied to the laws of marriage and descent. *Journal of the Royal Anthropological Institute, 18*(3), 245–272.

Vandenberg, R.J. (2002). Towards a further understanding of and improvement in measurement invariance methods and procedures. *Organisational Research Methods, 5*, 139–158.

Vandenberg, R.J., & Lance, C.E. (2000). A review and synthesis of the measurement invariance literature: suggestions, practices and recommendations for organisational research. *Organisational Research Methods, 3*(1), 1–69.

Villegas, J., & Shah, A. (2005). Lana o Bille?: *Humor appeal's effect in Mexican Americans and Cuban Americans explained by their attitude toward money retention.* American Academy of Advertising, Conference Proceedings, pp. 112–113 .

Webster, L. (1966). Comparability in multi-country surveys. *Journal of Advertising Research, 6,* 14–18.

Whiting, J.W.M. (1968). Methods and problems in cross-cultural research. In G. Lindzey & E. Aronson (Eds.), *The handbook of social psychology* (2nd ed., Vol. 2, pp. 693–728). Reading, MA: Addison-Wesley.

Wilson, A., & Laskey, N. (2003). Internet based marketing research: A serious alternative to traditional research methods? *Marketing Intelligence and Planning, 21*(2), 79–84.

Woodside, A.G. (2005). Advancing hermeneutic research for interpreting interfirm new product development. *The Journal of Business and Industrial Marketing, 20*(7), 364–378.

Yeganeh, H., Su, Z., & Chrysostome, E.V.M. (2004). A critical review of epistemological and methodological issues in cross-cultural research. *Journal of Comparative International Management, 7*(2), 66–86.

# Index

Page numbers in *Italics* represent tables.
Page numbers in **Bold** represent figures.